THE ILLUSTRATED
DINOSAUR
DICTIONARY

THE ILLUSTRATED DINOSAUR DICTIONARY

by Helen Roney Sattler

With a foreword by
John H. Ostrom, Ph.D.
Curator of Vertebrate Paleontology
Peabody Museum of Natural History
Yale University

Illustrated by Pamela Carroll

Color insert by Anthony Rao and
Christopher Santoro

LOTHROP, LEE & SHEPARD BOOKS
NEW YORK

First Edition
1 2 3 4 5 6 7 8 9 10

Library of Congress Cataloging in Publication Data

Sattler, Helen Roney.
The illustrated dinosaur dictionary.

Bibliography: p.
Summary: A dictionary with entries for all known dinosaurs, about 300 at
last count, and other animals of the Mesozoic Era, as well as general topics
relating to dinosaurs, from Acanthopholis to Zigongosaurus.   1. Dinosaurs—
ictionaries. [1. Dinosaurs—Dictionaries.   2. Extinct animals—Dictionaries]
. Carroll, Pamela, ill.   II. Rao, Anthony, ill.   III. Santoro, Christopher, ill.
Title.   QE862.D5S226 1983   567.9′1′0321   82-23947   ISBN 0-688-00479-2

Acknowledgments

I would like to express my deepest appreciation and thanks to John H. Ostrom, Curator of Vertebrate Paleontology, Peabody Museum of Natural History, Yale University, for reading the completed manuscript and for his many valuable comments and criticisms along the way, as well as for checking the drawings for accuracy.

I also extend thanks to Donald Baird, Edwin H. Colbert, Walter P. Coombs, John Horner, James Jensen, Wann Langston, Jr., James Madsen, Jr., Walter L. Manger, George Olshevsky, and Dale A. Russell for their contributions by way of conversations or correspondence. I am grateful also to the following authors for information gleaned from their papers published in scientific journals and books: R. M. Alexander, Luis Alvarez, Walter Alvarez, Donald Baird, Robert T. Bakker, Rinchen Barsbold, J. F. Bonaparte, M. K. Brett-Surman, A. J. Charig, Sankar Chatterjee, Edwin Colbert, Walter P. Coombs, Jr., W. W. Crompton, Philip J. Currie, Peter Dodson, James O. Farlow, Peter Galton, Stephen Jay Gould, M. J. Heaton, John Horner, Sohan L. Jain, James A. Jensen, M. John Kaye, Richard A. Kerr, S. M. K Kurzanov, Wann Langston, Jr., Douglas A. Lawson, John S. McIntosh, James H. Madsen, Jr., Jean L. Marx, Ralph E. Molnar, William J. Morris, Elizabeth Nicholls, George Olshevsky, Halszka Osmolska, John H. Ostrom, Jaime Eduardo Powell, A. K. Rozhdestvensky, Dale A. Russell, Loris S. Russell, Albert Santa Luca, William Lee Stokes, John E. Storer, J. Willis Stovall, Hans-Sieter Sues, William Swinton, Samuel P. Welles, Ruport Wild, P. Yadagiri, Zi-kui Zhao, and others too numerous to mention. I also thank Carol Gill, Rosalia Purdum, Malinda Shirley-Sattler, and Robert Sattler for their tireless assistance in obtaining reference material.

CONTENTS

Foreword

Why a dictionary of dinosaurs? This question can be answered easily. The answer, of course, is that there are so many people of all ages all over the world who are fascinated with dinosaurs. Dinosaur enthusiasts need a handy, quick reference book that will tell them the difference between *Tyrannosaurus* and *Scutellosaurus* or *Secernosaurus.* If you have not heard of either of these, or of *Minmi* and *Mussaurus,* one of the main reasons you will enjoy this book is obvious. It tells you about these and many other recently identified dinosaur kinds that have yet to be "discovered" by other writers of popular dinosaur books.

Helen Sattler's diligent research has produced the most comprehensive book on dinosaurs for the nonscientist that I know of. She has done a superb job of tracking down all the latest discoveries from places like Argentina, China, Mongolia, Brazil, and many others. This book can be depended on to give you accurate, up-to-the-minute information on the subject. And, though dictionaries are not usually purchased for casual reading, it is an additional bonus that *The Illustrated Dinosaur Dictionary* is both an up-to-date reference and a readable book.

Dinosaurs have been known to the world for only a little more than a century and a half, and new discoveries, new knowledge, and new hypotheses come forward almost every day. Of the approximately three hundred dinosaur kinds included in this dictionary, *almost one hundred were discovered and named in just the last twenty years.* These

latest discoveries, and all those that were made before, were
the result of strenuous and costly expeditions to many parts
of the world. The search for new dinosaurs and other forms
of ancient life will continue as long as the public and the
scientist are intrigued by the curious creatures of the past.
Indeed, the curiosity of the paleontologist, and the excite-
ment of search and discovery, guarantee future finds.

John H. Ostrom, Ph. D.
Curator of Vertebrate Paleontology
Peabody Museum of Natural History
Yale University

Introduction

In this book you will find an alphabetical listing of your favorite dinosaurs, plus information on many that will be new to you. You will also find the names of some of the animals that lived with the dinosaurs, or are mistaken for dinosaurs, and definitions of some of the terms that you come across when reading about dinosaurs and can't find in a regular dictionary. In fact, in this book you can find out just about anything there is to know about dinosaurs.

The word "dinosaur" means "terrible lizard" (it comes from the Greek words *deinos,* "terrible," and *sauros,* "lizard"). These prehistoric animals were originally thought to be gigantic reptiles. Today the word *dinosaur* is used to name a group of extinct animals classed as reptiles because of their reptilian skulls. However, some scientists now think that it is possible that dinosaurs were not true reptiles —at least not in the sense of modern reptiles such as lizards and turtles.

Dinosaurs were actually two kinds of animals, *Saurischia* and *Ornithischia.* The two were no more closely related to each other than they were to crocodiles or to the extinct flying reptiles (pterosaurs). Both the saurischian and the ornithischian dinosaurs are thought to have evolved from reptilian ancestors called thecodonts. Dinosaurs in both groups probably were scaly, egg-laying animals that walked in an erect posture like mammals. They did not crawl along close to the ground like modern reptiles. Some scientists now think that dinosaurs were warm-blooded, like today's mammals and birds, and capable of rapid movement. Today's reptiles are cold-blooded and generally slow-moving. There is evidence suggesting the possibility that many dinosaurs gave some kind of care to their young. Some scientists have proposed that dinosaurs should be removed from the class *Reptilia* and placed in a separate class called *Dinosauria* or *Archosauria.*

The saurischians, or "lizard-hipped" dinosaurs, are divided into three groups. Theropods were bipedal (two-legged) meat-eaters. Sauropods were gigantic quadrupedal (four-legged) plant-eaters. Prosauropods were sometimes bipedal and sometimes quadrupedal. Most prosauropods ate plants, but some may have eaten meat also.

There were four kinds of ornithischians, or "bird-hipped" dinosaurs. Those that walked on two legs most of the time are called ornithopods. The plated dinosaurs are called stegosaurs, the armored dinosaurs are called ankylosaurs, and the horned dinosaurs are called ceratopsians. Some scientists separate the ornithischians into five groups instead of four. They put the dome-headed dinosaurs, or pachycephalosaurs, in a group by themselves. Other scientists consider the pachycephalosaurs to be a subdivision (family) of the ornithopods.

The period of the earth's history in which dinosaurs lived is called the Mesozoic Era. It began 225 million years ago and ended 65 million years ago. This era is divided into three periods: the Triassic (the earliest), the Jurassic, and the Cretaceous (the latest). Dinosaurs evolved around the middle of the Triassic Period and became extinct at the close of the Cretaceous Period.

During the 140 million years that dinosaurs existed, many different kinds evolved. We know this because we have found their fossilized remains and tracks. In this book you will find the names of about three hundred different dinosaurs. The meaning of each name and a guide to its pronunciation follows. Each entry also tells which group a

Classification of Dinosaurs

CLASS REPTILIA

Subclass *Archosauria*   Triassic to present

  Order *Thecodontia*   Triassic
    Suborder *Proterosuchia*   Primitive thecodonts;
                     Early Triassic

    Suborder *Pseudosuchia*   Dinosaur ancestors; Triassic
    Suborder *Aetosauria*   Heavily armored plant-eaters;
                     Triassic

    Suborder *Phytosauria*   Phytosaurs; Triassic

  Order *Crocodilia*   Crocodiles; Triassic to present

  Order *Pterosauria*   Flying reptiles;
                     Jurassic to Late Cretaceous

  Order *Saurischia*   "Lizard-hipped" dinosaurs;
                     Triassic through Cretaceous

    Suborder *Theropoda*   Bipedal meat-eaters;
                     Triassic through Cretaceous

      Infraorder *Coelurosauria*   Small theropods
      Infraorder *Carnosauria*   Large theropods
    Suborder *Sauropodomorpha*   Triassic to Cretaceous
      Infraorder *Prosauropoda*   Forerunners of the *Sauropoda*
      Infraorder *Sauropoda*   Huge quadrupedal plant-eaters

  Order *Ornithischia*   "Bird-hipped" dinosaurs;
                     mainly plant-eaters

    Suborder *Ornithopoda*   All bipedal; some duck-billed;
                     Triassic to Cretaceous

    Suborder *Stegosauria*   Plated; quadrupedal;
                     Jurassic and Cretaceous

    Suborder *Ankylosauria*   Armored; quadrupedal;
                     Cretaceous

    Suborder *Ceratopsia*   Horned; quadrupedal;
                     Late Cretaceous

    Suborder *Pachycephalosauria*   Dome-headed; bipedal;
                     Late Cretaceous

dinosaur belongs to, when it lived, and what it looked like.

This is an exciting time in the history of dinosaur study. New discoveries are made every year; new facts are unearthed almost daily. Two brand-new dinosaur grave-yards have just recently been found: one in China and the other in Alberta, Canada. It will take many years for scientists to dig out all the fossils, and it will take many more years to clean them and fit them together like the pieces of giant jigsaw puzzles. But when the work is finished, you can be sure there will be many more new and interesting dinosaurs to read about.

You can also be sure that new facts about old dinosaurs will be uncovered, giving us a better understanding of some that are now poorly known. New information about well-known dinosaurs may cause scientists to change their thinking about some of them, just as new information in the past changed scientific opinions. We know a great deal about dinosaurs now, but there is much more to be learned.

Helen Roney Sattler

How to Use
This Book

Just about everything there is to know about dinosaurs can be found in this book, which has been organized to make the information as readily accessible as possible. All the dinosaurs that have been named to date and many of the animals that are sometimes confused with dinosaurs are listed alphabetically in bold-face capital letters. The meaning of each animal name and a guide to its pronunciation are given. In addition to classification and detailed description, there is also information on the amount of evidence we have on each of the creatures. It's interesting as well as important to know if assumptions and theories have been based on the discovery of an entire skeleton or on a small fragment of bone or a footprint.

There are also definitions of terms frequently encountered when reading about dinosaurs that either aren't in regular dictionaries or may not be defined in a way to reveal the term's relationship to dinosaurs, as is the case with *endotherm*. You may also look up specific items, such as *feet*, *hands*, *extinction, young*, or *parental care*, and find discussions of facts and theories concerning them.

For your convenience, the dictionary is cross-referenced. You can find more information about the terms that are set in small capital letters within an entry by referring to the separate entries for those terms.

Black-and-white line drawings accompany the dinosaur entries as well as the entries for many of the other animals discussed. These drawings are stylized to point up the distinguishing features of each animal. Dinosaurs, however, were flesh-and-blood animals that lived and breathed and interacted with the flora and fauna in their territories in much the same way animals in the wild do today. The Pictorial Age of the Dinosaurs that immediately follows will help you visualize dinosaurs as creatures living in their natural habitats. These color pages contain a chart showing animal relationships from the Paleolithic to the present, with special emphasis on the Mesozoic Era. There is also a page of maps showing the positions of the continents during these ancient times.

The Reference, by Location, of Dinosaur Discoveries contains entries for continents, countries, and individual states, provinces, or regions. This index will be of special value to anyone who wants to know the names of dinosaurs that have been discovered in a particular area.

Relationships of Mesozoic Animals

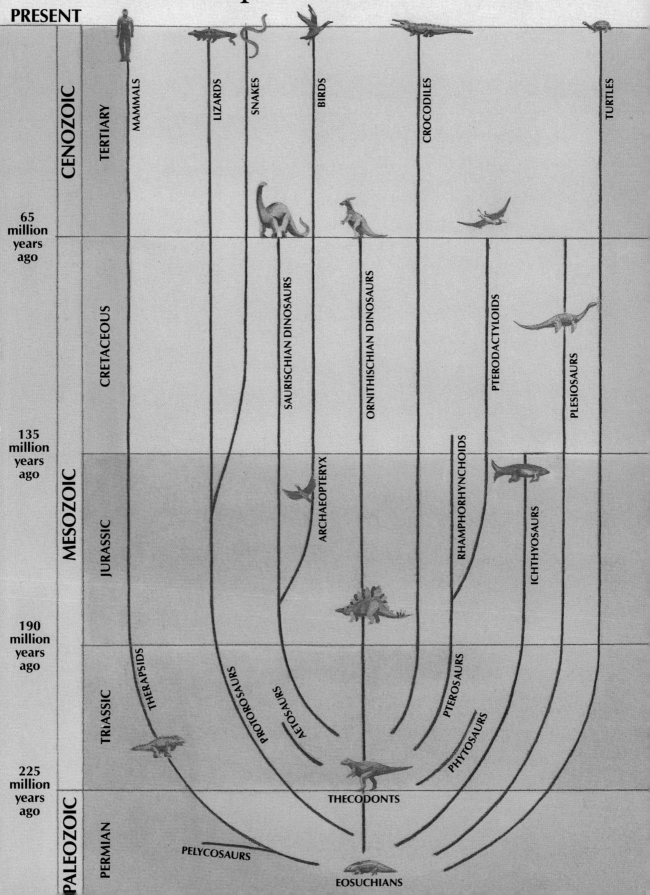

These pelycosaurs were extinct millions of years before dinosaurs lived. They lived during the **Permian,** the last period before the Triassic.

EDAPHOSAURUS

OPHIACODON

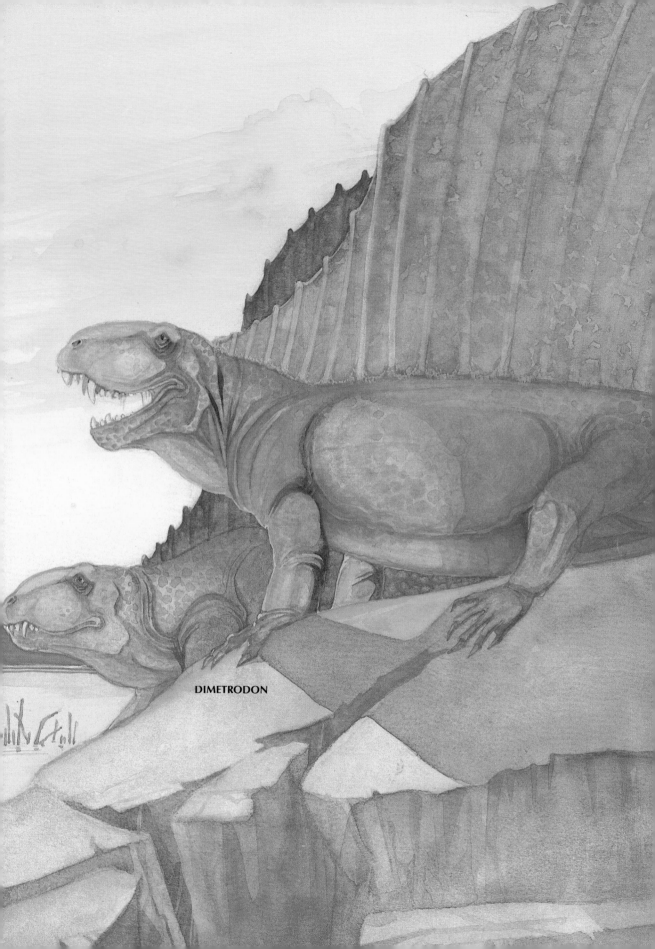

DIMETRODON

During the **Triassic,** Plateosaurus, one of the largest of the saurischian dinosaurs, and Procompsognathus, a primitive coelurosaur, sometimes lived near the crocodile-like phytosaur.

PLATEOSAURUS

PROCOMPSOGNATHUS

PHYTOSAUR

Though they may not have gathered around the same waterhole at the same time, all these animals lived near one another during the **Jurassic.** All except Rhamphorhynchus are dinosaurs.

APATOSAURUS

STEGOSAURUS

CAMPTOSAURUS

RHAMPHORHYNCHUS

DIPLODOCUS

ALLOSAURUS

COMPSOGNATHUS

PTERODACTYL

ACANTHOPHOLIS

These creatures lived during the **Early Cretaceous.** Some of the plant-eating dinosaurs were armed with spikes that may have helped protect them.

IGUANODON

These dinosaurs all lived in western
North America in **Late Cretaceous** times.

PARASAUROLOPHUS

ANKYLOSAURUS

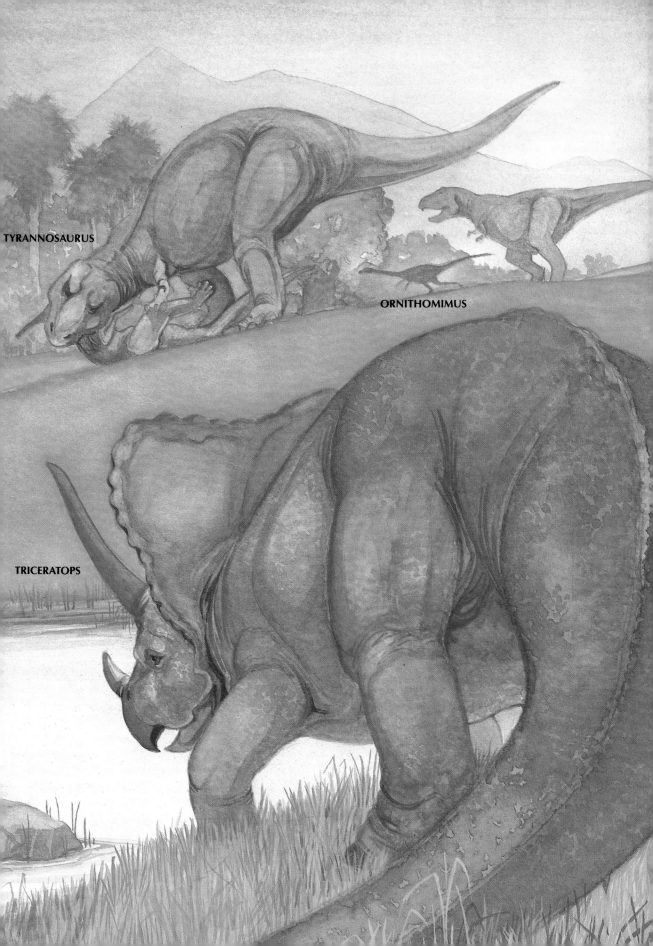

TYRANNOSAURUS

ORNITHOMIMUS

TRICERATOPS

The Mesozoic Era

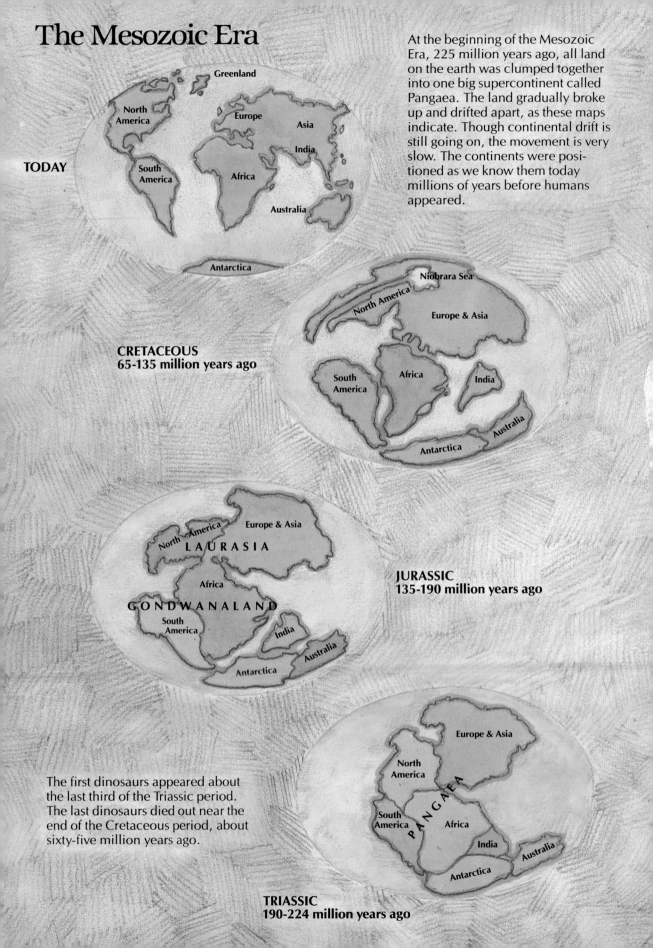

At the beginning of the Mesozoic Era, 225 million years ago, all land on the earth was clumped together into one big supercontinent called Pangaea. The land gradually broke up and drifted apart, as these maps indicate. Though continental drift is still going on, the movement is very slow. The continents were positioned as we know them today millions of years before humans appeared.

TODAY

Greenland
North America
Europe
Asia
India
South America
Africa
Australia
Antarctica

**CRETACEOUS
65-135 million years ago**

North America
Niobrara Sea
Europe & Asia
South America
Africa
India
Antarctica
Australia

**JURASSIC
135-190 million years ago**

North America
Europe & Asia
LAURASIA
Africa
GONDWANALAND
South America
India
Australia
Antarctica

The first dinosaurs appeared about the last third of the Triassic period. The last dinosaurs died out near the end of the Cretaceous period, about sixty-five million years ago.

**TRIASSIC
190-224 million years ago**

Europe & Asia
North America
South America
PANGAEA
Africa
India
Antarctica
Australia

A

ACANTHOPHOLIS (ā-kan-THOF-o-liss) "Prickly Scales" (Greek *akantha* = prickly + *pholis* = scale, referring to its armor.)

A small Early Cretaceous ANKYLOSAUR (armored dinosaur). The slim body of this animal was covered with small plates like those on a turtle's back. Its neck and shoulders were armed with spikes; the tail was clubless. This four-legged plant-eater may have grown to be 14 feet (4.2 m) long. It is known only from a fragmentary skeleton found in southern England.

Classification: Nodosauridae, Ankylosauria, Ornithischia

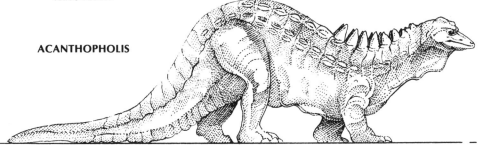

ACANTHOPHOLIS

ACROCANTHOSAURUS (ak-ro-KANTH-uh-sawr-us) "High-spined Lizard" (Greek *akro* = high + *akantha* = spine + *sauros* = lizard, referring to the spines on its vertebrae.)

A CARNOSAUR of Early Cretaceous North America. This

40-foot (12-m) meat-eating relative of ALLOSAURUS walked on two legs. It had a large head with sharp, saw-like teeth. Projections up to 17 inches (43 cm) long grew on its vertebrae. These spines were probably embedded in a thick ridge of muscle. *Acrocanthosaurus* is the only known American dinosaur with such high spines. It is known from a skull and partial skeleton found in Oklahoma and Texas.

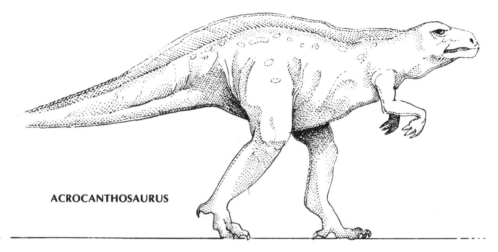

ACROCANTHOSAURUS

A recent flood in Texas uncovered some footprints that scientists think were made by *Acrocanthosaurus*. *Acrocanthosaurus* fossils have been found in similar rock nearby. The three-toed footprints were made by 15 individuals traveling at a high speed. Scientists have calculated that they were running about 25 miles (40 km) per hour. These tracks provide evidence that *Acrocanthosaurus* traveled in herds.

Classification: Carnosauria, Theropoda, Saurischia

AEGYPTOSAURUS (ee-JIP-tuh-sawr-us) "Egyptian Lizard" (Named for Egypt, where it was found.)

A name given to a few SAUROPOD bones found in Late

Cretaceous rock in Egypt. This huge four-legged plant-eater is thought to have been quite similar to DIPLODOCUS. Although its bones were destroyed in World War II, its discovery is important because it shows that sauropods were living on the African continent in Late Cretaceous times.

Classification: Sauropoda, Sauropodomorpha, Saurischia

AETONYX (eye-TON-ix) "Old Claw" (Latin *aetatis* = old + Greek *onyx* = claw, because it was a very early dinosaur.)

A primitive Late Triassic PROSAUROPOD similar to THECODONTOSAURUS. It is known only from fragments found in South Africa. This relatively small dinosaur had a long neck and tail. It was probably QUADRUPEDAL, but might have been capable of walking BIPEDALLY. It was a plant-eater, but possibly also ate meat.

Classification: Prosauropoda, Sauropodomorpha, Saurischia

aetosaurs or **Aetosauria** (eye-ee-tuh-SAWR-ee-uh) "Old Lizards" (Latin *aetatis* = old + Greek *sauros* = lizard, because they were very early reptiles.)

Not dinosaurs, but a suborder of THECODONTS. Aetosaurs were heavily armored reptiles that lived during the Triassic Period. Their crocodile-shaped bodies were covered with armadillo-like bony plates, and curved, serrated spikes protruded from their sides. They were four-legged OMNIVORES with pig-like snouts. Aetosaurs probably roamed throughout LAURASIA. They have been found in Germany, Scotland, and western United States. They ranged in size from the 3- to 4-foot (90- to 120-cm) AETOSAURUS to a 15-foot (4.5-m) DESMATOSUCHUS, that was found in Arizona. STAGONOLEPIS was about 9 feet (2.5 m) long. This animal was found in Scotland.

AETOSAURUS
See AETOSAURS.

age
No one knows for sure how old dinosaurs lived to be. Some scientists think they lived to a great age—possibly until they were 100 or 200 years old. These scientists think that the huge dinosaurs may have continued to grow throughout their lives and that that is why they got so large. Growth rings on dinosaur bones show that some were 120 years old when they died.

AGROSAURUS (AG-ruh-sawr-us) "Field Lizard" (Greek *agros* = field + *sauros* = lizard, referring to the place where it was found.)
An Early Jurassic COELUROSAUR. This small meat-eating dinosaur is known only from a few bones, a claw, and a broken tooth found in Queensland, Australia. It was BIPEDAL and probably resembled COELURUS. Its exact size is unknown.
Classification: Coelurosauria, Theropoda, Saurischia

ALAMOSAURUS (AL-uh-mo-sawr-us) "Alamo Lizard" (Named for the Ojo Alamo rock formation, where it was found + Greek *sauros* = lizard.)

ALAMOSAURUS

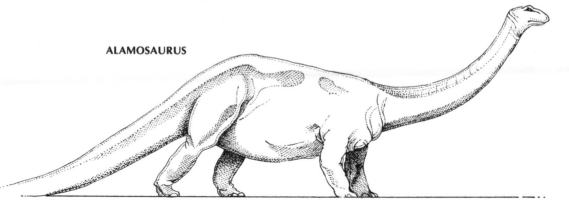

A SAUROPOD whose fossils have been found in western Texas, New Mexico, and Utah. This huge four-legged plant-eater lived in Late Cretaceous times; it was one of the last of the sauropods to live in North America. (See EXTINCTION.) It is known only from a few bones, but scientists think it resembled DIPLODOCUS. It may have grown to be 50 feet (15 m) long.

Classification: Sauropoda, Sauropodomorpha, Saurischia

ALBERTOSAURUS (al-BER-tuh-sawr-us) "Alberta Lizard" (Named for Alberta, Canada, where it was first found + Greek *sauros* = lizard.) Also called GORGOSAURUS.

A large CARNOSAUR of Late Cretaceous North America. This dinosaur is better known as *Gorgosaurus,* but *Albertosaurus* is the preferred name (even though it was given to just a partial skull), because it is the older name. The two are now considered to be the same animal, although *Gorgosaurus* may be a smaller species.

ALBERTOSAURUS

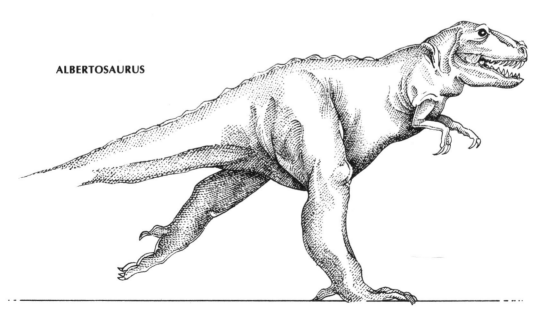

Albertosaurus was a close relative of TYRANNOSAURUS, but was smaller and lived several million years earlier. *Albertosaurus* weighed 3 tons (2.7 metric tons), stood 11 feet (3.3 m) tall at the hips, and measured 30 feet (9 m) from its snout to the tip of its tail. Like *Tyrannosaurus,* it was a meat-eater with a huge head; long, sharp, saw-toothed teeth; and two-fingered hands. Its arms were quite short, but were longer than those of *Tyrannosaurus. Albertosaurus* ran on powerful hind legs and was probably swifter than *Tyrannosaurus.* Its feet were armed with long claws.

Scientists have found more fossils of *Albertosaurus* than of any other Late Cretaceous carnosaur. Remains of this animal have been discovered in various areas of the western United States and in Baja California, as well as in Alberta, Canada. Similar types of dinosaurs lived in Mongolia during Late Cretaceous times.

Classification: Carnosauria, Theropoda, Saurischia

ALECTROSAURUS (ah-LEK-truh-sawr-us) "Unmarried Lizard" (Greek *alektros* = unmarried or alone + *sauros*

ALECTROSAURUS

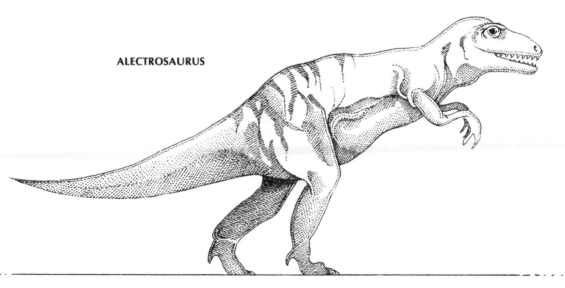

= lizard, because it was unlike any other Asian meat-eater known at the time.)

A large Late Cretaceous CARNOSAUR. This BIPEDAL meat-eater was closely related to TYRANNOSAURUS, but was more slender. It is known only from an upper arm, hand, shin, and foot found in Mongolia. It had very long finger claws. Its exact size is unknown.

Classification: Carnosauria, Theropoda, Saurischia

ALGOASAURUS (AL-go-uh-sawr-us) "Pain Lizard" (Greek *algos* = pain + *sauros* = lizard. The reason for this name is no longer known.)

An Early Cretaceous SAUROPOD whose fossils were found in South Africa. Only a few bones of this four-legged plant-eater have been found, but *Algoasaurus* is thought to be closely related to DIPLODOCUS, and was probably about the same size.

Classification: Sauropoda, Sauropodomorpha, Saurischia

ALIORAMUS (ah-lee-o-RAH-mus) "Different Branch" (Latin *alius* = different + *ramus* = branch, because it was a different kind of TYRANNOSAUR.)

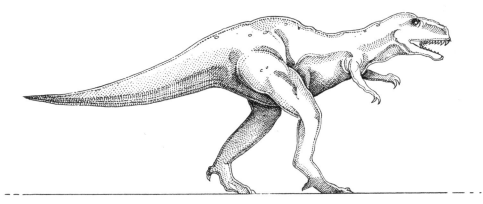

A Late Cretaceous CARNOSAUR whose fossils were found in Mongolia. This two-legged meat-eater was a close relative of TARBOSAURUS and resembled that dinosaur, but was smaller. *Alioramus* belonged to the tyrannosaur family, and like all tyrannosaurs, it had a large head, long teeth, and short arms with two-fingered hands. It was about 20 feet (6 m) long.

Classification: Carnosauria, Theropoda, Saurischia

allosaurids or **Allosauridae** (al-uh-SAWR-ih-dee) "Different Lizards" (Named after ALLOSAURUS.) Also commonly called ALLOSAURS.

A family of CARNOSAURS. These BIPEDAL meat-eaters were medium to very large in size—20 to 45 feet (6 to 13.5 m) long. They had strong heavy bodies and large narrow skulls with strong brow ridges. Their arms were quite short, but strong. The hands had three fingers and the feet three forward-pointing toes and a dewclaw. Allosaurids lived in North America and Asia during Late Jurassic and Early Cretaceous times. ACROCANTHOSAURUS, ALLOSAURUS, CHILANTAISAURUS, INDOSAURUS, and PIATNITZKYSAURUS are members of this family.

allosaurs (AL-uh-sawrz)

See ALLOSAURIDS or ALLOSAURIDAE.

ALLOSAURUS (AL-uh-sawr-us) "Different Lizard" (Greek *allos* = different + *sauros* = lizard, because its vertebrae were different from those of all other dinosaurs.) Also called ANTRODEMUS.

One of the largest Jurassic CARNOSAURS of North America. An average *Allosaurus* weighed about 4 tons (3.6 metric tons) and measured 35 feet (10.5 m) from the tip of its nose to the end of its tail. The largest known was 45 feet (13.5 m) long. When *Allosaurus* stood upright, it was 16.5 feet (5 m) tall.

Like all THEROPODS, *Allosaurus* walked on two legs with its heavy tail stretched out behind for balance. Its strong legs were built for speed; they had powerful muscles and heavy bones. Although its arms were short, each finger on its three-fingered hands was armed with a sharp claw that could be up to 6 inches (15 cm) long. The three long toes on its feet were equipped with eagle-like talons.

This savage meat-eater had a strong neck. Its huge, 3-foot (90 cm) long head had heavy bony knobs or ridges above its eyes; its enormously powerful jaws were filled with saber-like teeth 2 to 4 inches (5 to 10 cm) long. The jaws were hinged like those of a snake, so *Allosaurus* would have been able to swallow huge hunks of meat whole. Scientists have found APATOSAURUS vertebrae with *Allosaurus* tooth marks on them, evidence of a Jurassic feast!

Allosaurus remains have been found in North America; fossils found in Africa and Asia may also be those of *Allosaurus.* It is one of the best known carnosaurs. Sixty individuals—from juveniles to adults—were found at one site in Utah.

Classification: Carnosauria, Theropoda, Saurischia

ALLOSAURUS

ALTISPINAX (al-tuh-SPY-nax) "High Spines" (Latin *altus* = high + *spina* = spine, referring to the high spines on its vertebrae.)

The first CARNOSAUR with a fin on its back to be discovered. It is known only from some worn teeth and three mid-back vertebrae. On these vertebrae were very long projections similar to, but shorter than, those of SPINOSAURUS. They were, however, somewhat longer than those of ACROCANTHOSAURUS. This two-legged meat-eater lived in England in Early Cretaceous times.

Classification: Carnosauria, Theropoda, Saurischia

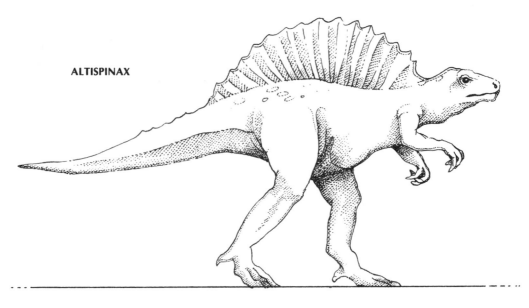

ALTISPINAX

AMBLYDACTYLUS (am-bly-DAK-tih-lus) "Blunt Finger" (Greek *amblys* = blunt + *daktylos* = finger, because the fingers were short.)

Name given to HADROSAUR footprints found in British Columbia, Alberta, and Utah. The prints of the hands show the webbing between the fingers. These are the most abundant footprints found in British Columbia.

AMMONITE (AM-uh-nite) "Horn of Ammon" (From Latin, because its shape resembles that of the horns of Ammon, an Egyptian god.)

Not a dinosaur, but a flat, coiled mollusk that lived in the oceans of the MESOZOIC ERA. This relative of the modern nautilus, octopus, and squid ranged in size from less than an inch to 6 feet (1.8 m) in diameter. These sea animals disappeared at the end of the era along with the dinosaurs and many other life forms. (See EXTINCTION.) Its fossils have been found in many Mesozoic marine deposits around the world.

AMMOSAURUS (AM-o-sawr-us) "Sand Lizard" (Greek *ammos* = sand + *sauros* = lizard, because it was found in sandstone.)

An early North American PROSAUROPOD. It had a long neck and tail. Its head was small, and its teeth were flat or peg-like. Its feet were broad. Most of the time this 7-foot (2-m) plant-eater walked on all fours, but it was capable of walking on two legs. It is one of the earliest known

AMMOSAURUS

North American dinosaurs. *Ammosaurus* probably lived all over North America during very late Triassic or Early Jurassic times. It is known from fairly complete material; remains have been found in both Connecticut and Arizona.

Classification: Prosauropoda, Sauropodomorpha, Saurischia

AMTOSAURUS (AHM-toe-sawr-us) "Amtgay Lizard" (Named for the Amtgay site, where it was discovered + Greek *sauros* = lizard.)

A large ANKYLOSAUR whose fossils were recently found in Mongolia. This creature lived during the Late Cretaceous Period. Like all ankylosaurs, it walked on four legs, ate plants, and its back was covered with bony "armor" plates. Its tail is unknown. This dinosaur is known only from a partial braincase and the back of a skull. It was a contemporary of TALARURUS and was probably closely related to that dinosaur, but was somewhat larger.

Classification: Ankylosauridae, Ankylosauria, Ornithischia

AMYGDALODON (ah-MIG-duh-lo-don) "Almond Tooth" (Greek *amygdale* = almond + *odon* = tooth, because its teeth were almond-shaped.)

One of the earliest known SAUROPODS. This giant four-footed plant-eater had a long neck and tail. It lived in southern Argentina during Middle Jurassic times. Little is known about it because a complete skeleton has not been found, but from the few bones that have been recovered, it appears that this dinosaur was a member of the CETIOSAURID family and was somewhat larger than TITANOSAURUS. It is one of the only certainly known Jurassic dinosaurs from South America.

Classification: Sauropoda, Sauropodomorpha, Saurischia

ANATOSAURUS (ah-NAT-uh-sawr-us) "Duck Lizard" (Latin *anatos* = duck + *sauros* = lizard, because it had a wide, duck-like bill.) Also called TRACHODON.

A Late Cretaceous HADROSAUR. This duck-billed dinosaur is one of the best known dinosaurs—only its color is unknown. Many skeletons and several SKIN impressions have been found. The skin had a rough pebbly texture. Fossilized stomach contents show that it ate shrubs, evergreen needles, fruits, and seeds. This indicates that *Anatosaurus* was a land dweller, rather than a water dweller, as scientists first thought. It ran on two legs with its body held horizontally, balanced by a long tail stretched out behind.

ANATOSAURUS

Anatosaurus belonged to the HADROSAURINE group of hadrosaurs. It had a flat head, webbed forefeet, and up to 1,000 closely packed teeth in its horny bill. It grew to be 14 feet (4.3 m) tall and 30 feet (9 m) long. It weighed up to 3.5 tons (3.2 metric tons). *Anatosaurus* lived in North America and in England, and was one of the last of the duckbills to become extinct. (See EXTINCTION.)

Classification: Hadrosauridae, Ornithopoda, Ornithischia

ANCHICERATOPS (ANG-kee-sair-a-tops) "Similar Horned Face" (Greek *anchion* = similar + *keratops* = horned face, because it was similar to other CERATOPSIANS.)

A Late Cretaceous ceratopsian. This 16-foot (4.8-m) OR-NITHISCHIAN had a horny beak and three horns on its face —a short stubby one on its nose and two long ones above its eyes. *Anchiceratops* was a long-frilled ceratopsian. Its bony frill covered the neck to the shoulders. This four-legged plant-eater was very common in Alberta, Canada.

Classification: Ceratopsidae, Ceratopsia, Ornithischia

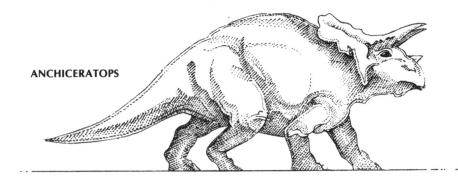

ANCHICERATOPS

anchisaurids or **Anchisauridae** (ang-kee-SAWR-ih-dee) "Near Lizards" (Named after ANCHISAURUS.)

A primitive family of PROSAUROPODS. They were relatively small, 8 to 10 feet (2.5 to 3 m) long and were lightly built. They had lightweight bones; long necks and tails; and long, slender fingers and toes. Anchisaurids could walk on either two or four legs. They may have eaten both meat and plants; they had blade-like teeth suitable for tearing meat and teeth suitable only for grinding plants. Anchisaurids lived from Middle to Late Triassic times and have been found almost all over the world. AN-CHISAURUS, EFRAASIA, and THECODONTOSAURUS were members of this family.

ANCHISAURIPUS (ANG-kee-sawr-ih-pus) "Near Lizard Foot" (Greek *anchion* = near + *sauripous* = lizard foot, because it was originally believed that these footprints were made by ANCHISAURUS.)

A name given to three-toed footprints made by a small, 12-foot (3.5-m), BIPEDAL meat-eating dinosaur as it walked from the shore into shallow water during Early Jurassic times 180 million years ago. These footprints were found in the Connecticut Valley in eastern United States. Scientists now know the prints could not have been made by *Anchisaurus*, because *Anchisaurus* was a PROSAUROPOD. These footprints are typical of THEROPODS; the middle toe is longer than the other two. Prosauropods have four, forward-pointing toes; the first toe is quite short, and toe number three is slightly longer than two and four.

ANCHISAURIPUS TRACKS

ANCHISAURUS (ANG-kee-sawr-us) "Near Lizard" (Greek *anchion* = near or close to + *sauros* = lizard, because it was an early dinosaur and was close to the reptilian ancestors.) Sometimes called YALEOSAURUS.

A PROSAUROPOD resembling AMMOSAURUS, but with narrower feet and a slightly smaller head. It was about 8 feet (2.5 m) long. *Anchisaurus* was basically QUADRUPEDAL, but may sometimes have run two-legged. It may have eaten both plants and meat. Fossils of this dinosaur have been found in Connecticut, Arizona, South Africa, and Germany. It probably lived all over the world from Late Triassic to Early Jurassic times. It was one of the oldest dinosaurs in geological time to be discovered in North

America, and it is known from very complete material. At one time it was thought that this dinosaur was a THEROPOD, because of its thin-walled bones and serrated teeth.

Classification: Prosauropoda, Sauropodomorpha, Saurischia

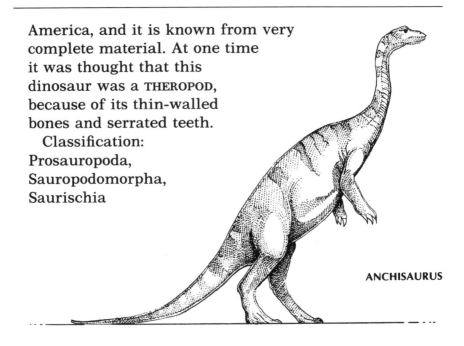

ANCHISAURUS

ankylosaurids or **Ankylosauridae** (ang-kile-uh-SAWR-ih-dee) "Armored Lizards" (Named after ANKYLOSAURUS.)

One of the two families of ANKYLOSAURS. The backs, heads, and tails of these four-legged plant-eaters were covered with thin bony plates, or scutes. Ankylosauridae ranged in size from 15 to 30 feet (4.5 to 9 m) long. They have been found in North America and Asia. This group had triangular heads, small spikes on their sides (or none at all), and clubbed tails. AMTOSAURUS, ANKYLOSAURUS, EUOPLOCEPHALUS, PINACOSAURUS, SAICHANIA, SAUROPLITES, TALARURUS, and TARCHIA were ankylosaurids.

ankylosaurs or **Ankylosauria** (ang-kile-uh-SAWR-ee-ah) "Armored Lizards" (Named after ANKYLOSAURUS.)

The suborder of armored ORNITHISCHIAN dinosaurs. It consisted of two families—ANKYLOSAURIDAE and NODOSAURIDAE. They ranged in size from 6 feet (1.8 m) to 30 feet (9 m) long. These four-legged plant-eaters lived in

Europe, Asia, Australia, and North America throughout the Cretaceous Period. Their backs, heads, and tails were covered with bony plates, or scutes, somewhat like those of a turtle, but they were flexible except over the shoulders and hips. The Nodosauridae—the most primitive—had thick scutes, pear-shaped heads, large spikes on their sides, and clubless tails. Ankylosauridae had thin oval scutes, triangular heads, small spikes on their sides (or none at all), and clubbed tails.

ANKYLOSAURUS (ang-KILE-uh-sawr-us) "Stiffened Lizard" (Greek *ankyloein* = stiffen + *sauros* = lizard, because of its stiffened dermal armor.) Sometimes mistakenly called EUOPLOCEPHALUS.

One of the largest and best known of the ANKYLOSAURS.

ANKYLOSAURUS

The body, head, and tail of this "reptilian tank" were covered with bony plates set close together in thick, leathery SKIN. A row of short spikes protected each side of the body. The tail was short and thick and ended in a bony club. This peaceful plant-eater lived in western North America during the Cretaceous Period. It was 25 feet (7.5 m) long, 6 feet (1.8 m) wide, and over 4 feet (1.2 m) tall. It weighed about 5 tons (4.5 metric tons). *Ankylosaurus* was one of the very last kinds of dinosaurs to die out. (See EXTINCTION.) It is known from fairly complete material found in Montana.

Ankylosaurus is sometimes called *Euoplocephalus,* but it is now believed that these were two different animals.

Classification: Ankylosauridae, Ankylosauria, Ornithischia

ANODONTOSAURUS (an-uh-don-tuh-SAWR-us) "Toothless Lizard" (Greek *an* = without + *odontos* = teeth + *sauros* = lizard, because its jaw was without teeth.)

A very primitive toothless ANKYLOSAUR of the NODOSAURIDAE family found in Late Cretaceous rock in Alberta, Canada. It is known only from a skull, jaw, and several scutes. The skull is 1.25 feet (40 cm) long and 1 foot (30 cm) wide. This armored dinosaur is now considered by some to be the same as EUOPLOCEPHALUS.

Classification: Nodosauridae, Ankylosauria, Ornithischia

ANOMOEPUS (an-o-MEE-pus) "Different Foot" (Greek *anomoios* = different + *pous* = foot, because these footprints were different from others found in the same area.)

Name given to Late Triassic or Early Jurassic dinosaur footprints found in the Newark Basin of Connecticut; in Glen Canyon, Arizona; and in Europe. Both the three-toed hind feet and five-fingered forefeet left impressions, indicating the animal that made them was at least sometimes QUADRUPEDAL. Scientists believe the TRACKS were made by an ORNITHOPOD because there are no claw marks. When found, these tracks were important, because no ORNITHISCHIAN dinosaur bones and only a few isolated teeth had been found in Triassic rock in North America. But now a recent discovery in Arizona has changed that. SCUTELLOSAURUS has been identified as a Late Triassic ornithischian.

ANOMOEPUS TRACKS

ANTARCTOSAURUS (ant-ARK-tuh-sawr-us) "Southern Lizard" (Greek *antarktikos* = southern + *sauros* = lizard, because it was found at the southern tip of South America.)

A Late Cretaceous SAUROPOD. This plant-eating QUAD-RUPED has been found in India as well as in South America. A nearly complete skeleton was found in Argentina. It was about the size of APATOSAURUS, but was more similar in build to DIPLODOCUS. The skull is over 2 feet (60 cm) long. The presence of *Antarctosaurus* in both India and South America raises an interesting question as to when these two continents separated. (See GONDWANALAND.)

Classification: Sauropoda, Sauropodomorpha, Saurischia

ANTARCTOSAURUS

ANTRODEMUS (an-tro-DEE-mus) "Cavern-framed" (Greek *antron* = cavern + *demas* = frame, referring to the hollows in its vertebrae.)

Another name frequently used for ALLOSAURUS. Actually there is disagreement among scientists as to whether *Antrodemus* and *Allosaurus* are the same animal. The name *Antrodemus* was based on such scanty material, it is difficult to determine for sure.

Classification: Carnosauria, Theropoda, Saurischia.

APATOSAURUS

APATOSAURUS (ah-PAT-uh-sawr-us) "Deceptive Lizard" (Greek *apatelos* = deceptive + *sauros* = lizard, because it was easily confused with other SAUROPODS.) Also called BRONTOSAURUS.

One of the largest of the Late Jurassic sauropods. This giant four-legged plant-eater had a long neck and tail. It measured 75 feet (23 m) from the tip of its nose to the end of its 30-foot (9-m), whip-like tail. It stood 15 feet (4.5 m) tall at the hips and weighed about 30 tons (27 metric tons). It had a small, long-snouted, horse-like head, and elephant-like feet and legs. The front legs were shorter than the hind legs. The teeth were small and peg-like. The BRAIN was about the size of an adult human's fist.

For a long time scientists thought *Apatosaurus* was too heavy to walk on land and assumed that it was a water dweller. However, recent bone studies prove that its legs could have supported its weight. It was probably a plains and forest dweller, and it probably traveled in herds. It ate twigs and the needles of pine, fir, and sequoia trees. Its 20-foot (6-m) neck—which had 14 or 15 vertebrae and was longer than its body—allowed it to browse on the very tops of trees.

For protection *Apatosaurus* relied on its size and tough, leathery SKIN. It lived in many areas of western North

America from Montana to Baja California, as well as in Europe. Several nearly complete skeletons have been found, but only one head.

Classification: Sauropoda, Sauropodomorpha, Saurischia

ARALOSAURUS   (ar-al-uh-SAWR-us) "Aral Lizard" (Named for the U.S.S.R.'s Aral Lake + Greek *sauros* = lizard.)

A HADROSAUR (duck-billed dinosaur) that lived in what is now the U.S.S.R. during Late Cretaceous times. Very little is known about this BIPEDAL plant-eater, because only an incomplete skull has been found. However, it is important because from it scientists learned that the teeth in the upper and lower jaws of hadrosaurs were quite different from one another. This has made it possible to identify many teeth as hadrosaurian that were previously unidentifiable.

Classification: Hadrosauridae, Ornithopoda, Ornithischia

ARCHAEOPTERYX   (ar-kee-OP-ter-ix) "Ancient Wing" (Greek *archaio* = ancient + *pteryx* = wing, because it was an ancient bird.)

Not a dinosaur, but a crow-sized Jurassic bird—the old-

ARCHAEOPTERYX

est bird known. Many scientists believe *Archaeopteryx* was the first step in the evolution of birds from small COELUROSAURS. *Archaeopteryx* looked very much like a tiny dinosaur with feathers and wings. It probably could fly, but not far. Three clawed fingers extended from the front of each wing. The tail was long and bony, and the jaws were lined with teeth. *Archaeopteryx* probably ate insects. Its fossils have been found in West Germany. These fossils were formed in fine-grained limestone; they clearly show the impressions of the long feathers on the wings and tail. The first *Archaeopteryx* specimen ever found is owned by the Natural History Museum in London. It is considered the most valuable fossil in the world.

ARCHAEORNITHOMIMUS (ar-kee-or-NITH-uh-my-mus) "Ancient Bird Mimic" (Greek *archaio* = ancient + *ornithos* = bird + *mimos* = mimic, because it was bird-like.)

An early ORNITHOMIMID ("ostrich dinosaur"). It lived during Late Cretaceous times. This dinosaur was BIPEDAL; it had three-fingered hands with nearly straight claws. The toe claws, however, were curved. *Archaeornithomimus* probably ate insects and small animals. Its fossils have been found in both the eastern United States and Mongolia, but it is known only from fragments and its size is unknown.

Classification: Coelurosauria, Theropoda, Saurischia

ARCHELON (AR-kee-lon) "Ruler Tortoise" (Greek *archos* = ruler + *chelone* = tortoise, because it is the largest known turtle.)

Not a dinosaur, but a giant turtle that lived in an inland sea that covered the middle of North America in Cretaceous times. *Archelon* ate fish. It was about 12 feet (3.5 m) long. Its fossils have been found in South Dakota.

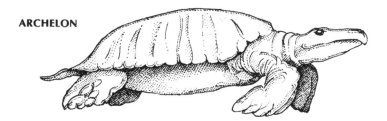

ARCHELON

archosaurs or **Archosauria** (ar-ko-SAWR-ee-ah) "Ruling Lizards" (Greek *archos* = ruler + *sauros* = lizard, because they were the dominant life form of the MESOZOIC ERA.)

A subclass of REPTILIA; a group of higher vertebrates (animals with backbones) including the CROCODILIANS, DINOSAURS, PTEROSAURS, and THECODONTS. Since birds are now thought to be descendants of dinosaurs, some scientists propose that Archosauria should be raised to class level and that it should include birds.

ARGYROSAURUS (ar-JYE-ruh-sawr-us) "Silver Lizard" (Greek *argyros* = silver + *sauros* = lizard, because it was found in Argentina, or "Silver Land.")

A massive SAUROPOD, larger than APATOSAURUS, that lived in Argentina during Late Cretaceous times. Only the legs and a few vertebrae have been recovered, but these are quite similar to those of DIPLODOCUS, and *Argyrosaurus* may be a Cretaceous descendant of that dinosaur. Like all sauropods, *Argyrosaurus* was a four-legged plant-eater.

Classification: Sauropoda, Sauropodomorpha, Saurischia

ARISTOSUCHUS (ah-RISS-tuh-sook-us) "Best Crocodile" (Greek *aristos* = best + *souchos* = crocodile, because at first it was thought to be CROCODILIAN.)

A small COELUROSAUR. This two-legged meat-eater lived during Late Jurassic or Early Cretaceous times. It is known only from fragments found on the Isle of Wight, but it is thought to be closely related to COELURUS or ORNITHOLESTES, and probably resembled them.

Classification: Coelurosauria, Theropoda, Saurischia

ARKANOSAURUS (ar-KAN-uh-sawr-us) "Arkansas Lizard" (Named for the state in which it was found + Greek *sauros* = lizard.)

The name given to the foot bones of a dinosaur found in Cretaceous sediments in Arkansas. Arkansas was covered by a shallow sea at this time. The bones were probably washed into the sea by flood waters. This dinosaur was a BIPEDAL meat-eater that probably resembled ORNITHOMIMUS. Although *Arkanosaurus* has been named and classified as an ORNITHOMIMID, it has not, at this time, been certified.

Classification: Coelurosauria, Theropoda, Saurischia

armor plating

The bodies of ANKYLOSAURS were covered with rows of plates, or scutes, that were made of hard, bony material and keeled like the bottom of a boat. In the ANKYLOSAURIDAE these plates were oval and were hollowed out underneath, so they were relatively thin and light. Some rose to form low pointed cones. These plates did not touch one another. The plates of the NODOSAURIDAE were thicker and heavier than those of the Ankylosauridae. They were solid and flat (or nearly flat) underneath. Some rose to form tall conical spikes. The plates, or scutes, of Nodosauridae contacted or touched each other and were rectangular or square in outline, rather than oval.

There is evidence that some ORNITHOPODS and some SAUROPODS (TITANOSAURIDS) had bony, armor plates, similar to those of the ankylosaurids, attached to their SKIN.

STEGOSAURS had two rows of large, thin, leaf-shaped bony plates running down the middle of their backs. Although these were once thought to be defense mechanisms, it is now believed that they regulated the body temperature. These plates contained blood vessels. Wind flowing across the plates would cool the blood flowing through the blood vessels.

armored dinosaurs

See ANKYLOSAURS.

ARRHINOCERATOPS (ah-RHINE-o-sair-tops) "Without a Nose-horn Face" (Greek *a* = without + *rhinokerat* = nose-horn + *ops* = face, referring to the small nose-horn.)

A Late Cretaceous CERATOPSIAN with a very short nose horn and two long, slightly forward-curving brow horns. Its long neck shield was armed with spikes, and its snout ended in a short, horny beak. This four-legged plant-eater is known from a skull found in Alberta, Canada.

Classification:
Ceratopsidae,
Ceratopsia,
Ornithischia

ARRHINOCERATOPS

ASTRODON (ASS-tro-don) "Star Tooth" (Greek *astro* = star + *don* = tooth)

Same as PLEUROCOELUS.

Classification: Sauropoda, Sauropodomorpha, Saurischia

atlantosaurids or **Atlantosauridae** (at-lan-tuh-SAWR-ih-dee) "Southern Lizards" (Named after ATLANTOSAURUS.)

A name sometimes used for one of the two major divisions of SAUROPODS. Most paleontologists now prefer to use the name TITANOSAURIDAE for this group, because *Atlantosaurus* is no longer considered a valid name for a dinosaur.

Atlantosaurinae (at-lan-tuh-SAWR-ih-nee) "Southern Lizards" (Named after ATLANTOSAURUS.)

One of the subfamilies of the TITANOSAURIDAE (ATLANTOSAURIDAE) SAUROPODS. APATOSAURUS was the only member of this family, and it is now placed in the new DIPLODOCIDAE family.

ATLANTOSAURUS (at-lan-tuh-SAWR-us) "Strong Lizard" (Named for Atlantis, god of strength in Greek and Latin mythology + Greek *sauros* = lizard.)

Name given to the fossils of the first four-footed dinosaur to be discovered in North America. This dinosaur was originally called TITANOSAURUS, but this name had already been given to another dinosaur, so the name was changed to *Atlantosaurus.* However, it is known from very fragmentary material. Some think it is the same as APATOSAURUS, but there is not enough material to make a definite identification.

Classification: Sauropoda, Sauropodomorpha, Saurischia

AUSTROSAURUS (OSS-tro-sawr-us) "Southern Lizard" (Latin *auster* = south + Greek *sauros* = lizard, because it was found in Australia.)

An Early Cretaceous SAUROPOD. This giant, four-legged plant-eater was closely related to CETIOSAURUS and probably resembled that dinosaur. It was probably about the same size—about 50 feet (15 m) long, but its forelegs were slightly longer than those of *Cetiosaurus*. Although this dinosaur is known from very fragmentary material, it is important, because it shows that sauropods were living in Australia in Early Cretaceous times. It may have survived into Late Cretaceous times.

Classification: Sauropoda, Sauropodomorpha, Saurischia

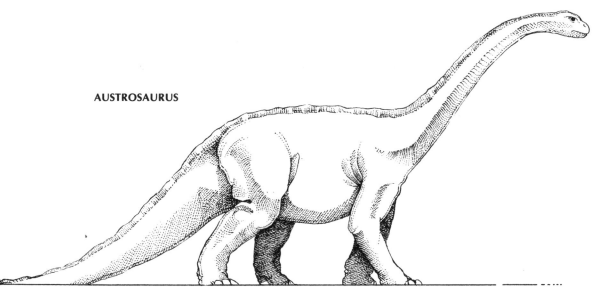

AUSTROSAURUS

AVIMIMUS (a-vee-MY-mus) "Bird Mimic" (Latin *avis* = bird + Greek *mimos* = mimic, because it was bird-like.)

A small Late Cretaceous COELUROSAUR discovered in Mongolia. It is known from a partial skeleton of one individual and fragments of another. This BIPEDAL dinosaur is estimated to be 3.5 to 5 feet (1 to 1.5 m) long, including its long tail. It probably ate lizards and insects.

Classification: Coelurosauria, Theropoda, Saurischia

B

BACTROSAURUS (BAK-truh-sawr-us) "Staff Lizard" (Greek *baktron* = staff + *sauros* = lizard, because it was the staff, or beginning, of a new line of dinosaurs.)

One of the earliest known HADROSAURS (duck-billed dinosaurs). It is known from a nearly complete skeleton and a partial skull. Although we don't know what the top of its head looked like, scientists think that *Bactrosaurus* was close to (if not the) ancestor of the hollow-crested duckbills (the LAMBEOSAURINES). It had robust limbs, high spines on its pelvic vertebrae, and other features that are similar to those of the lambeosaurines. This BIPEDAL plant-eater evolved in Mongolia about the middle of the Cretaceous Period.

Bactrosaurus was 13 feet (4 m) long and 6.5 feet (1.9 m) tall at the hips. It had fewer teeth than later hadrosaurs.

Classification: Hadrosauridae, Ornithopoda, Ornithischia

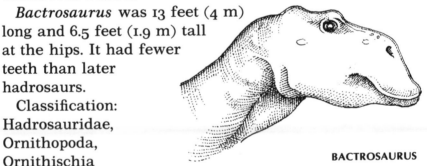

BACTROSAURUS

BAGACERATOPS (bah-gah-SAIR-uh-tops) "Small Horned Face" (Mongolian *baga* = small + Greek *keratops* = horned face, referring to its overall size.)

A tiny Late Cretaceous PROTOCERATOPSIAN. This four-legged plant-eater was only 3 feet (90 cm) long. It had a small horn on its nose and a short frill or shield that protected its neck. Its fossils were found in Mongolia.

Classification: Protoceratopsidae, Ceratopsia, Ornithischia

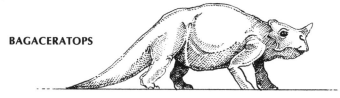

BAGACERATOPS

BAHARIASAURUS (bah-ha-REE-uh-sawr-us) "Baharije Lizard" (Named for Baharije Oasis, near where it was found + Greek *sauros* = lizard.)

Name given to a few bones of a large CARNOSAUR found in Late Cretaceous deposits in Egypt. This BIPEDAL meat-eater belonged to the same family as MEGALOSAURUS, and probably resembled that dinosaur.

Classification: Carnosauria, Theropoda, Saurischia

BARAPASAURUS (bah-RAH-puh-sawr-us) "Big Leg Lizard" (Indian *bara* = big or massive + *pas* = leg + Greek *sauros* = lizard, referring to the size of the leg bone.)

BARAPASAURUS

One of the earliest known SAUROPODS. This giant four-legged plant-eater was only slightly smaller than DI-PLODOCUS. Unlike most sauropods, it had rather slender limbs. Its teeth were spoon-shaped. It probably resembled CAMARASAURUS or *Diplodocus* in shape. It is known from well-preserved material of at least eight or nine individuals. These individuals varied greatly in size, the largest being nearly twice as large as the smallest, suggesting that YOUNG and older animals HERDED together. These fossils were found in Early Jurassic sediments in India.

Classification: Sauropoda, Sauropodomorpha, Saurischia

BAROSAURUS (BAR-uh-sawr-us) "Heavy Lizard" (Greek *baros* = heavy + *sauros* = lizard, referring to its heavy neck bones.)

BAROSAURUS

A SAUROPOD that resembled DIPLODOCUS. *Barosaurus* was the same overall length as *Diplodocus,* but had a shorter tail and a longer neck. This four-legged plant-eater measured 90 feet (27 m) from snout to the tip of its tail. Its neck was 30 feet (9 m) long. *Barosaurus* lived in western North America and east Africa in Late Jurassic times. Three nearly complete skeletons have been found at the Dinosaur National Monument in Utah. Seven GAS-TROLITHS were found with the bones of one specimen, giving evidence that these animals swallowed food whole and swallowed stones to grind it up.

Classification: Sauropoda, Sauropodomorpha, Saurischia

BAVARISAURUS (bah-VAR-eh-sawr-us) "Bavaria Lizard" (Named for Bavaria in Germany, where it was found + Greek *sauros* = lizard.)

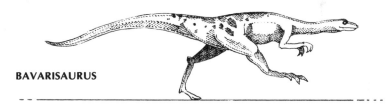

BAVARISAURUS

Not a dinosaur, but a small, fast-running ground lizard of Late Jurassic Germany. This animal had a very long tail and short forelimbs. It probably ran on two legs. A nearly complete specimen of this lizard was found within the skeleton of a COMPSOGNATHUS. It was once thought that this skeleton was an unborn baby *Compsognathus.* We now know it was the last dinner of the little dinosaur, giving proof that *Compsognathus* preyed upon small lizards.

Beringia (ber-ING-ee-a)   (Named after the land bridge that spanned the Bering Straight.)

During the Cretaceous Period, the western part of North America was separated from the eastern part of the continent by a wide, shallow sea. However, the western part of North America was connected with the eastern part of Asia. This land mass is called Beringia.

biped (BY-ped)   "Two feet" (Latin *bi* = two + *ped* = foot.)

Any animal that stands or walks on its two hind legs. "Bipedal" means two-footed. THEROPODS were bipeds; so were ORNITHOPODS such as HADROSAURS and IGUANODONTS. Human beings and birds are also bipeds. Compare with QUADRUPED.

bipedal

See BIPED.

bird-hipped dinosaurs

See ORNITHISCHIANS.

BOTHRIOSPONDYLUS   (bah-three-uh-SPON-dih-lus)

"Trench Vertebrae" (Greek *bothrion* = trench + Latin *spondylus* = vertebrae, referring to the grooves in its vertebrae.)

A large Late Jurassic SAUROPOD. This four-legged planteater was similar to CAMARASAURUS. Its forelegs were about as long as its hind legs. It is estimated that this dinosaur was about 65 feet (19.8 m) long. It had large teeth, and like all sauropods had a long neck and tail. It is known only from a few teeth and vertebrae. Its fossils have been found in England and Madagascar.

Classification: Sauropoda, Sauropodomorpha, Saurischia

brachiosaurids or **Brachiosauridae** (brak-ee-uh-SAWR-ih-dee) "Arm Lizard" (Named after BRACHIOSAURUS.) Sometimes called CAMARASAURIDAE.

A family of SAUROPODS with spatulate (or spoon-shaped) teeth and forelimbs as long or longer than the hind. Dinosaurs in this group had only four vertebrae in their pelvic area. These plant-eaters were the largest of the dinosaurs —some may have been as much as 100 feet (30 m) long or more. Brachiosauridae lived worldwide during the Jurassic and Cretaceous times. This family is divided into four subfamilies: CETIOSAURINAE, BRACHIOSAURINAE, CAMARASAURINAE, and EUHELOPODINAE. It has been proposed that these subfamilies be raised to family status. A study is being made to do that.

Brachiosaurinae (brak-ee-uh-SAWR-ih-nee) "Arm Lizards" (Named after BRACHIOSAURUS.)

A subfamily of brachiosaurid SAUROPODS. In this group the forelegs were longer than the hind. They lived in North America, Europe, Africa, and Asia. BOTHRIOSPONDYLUS, BRACHIOSAURUS, PLEUROCOELUS, REBBACHISAURUS, ZIGONGOSAURUS, and possibly "ULTRASAURUS" were members of this subfamily. This subfamily may soon be raised to the family level.

brachiosaurs (BRAK-ee-uh-sawrs) "Arm Lizards" (Named after BRACHIOSAURUS.)

Same as BRACHIOSAURIDS or BRACHIOSAURINAE. This is just a shortened form of the other two names.

BRACHIOSAURUS (BRAK-ee-uh-sawr-us) "Arm Lizard" (Latin *bracchium* = arm + Greek *sauros* = lizard, referring to its long forelegs.)

A gigantic Jurassic SAUROPOD, one of the largest known land animals. A complete skeleton found in Tanzania, now at the Humboldt University Natural History Museum in East Berlin, stands 40 feet (12 m) tall—taller than a four-story building—and is 85 feet (26 m) long. A live *Brachiosaurus* probably weighed 70 or 80 tons (63 to 72 metric tons). Its body was more massive than that of any other sauropod. Its neck was 28 feet (8.5 m) long, but its tail was short. Unlike most sauropods, *Brachiosaurus* had longer forelegs than hind legs. Its shoulders towered 19 feet (5.8 m) above the ground.

BRACHIOSAURUS

This four-legged dinosaur roamed the forests of the Jurassic world eating the tops from tall trees. Contrary to popular belief, it could not have lived in deep water—it would not have been able to breathe. The pressure of the water on the lungs would have been too great.

The remains of *Brachiosaurus* have been found in the western United States as well as in Africa and Europe.

Classification: Sauropoda, Sauropodomorpha, Saurischia

BRACHYCERATOPS (brak-ee-SAIR-uh-tops) "Short Horned Face" (Greek *brachys* = short + *keratops* = horned face, because it was a short-faced CERATOPSIAN.)

Name given to the fossils of five small, short-frilled ceratopsians that were found together in Montana. These horned dinosaurs were only 6 feet (1.8 m) long, and are believed to be juveniles. It was first thought that they were young specimens of CENTROSAURUS or MONOCLONIUS, but then a few bones and the skull of an adult ceratopsian were found near the same site. The bones of the adult were nearly twice as large as those of the five juveniles. The adult represented a new genus. It had a very large horn on its nose, short brow horns, and a short knobbed frill. The horns and frills of the juveniles more closely resembled those of the adult than those of *Centrosaurus* or *Monoclonius* and were therefore assigned to the same genus.

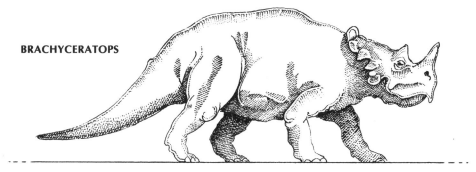

BRACHYCERATOPS

Finding five half-grown ceratopsians together near an adult suggests to some scientists that the YOUNG may have received some kind of PARENTAL CARE.

These four-legged plant-eaters lived during Late Cretaceous times.

Classification: Ceratopsidae, Ceratopsia, Ornithischia

BRACHYLOPHOSAURUS (brak-ee-LO-fuh-sawr-us) "Short-crested Lizard" (Greek *brachys* = short + *lophos* = crest + *sauros* = lizard, referring to its small crest.)

A Late Cretaceous HADROSAUR (duck-billed dinosaur). *Brachylophosaurus* had a small hump on its nose and a small, thin, bony crest over the top of its head. It belonged to the HADROSAURINE group of hadrosaurs. This two-legged plant-eater was about 16.5 feet (5 m) tall, and, like all hadrosaurs, it ran with its body horizontal and its tail extended for balance. *Brachylophosaurus* lived in forests, browsing on leaves and flowering plants. It is known from fairly complete material found in Alberta, Canada.

Classification: Hadrosauridae, Ornithopoda, Ornithischia

BRACHYLOPHOSAURUS

brains

Scientists have not found dinosaur brains, but they know how large some of them were. Casts formed when mud filled the brain cavities of dead dinosaurs are almost the same size and shape as the dinosaurs' brains. These casts also show the roots of nerves in the brains, and help us to understand how well a particular dinosaur could smell or hear. (See SENSORY PERCEPTION.)

Most dinosaurs (like modern reptiles) had rather small brains in comparison to their body size. The brains of huge SAUROPODS, for example, were only about the size of a modern dog's brain. STEGOSAURUS had a ridiculously small brain. It was only the size of a golf ball, and was the smallest, in comparison to the size of the animal, of all the dinosaurs' brains. However, sauropods and *Stegosaurus* were specially adapted to get along without large brains. Each animal had an enlargement in the spinal cord in the region of its hips. This nerve center was larger than the brain itself, and it controlled the dinosaur's hind legs and tail. (This nerve center has sometimes been called a second brain, but it was not.) The brains of ANKYLOSAURS were probably small also, because they had small heads.

Not all dinosaurs had tiny brains. The brains of CERA-TOPSIANS and THEROPODS were relatively large. Of all the dinosaurs, the DROMAEOSAURIDS ("emu lizards") had the largest brains, in comparison to their body size. The brain of STENONYCHOSAURUS was seven times as large as the brain of any living ARCHOSAUR of similar body weight. Its brain was larger than that of an ostrich, and it was probably at least as intelligent as an ostrich. (Also see INTELLI-GENCE.)

The brains of ORNITHOPODS were somewhat larger than those of the ankylosaurs and the ceratopsians.

brontosaurs   (BRON-tuh-sawrz)   "Thunder Lizards" (Named after BRONTOSAURUS.)

Another name for SAUROPODS, the largest land animals that ever lived. Any giant, four-legged, plant-eating, land-dwelling SAURISCHIAN dinosaur may be called a brontosaur. These dinosaurs are also sometimes called CETIOSAURS.

BRONTOSAURUS (BRON-tuh-sawr-us) "Thunder Lizard" (Greek *bronte* = thunder + *sauros* = lizard, perhaps because its discoverer thought its footfalls would have been thunderous.)

The best known of the dinosaurs. Its correct name is APATOSAURUS, because that name was given first. The fossil bones that were named *Apatosaurus,* in 1877, belong to the same kind of animal as those discovered later, in 1879, and named *Brontosaurus.*

Classification: Sauropoda, Sauropodomorpha, Saurischia

C

CALLOVOSAURUS (cal-LOW-vuh-sawr-us) "Callovian Lizard" (Named for the Callovian Rock Formation, from which it was recovered + Greek *sauros* = lizard.)

An ORNITHOPOD of the CAMPTOSAURID family. It lived during Mid-Jurassic times in England. This BIPEDAL plant-eater was about 9 feet (2.75 m) long and possibly weighed 125 pounds (56.8 kg). It is known from incomplete material, and was once thought to be a species of CAMPTOSAURUS.

Classification: Iguanodontidae or Camptosauridae, Ornithopoda, Ornithischia

camarasaurids or **Camarasauridae** (kam-uh-ruh-SAWR-ih-dee) "Chambered Lizards" (Named after CAMARASAURUS.) Also commonly called CAMARASAURS.

A name sometimes used for the family of spatulate-toothed (spoon-shaped teeth) SAUROPODS whose forelimbs were as long as or longer than the hind legs. This group is more frequently called the BRACHIOSAURIDAE.

Camarasaurinae (kam-uh-ruh-SAWR-ih-nee) "Chambered Lizards" (Named after CAMARASAURUS.) Sometimes called CAMARASAURS.

A subfamily of BRACHIOSAURID SAUROPODS whose forelimbs and hind limbs were nearly equal. Their skulls were large, but the snouts were shorter than those of other sauropods. The necks and tails were relatively shorter. These four-legged plant-eaters were from 30 to 60 feet (9 to 18 m) long. They lived in North America and Europe from Mid-Jurassic to Early Cretaceous. *Camarasaurus* is the only certainly known member of this family.

camarasaurs (KAM-uh-ruh-sawrz)

A name commonly used in the place of CAMARASAURIDAE or CAMARASAURINAE.

CAMARASAURUS (KAM-uh-ruh-sawr-us) "Chambered Lizard" (Greek *kamara* = chamber + *sauros* = lizard, referring to the holes in its vertebrae.)

The most common SAUROPOD in North America during Middle and Late Jurassic times. It also lived in Europe where it survived into Early Cretaceous times. *Camarasaurus* was one of the smallest sauropods. Its neck was shorter, and its tail was *much* shorter than those of most, but the tail was more powerful than the tails of other sauropods. *Camarasaurus* grew to be 30 to

60 feet (9 to 18 m) long and 15 feet (4.5 m) high at the hips. There were holes in the vertebrae to lighten the weight of the backbone. Its forelegs were nearly as long as its hind legs, making the back almost level. The head of this peaceful plant-eater was larger and shorter than those of most sauropods. Many skeletons of this dinosaur have been found in western United States. A complete skeleton of a 17-foot (5.2 m) long juvenile in nearly perfect condition was found in Utah.

Classification: Sauropoda, Sauropodomorpha, Saurischia

CAMARASAURUS

camptosaurids or **Camptosauridae** (kamp-tuh-SAWR-ih-dee) "Bent Lizards" (Named after CAMPTOSAURUS.) Also called CAMPTOSAURS.

A family of ORNITHOPODS sometimes listed as a subfamily of IGUANODONTIDS. Their forelegs were much shorter than the hind legs, but they were stout, and the five-fingered hands were strong. This makes scientists believe that although these plant-eaters were basically BIPEDAL, they probably grazed on all fours. The feet had four toes. Both fingers and toes were tipped with hoof-like

68

nails. Camptosaurid snouts ended in horny beaks. Camptosaurids were very common in North America from Middle Jurassic to possibly Early Cretaceous times. They also lived in England. They ranged from turkey-sized up to 17 feet (5.2 m). Camptosaurids were quite similar to iguanodontids and were possibly ancestors of that dinosaur family. Two GENERA of Camptosauridae are known: CALLOVOSAURUS and CAMPTOSAURUS.

camptosaurs (KAMP-tuh-sawrz)
A shortened version commonly used for CAMPTOSAURIDS.

CAMPTOSAURUS (KAMP-tuh-sawr-us) "Bent Lizard" (Greek *kamptos* = bent + *sauros* = lizard, because when it grazed on all fours, its body had to have been bent.)

An early ORNITHOPOD (a two-legged, plant-eating ORNITHISCHIAN). It was an ancestor of the HADROSAURS (duck-billed dinosaurs). Large numbers lived in North America and Europe during the Jurassic Period, and a few may have lived until Early Cretaceous times. There were many species of *Camptosaurus*. Their sizes ranged from turkey-sized to 17 feet (5.2 m) long and 7 feet (2 m) tall at the hips. This plant-eater usually walked on two legs with its body held horizontally, but probably grazed on all fours. Although the forelegs were quite short, they were strong. The hands had five fingers and the snout ended in

CAMPTOSAURUS

a horny beak. Many skeletons have been found in Wyoming, Colorado, and Utah.

Classification: Iguanodontidae? or Camptosauridae?, Ornithopoda, Ornithischia

CARCHARODONTOSAURUS (kar-kar-o-DON-tuh-sawr-us) "Sharp-toothed Lizard" (Greek *karcharo* = sharp-pointed + *odontos* = teeth + *sauros* = lizard.)

An Early Cretaceous CARNOSAUR whose fossils were found in Northern Africa. This two-legged meat-eater is known only from a few bones and teeth. It probably resembled MEGALOSAURUS, but it was somewhat smaller— about 26 feet (8 m) long. It had elongated spines on its neck vertebrae which may have served as places of attachment for the extra strong muscles needed to hold up its enormous head. Its teeth were less curved than those of most carnosaurs.

Classification: Carnosauria, Theropoda, Saurischia

carnivore (KAR-nih-vor) "Meat-eater" (Latin *carnis* = flesh + *vorare* = to devour.)

Any animal that eats mainly meat. Modern cats, dogs, and bears are carnivores. Carnivores have large, sharp teeth and powerful jaws. Some may, on occasion, eat plant food such as berries or grass. COELUROSAURS and CARNOSAURS were meat-eating (carnivorous) dinosaurs. Compare HERBIVORE; OMNIVORE.

carnivorous (kar-NIV-or-us)

See CARNIVORE.

carnosaurs or **Carnosauria** (kar-nuh-SAWR-ee-ah) "Meat-eating Lizards" (Latin *carnis* = flesh + Greek *sauros* = lizard.)

The infraorder of large THEROPODS. All were BIPEDAL

meat-eaters; all had huge skulls, short necks, heavy bones, chicken-like feet, powerful tails, knife-like teeth, and (except for the DEINOCHEIRIDS) short front legs. Some scientists think that carnosaurs may have been ENDOTHERMIC (warm-blooded). Carnosaurs lived from Late Triassic to Late Cretaceous times. They have been found on every continent except Antarctica.

There is not complete agreement on how carnosaurs should be divided. In the past, they were divided into four families: MEGALOSAURIDAE, SPINOSAURIDAE, DEINOCHEIRIDAE, and TYRANNOSAURIDAE.

Many scientists think that the Deinocheiridae should be classed as an infraorder rather than a family of carnosaurs, because unlike all other carnosaurs, they had very long arms and huge claws on their fingers. They have been found only in Cretaceous deposits in Mongolia. Only two are known—DEINOCHEIRUS and THERIZINOSAURUS.

It seems that any carnosaur that could not specifically be identified as belonging to one of the other families was placed in the Megalosauridae. Most of these were known from very fragmentary material. However, many dinosaurs once classed as MEGALOSAURIDS are now much better known and have been placed in families of their own. Members left in this family ranged from 25 to 30 feet (7.5 to 9 m) long, had massive heads, three or more fingers, and some had elongated spines on their vertebrae, but the spines were not as long as those of the SPINOSAURIDS. They lived during the Jurassic and Cretaceous Periods in Europe, North America, Africa, Asia, South America, and Madagascar.

Three new families of carnosaurs have been formed from dinosaurs once classed as megalosaurids. The TERATOSAURIDAE—the earliest known carnosaurs—lived in Europe and South Africa during the Triassic Period. TERATOSAURUS is the best known of this group. The ALLOSAURIDAE had strong, heavy bodies; large, narrow skulls;

strong brow ridges, and three-fingered hands. They lived in North America and Asia during Late Jurassic and Early Cretaceous times. ACROCANTHOSAURUS, ALLOSAURUS, and CHILANTAISAURUS are examples of this family. The CERATOSAURIDAE had four fingers and a horn on the nose. CERATOSAURUS from Late Jurassic North America is the only known member of this family.

The TYRANNOSAURIDAE represents the culmination of carnosaur evolution. These dinosaurs had very short arms and only two fingers on their hands. They first appeared in Mongolia during the early part of Late Cretaceous times. However, most TYRANNOSAURIDS lived during the later part of the Late Cretaceous Period. They have been found in east Asia, western North America, and India. ALBERTOSAURUS, DASPLETOSAURUS, TARBOSAURUS, and TYRANNOSAURUS were Tyrannosauridae.

The SPINOSAURIDAE had very long spines on their vertebrae—some up to 6 feet (1.8 m) long. These spines may have supported a SKIN fold shaped like a fin that ran along the dinosaur's back. The spinosaurids lived in North Africa during the Cretaceous Period. SPINOSAURUS is the best known of these. Although some scientists place ALTISPINAX in this family group, it is so poorly known at this time that most scientists place it with the MEGALOSAURS.

Many recent discoveries do not fit neatly into any of these families and these have each been placed in separate families of their own.

Cenozoic (sen-uh-ZO-ik) **Era** "New Life" (Greek *kaino* = new + *zoikos* = life)

The "age of mammals"—the geological age following the MESOZOIC ERA. It began 65 million years ago and continues to the present. This is the time during which mammals became dominant. It is the era in which we are living.

CENTROSAURUS (SEN-truh-sawr-us) "Horned Lizard" (Greek *kentron* = horn or spike + *sauros* = lizard, because of the horn on its nose.)

A CERATOPSIAN (horned dinosaur) of Late Cretaceous North America. This four-legged plant-eater was very similar to MONOCLONIUS, but the 18-inch (46-cm) horn on its nose curved forward rather than to the rear, as did the horn of *Monoclonius*. Its frill was knobbed, and in the center of the back edge there were two long, hook-like projections. Some scientists consider this dinosaur a species of *Monoclonius*. Eighteen separate individuals have been found in Alberta, Canada, suggesting that ceratopsians traveled in large HERDS.

Classification: Ceratopsidae, Ceratopsia, Ornithischia

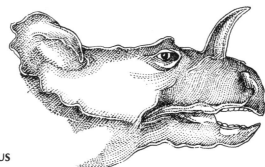

CENTROSAURUS

CERATOPS (SAIR-uh-tops) "Horned Face" (Greek *keratos* = horned + *ops* = face, referring to the horns.)

Name given to a pair of small brow horns found in Late Cretaceous rocks in Montana. *Ceratops* is probably a juvenile specimen of another CERATOPSIAN.

Classification: Ceratopsidae, Ceratopsia, Ornithischia

ceratopsians or **Ceratopsia** (sair-uh-TOP-see-ah) "Horned Faces" (Named after CERATOPS.)

The suborder of ORNITHISCHIAN dinosaurs with horns on

their faces. Ceratopsians resembled rhinoceroses, and possibly ran like them. However, ceratopsians had neck frills, or shields, and much longer and heavier tails than rhinoceroses. Some ceratopsians were pig-sized; others were quite large. They probably ate cycad and palm leaves, nipping off leaves with their parrot-like beaks and chopping them up with their scissor-like teeth.

There were three families of ceratopsians: the PSIT-TACOSAURIDAE, the PROTOCERATOPSIDAE, and the CERATOP-SIDAE. The Psittacosauridae were the most primitive group and are thought to be the ancestors of all ceratopsians. They had parrot-like beaks, large heads, and the faintest hint of a frill. They were mainly BIPEDAL. The Protoceratopsidae were almost completely QUADRUPEDAL and were the smallest of the four-legged ceratopsians. They had very small horns on their noses, or none at all. They had very short neck frills. There were two kinds of Ceratopsidae. Some had short nose-horns, long brow horns, and long frills. Others had long nose-horns, short brow horns, and short frills.

The Ceratopsians seem to have EVOLVED in Mongolia. They were the last group of dinosaurs to evolve and were among the last to become extinct. (See EXTINCTION.) Most of these Late Cretaceous dinosaurs have been found in North America, but a few kinds have been found in Mongolia. PROTOCERATOPS, MONOCLONIUS, STYRACOSAURUS, TOROSAURUS, and TRICERATOPS are some of the best known of this group.

ceratopsids or **Ceratopsidae** (sair-uh-TOP-see-dee) "Horned Faces" (Named after CERATOPS.)

A family of the CERATOPSIA (horned dinosaurs). Members of this family had horns on either their snouts or their brows, and sometimes on both. They had frills extending back over their necks. These four-legged plant-eaters were from 12 to 25 feet (3.5 to 7.5 m) long. They lived in North America during the Late Cretaceous Period. There were two kinds of ceratopsids. One group, the short-frilled ceratopsians, had short shields that did not reach the shoulders, long nose-horns, and short brow horns. BRACHYCERATOPS, CENTROSAURUS, MONOCLONIUS, PACHYRHINOSAURUS, and STYRACOSAURUS were members of this group. Long-frilled ceratopsians had shields that extended back to or over the shoulders, short nose-horns, and long brow horns. ANCHICERATOPS, ARRHINOCERATOPS, CHASMOSAURUS, PENTACERATOPS, and TOROSAURUS were members of this group.

CERATOSAURUS (sair-AT-o-sawr-us) "Horned Lizard" (Greek *keratos* = horned + *sauros* = lizard, referring to its nose-horn.)

A 20-foot (6-m) Jurassic CARNOSAUR. It was related to ALLOSAURUS and resembled that dinosaur, but it had a blade-like horn on its nose, and four-fingered hands. *Ceratosaurus* is the only known SAURISCHIAN with a horn. Like *Allosaurus, Ceratosaurus* had a huge head, saber-like teeth, bony knobs above its eyes, and short front legs.

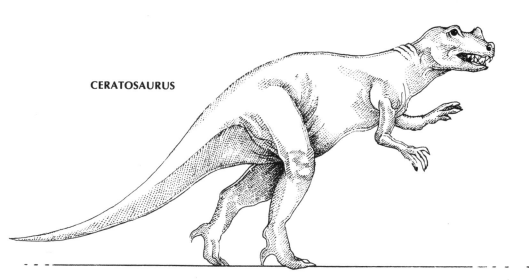

CERATOSAURUS

This powerful, savage hunter walked on two legs with its long, heavy tail extended to balance its head. Its fossils have been found in western North America and in Tanzania. A complete skeleton was found in Colorado.

Classification: Carnosauria, Theropoda, Saurischia

cetiosaurs or **Cetiosaurinae** (seet-ee-oh-SAWR-ih-nee) "Whale Lizards" (Named after CETIOSAURUS.)

A subfamily of BRACHIOSAURIDAE SAUROPODS. These were the most primitive sauropods. They lived from early Jurassic to Early Cretaceous times, and have been found in Europe, South America, North America, Africa, and Australia. They ranged in size from 45 to 72 feet (13.4 to 22 m) long. Their forelegs and hind legs were nearly equal in length. AMYGDALODON, AUSTROSAURUS, CETIOSAURUS, HAPLOCANTHOSAURUS, OHMDENOSAURUS, PATAGOSAURUS, and VOLKHEIMERIA were cetiosaurs.

CETIOSAURISCUS (SEET-ee-o-sawr-iss-kus) "Whale Lizard" (Modified from CETIOSAURUS, because it was once thought to be a species of CETIOSAURUS.)

A Late Jurassic SAUROPOD. It was a relative of DIPLODOCUS, and like that dinosaur, it had a long neck and a long whip-like tail. It grew to be 50 feet (15 m) long and weighed about 10 tons (9 metric tons). An incomplete skeleton was found in England. It was a four-legged plant-eater.

Classification: Sauropoda, Sauropodomorpha, Saurischia

CETIOSAURUS (SEET-ee-o-sawr-us) "Whale Lizard" (Greek *keteios* = sea monster + *sauros* = lizard, because scientists first thought it was a whale.)

A very early Middle Jurassic SAUROPOD from England,

Europe, and Africa. It was the first giant four-legged plant-eating SAURISCHIAN discovered. It resembled its relative, CAMARASAURUS, but its vertebrae were spongy instead of hollow as were those of later sauropods. It was 45 feet (13.5 m) long and weighed about 10 tons (9 metric tons). It is known from most of a skeleton.

Classification: Sauropoda, Sauropodomorpha, Saurischia

CETIOSAURUS

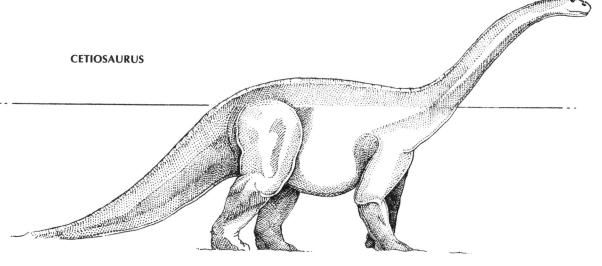

CHAMPSOSAURUS (CHAMP-suh-sawr-us) "Crocodile Lizard" (Latin *champsa* = crocodile + Greek *sauros* = lizard, because it resembled a crocodile.)

Not a dinosaur, but a large EOSUCHIAN. (Eosuchians were sprawling reptiles that resembled the gavials or

CHAMPSOSAURUS

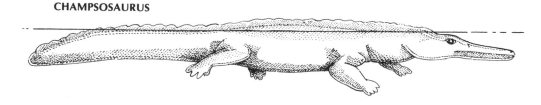

crocodiles of today, but were more closely related to lizards.) *Champsosaurus* lived in North American freshwater lakes and streams throughout the Cretaceous and into the TERTIARY PERIOD. It was 6 to 8 feet (1.8 to 2.5 m) long, and it was a meat-eater. It probably ate small dinosaurs.

CHASMOSAURUS (KAZ-muh-sawr-us) "Opening Lizard" (Latin *chasma* = opening + Greek *sauros* = lizard, referring to the openings in its frill.)

A medium-sized CERATOPSIAN. This horned dinosaur was about 16 feet (4.8 m) long and weighed about 2.5 tons (2.25 metric tons). It had a small horn on its nose and two fairly long, upward-curving horns on its brow. Very large holes through the bone lightened the weight of the very long frill or shield that stretched back over the neck and shoulders. These holes are technically called fenestrae. SKIN impressions show that *Chasmosaurus* had rows of button-like scales down its back. These scales were 2 inches (5 cm) across. This four-legged plant-eater ate ground plants that it cropped with a horny, parrot-like beak. Many fossils of *Chasmosaurus* have been discovered in Late Cretaceous sediments in Alberta, Canada.

Classification: Ceratopsidae, Ceratopsia, Ornithischia

CHASMOSAURUS

CHENEOSAURUS (KEEN-ee-uh-sawr-us) "Goose Lizard" (Greek *chen* = goose + *sauros* = lizard, referring to its goose-like bill.)

A small Late Cretaceous HADROSAUR whose fossils were found in Alberta, Canada. This duck-billed dinosaur had a rather large skull and a low, hollow crest. Some scientists believe it was a young HYPACROSAURUS or LAMBEOSAURUS. Others disagree; they believe it was a different dinosaur. This four-legged plant-eater is known only from a skull, some leg bones, and a few vertebrae.

Classification: Hadrosauridae, Ornithopoda, Ornithischia

CHIALINGOSAURUS (chye-ah-ling-uh-SAWR-us) "Chialing Lizard" (Named for the Chia-ling River, near which it was found + Greek *sauros* = lizard.)

A STEGOSAUR (plated dinosaur) that lived in China during Late Jurassic times. It was very similar to KENTROSAURUS, but perhaps was an earlier GENUS. It had smaller, more plate-like spikes than *Kentrosaurus* and was more slender. Like all stegosaurs, *Chialingosaurus* was a QUADRUPEDAL plant-eater. It is known from incomplete material.

Classification: Stegosauridae, Stegosauria, Ornithischia

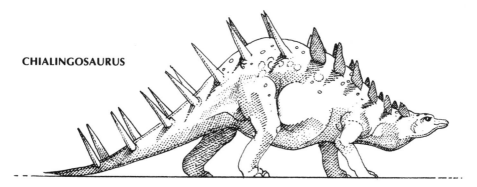

CHIALINGOSAURUS

CHILANTAISAURUS (CHYE-lan-tah-ee-sawr-us) "Chilantai Lizard" (Named for the Lake Chilantai in Inner Mongolia, near which it was found + Greek *sauros* = lizard.)

A CARNOSAUR with great hooked claws and three-fingered hands. This large BIPEDAL meat-eater was related to, and probably resembled, ALLOSAURUS or CERATOSAURUS; however, it had a less distinct brow ridge than those dinosaurs. *Chilantaisaurus* lived during Late Jurassic and Early Cretaceous times. It is known only from fragments found in Mongolia and China.

Classification: Carnosauria, Theropoda, Saurischia

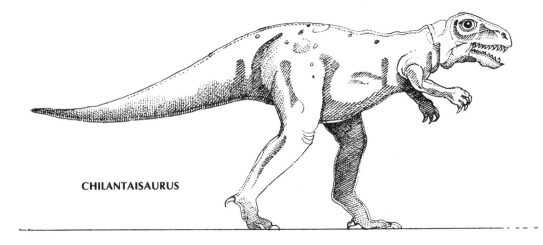

CHILANTAISAURUS

CHINGKANKOUSAURUS (ching-KANG-kow-sawr-us) "Chingkankou Lizard" (Named for the province in China, where it was found + Greek *sauros* = lizard.)

Name given to the shoulder blade of a large CARNOSAUR. This bone resembles the shoulder blade of TYRANNOSAURUS. It was found in Late Cretaceous deposits in eastern China. Like all carnosaurs, *Chingkankousaurus* was a BIPEDAL meat-eater.

Classification: Carnosauria, Theropoda, Saurischia

CHIROSTENOTES (kye-ROSS-ten-o-teez) "Narrow Hand"
(Greek *cheir* = hand + *steno* = narrow.)

A Late Cretaceous COELUROSAUR. It is known only from
fragments and a pair of hands similar to those of ORNI-
THOLESTES, but larger and narrower. The fossils of this
small meat-eater were found in Alberta, Canada.

Classification: Coelurosauria, Theropoda, Saurischia

CHUBUTISAURUS (choo-VOOT-uh-sawr-us) "Chubut Lizard" (Named for Chubut Province in Argentina, where it
was found + Greek *sauros* = lizard.)

A large Late Cretaceous SAUROPOD. It is known only
from fragments found in Argentina. It is important, because it shows that these huge animals were living in
South America in Late Cretaceous days. Like all sauropods, *Chubutisaurus* was a giant four-legged HERBIVORE
with a long neck and tail.

Classification: Sauropoda, Sauropodomorpha, Saurischia

CLAOSAURUS (CLAY-o-sawr-us) "Broken Lizard" (Greek
klao = broken + *sauros* = lizard, referring to the position of the skeleton when it was found.)

One of the oldest known North American HADROSAURS
(duck-billed dinosaurs.) It was much smaller than later
duckbills—only 12 feet (3.5 m) long. Its unusual feet and
teeth suggest that this HADROSAURINE (flat-headed hadrosaur) was one of the earliest. The small pointed teeth
were broader than those of later hadrosaurs and were set
in single rows rather than in banks. The hind feet had a
trace of a first toe as did the feet of IGUANODONTS.

Fossils of *Claosaurus* have been found in Kansas and
Wyoming. One complete skeleton found in Kansas shows
the animal frozen in what was apparently a running position, with the body held horizontally, the tail outstretched, and the head thrown back. This important dis-

covery provided strong evidence that hadrosaurs did run in this position, rather than upright, as had previously been thought. *Claosaurus* was a peaceful plant-eater. It lived during Late Cretaceous times.

Classification: Hadrosauridae, Ornithopoda, Ornithischia

CLAOSAURUS

claws

All dinosaurs had claws of some sort on their feet and hands. The THEROPODS had long sharp, talon-like claws similar to those of an eagle. These occurred on both the hands and the feet. The claws of CARNOSAURS often were quite long, ranging in length from 5 inches (13 cm) to 8 inches (20 cm). These claws were used to capture and hold prey, while being ripped apart by the enormous teeth. The DROMAEOSAURIDS such as DEINONYCHUS and VELOCIRAPTOR had a sickle-like claw on each foot. These were used to rip open the bellies of their prey, while the finger claws gripped the head or body. *Deinonychus*'s "switchblade" was 5 inches (13 cm) long. DEINOCHEIRUS had 12-inch (30-cm) claws.

The ORNITHOMIMIDS probably used their bear-like claws to dig up reptile EGGS, rip open logs, or rake leaves in search of insects and ground animals.

SAUROPODS had one or more long claws on each forefoot and three or more on their hind feet. These may have been used for digging their bowl-shaped NESTS in sand or mud.

ORNITHISCHIANS had blunt, hoof-like claws which served the same purpose of hoofed animals of today—to protect the ends of the toes. IGUANODON had a unique spike-like claw on each thumb. It was probably used as a defense weapon.

COELOPHYSIS (see-lo-FISE-iss) "Hollow Form" (Greek *koilos* = hollow + *physis* = form, referring to its hollow bones.)

A Late Triassic COELUROSAUR. This small two-legged meat-eater is one of the earliest and most primitive North American THEROPODS known. It was only 10 feet (3 m) long, counting the long slender tail that it carried stretched out behind. It stood 3 feet (90 cm) tall at the hips and weighed about 100 pounds (45 kg). Its head was small, but it had very long jaws. The neck was long and slender. The legs were also long and slender; the bones were hollow like those of a bird. The feet had three long forward-pointing toes and a dewclaw. The arms were short, like those of most other theropods, and the three-fingered hands could grip prey.

COELOPHYSIS

83

Some scientists think that *Coelophysis* was warm-blooded because it was apparently an active animal and capable of running very swiftly. *Coelophysis* probably lived in family groups. Whole families—from very small juveniles to adults—have been found together in New Mexico. This seems to indicate that the parents gave some care to their YOUNG. Two adult skeletons were found with the remains of tiny *Coelophysis* skeletons inside their rib cages. This may mean that *Coelophysis* gave birth to live young, but more likely it means that adults sometimes ate the young. Traces of *Coelophysis* have been found in the eastern United States as well as in New Mexico. PODOKESAURUS may be the same as this dinosaur.

Classification: Coelurosauria, Theropoda, Saurischia

coelurids or **Coeluridae** (see-LURE-ih-dee)   "Hollow Bones" (Named after COELURUS.)

A family of small, lightweight COELUROSAURS. This group were 2.5 to 6 feet (.76 to 1.8 m) long. They had hollow bones; their forelegs were long and slender. These BIPEDAL meat-eaters lived from Late Jurassic to Early Cretaceous times in North America, England, and possibly Australia. COELURUS, ORNITHOLESTES, and MICROVENATOR were members of this family.

coelurosaurs or **Coelurosauria** (see-lure-uh-SAWR-ee-ah) "Hollow Lizards" (Named after COELURUS + Greek *sauros* = lizard, referring to their hollow bones.)

The infraorder of small THEROPODS. Some scientists believe that these BIPEDAL meat-eaters were the ancestors of birds. They had hollow bones like birds, were fleet-footed, and had delicate, bird-like builds. Most had three-fingered hands. Some had quite large BRAINS in comparison to their body size, and these were the most intelligent of the dinosaurs. Some scientists believe that coelurosaurs were ENDOTHERMIC (warm-blooded).

Many kinds of coelurosaurs lived throughout the world, and they existed through most of the MESOZOIC ERA. This was the longest-lived of all dinosaur groups. Some coelurosaurs were no larger than a chicken, and others were larger than ostriches.

The Coelurosauria have been divided into eight families. The PROCOMPSOGNATHIDAE was the most primitive group. They were about 4 feet (1.2 m) long and had four-fingered hands and four toes. Their necks were long and flexible. They have been found in Late Triassic Germany. PROCOMPSOGNATHUS is the best known member of this family.

The PODOKESAURIDAE were small, very early coelurosaurs. They had short necks and forelegs. Their hands had five fingers. Their hind legs were long. Podokesauridae ranged from cat-sized to 10 feet (3 m) long or more. This family lived from the very earliest Late Triassic times to very early Jurassic times. They have been found in North America, South America, Africa, Europe, and Asia. COELOPHYSIS, HALTICOSAURUS, and PODOKESAURUS were members of this family, and some people think DILOPHOSAURUS belongs in this family instead of in the CARNOSAURS.

The SEGISAURIDAE were quite similar to the COELURIDAE, but were more primitive and had collar bones. Their vertebrae and the long bones of their body were solid instead of hollow. Segisauridae were rabbit-sized and in many respects resembled THECODONTS. They lived during Late Triassic and Early Jurassic times.

The Coeluridae were small and lightweight, because they had hollow bones. Their front legs were long and slender. Coeluridae ranged from 30 inches to 6 feet (76 cm to 8 m) long. They lived from Late Triassic to Early Cretaceous in North America, England, and possibly Australia. COELURUS, ORNITHOLESTES, and MICROVENATOR are members of this family.

The COMPSOGNATHIDAE had small pointed heads, flexible necks, hollow bones, and two-fingered hands. They were about the size of a chicken. They lived in Europe in Late Jurassic times. COMPSOGNATHUS is the best known member of this family.

The ORNITHOMIMIDAE resembled ostriches in shape, but had long tails, three toes instead of two, and arms instead of wings. They ranged from ostrich-sized to 20 feet (6 m) long and lived in North America, Israel, Asia, and Africa in Late Cretaceous times. DROMICEIOMIMUS, GALLIMIMUS, and STRUTHIOMIMUS were members of this family.

The DROMAEOSAURIDAE were advanced coelurosaurs. They had large brains, huge eyes, and sickle-like claws on their inner toes. They were about man-sized and lived in North America, South America, and Asia during Cretaceous times. DEINONYCHUS, DROMAEOSAURUS, STENONYCHOSAURUS, and VELOCIRAPTOR were members of this family. It has been proposed that this family be raised to infraorder—the DEINONYCHOSAURIA—because they are so different from other coelurosauria.

The OVIRAPTORIDAE closely resembled birds. They were toothless and were lightly built with hollow bones. Their skulls were unusually short and deep and had large brain cavities. They were about 5 feet (1.5 m) long and lived during Cretaceous times in Mongolia. OVIRAPTOR is the best known of this family.

Several new discoveries have been placed in separate families of their own.

COELUROSAURUS (see-LURE-uh-sawr-us) "Hollow Lizard" (Greek *koilos* = hollow + *sauros* = lizard, referring to its hollow bones.)

A Late Cretaceous COELUROSAUR. This two-legged meat-eater is known only from a few fossil bones found in New Jersey. It may be the same as STRUTHIOMIMUS.

Classification: Coelurosauria, Theropoda, Saurischia

COELURUS (see-LURE-us) "Hollow Bones" (Greek *koilos* = hollow, referring to the hollow vertebrae in its tail.)

A small COELUROSAUR of Late Jurassic North America. This BIPEDAL meat-eater has long been considered to be the same as ORNITHOLESTES. However, new studies of several more fossil bones of *Coelurus* show that the two are probably different GENERA. The tail bones of *Coelurus* were more hollow than those of *Ornitholestes* and some of the vertebrae and foot bones were longer and more complex.

It is estimated that *Coelurus* was 6 feet (1.8 m) long and 3 feet (90 cm) tall. It is known only from several vertebrae, foot and leg bones, and parts of the pelvis found in Wyoming.

Classification: Coelurosauria, Theropoda, Saurischia

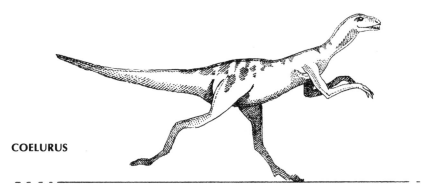

COELURUS

COLUMBOSAURIPUS (ko-lum-bo-SAWR-ih-pus) "Columbian Lizard Foot" (Named for British Columbia, where it was found + Greek *sauripous* = lizard foot.)

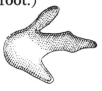

COLUMBOSAURIPUS TRACKS

Name given to COELUROSAUR footprints found in Early Cretaceous deposits of British Columbia, Canada. The feet that made these TRACKS had three toes. The toes were tapered and ended in long claws, similar to those of ORNITHOMIMIDS. Only hind feet left tracks so the animal was obviously BIPEDAL.

coloration

Scientists know almost everything about how dinosaurs looked except their color. They think that some dinosaurs may have been dull greens or browns similar to living crocodiles and alligators. Some may have been brightly colored like modern monitor lizards, Gila monsters, and iguanas. Their SKIN texture was quite similar to that of these animals.

COMPSOGNATHUS (komp-so-NAY-thus) "Elegant Jaw" (Greek *kompos* = elegant + *gnathos* = jaw.)

Until recently, the smallest known dinosaur. *Compsognathus* was about the size of a chicken. Only baby dinosaurs are smaller. This tiny COELUROSAUR lived in Europe during the Late Jurassic Period. It was BIPEDAL and had long, delicate, bird-like legs; a small, pointed head; and a flexible neck. Like all coelurosaurs, it had hollow bones and was fleet-footed. Its teeth were sharp, and its short arms were equipped with two-fingered hands with which it could catch and hold prey. It probably ate insects and small reptiles or mouse-like mammals. This coelurosaur was very bird-like, and it is possible that it had feathers.

COMPSOGNATHUS

A complete skeleton of *Compsognathus* was found in Germany. It had the skeleton of a smaller reptile within its body. Scientists once believed that this skeleton was a baby *Compsognathus*. It has now been shown that the skeleton was a young BAVARISAURUS—a small, fast-running ground lizard—which was the last meal for the *Compsognathus*. This discovery provides proof of the agility and swiftness of this little predator.

Classification: Coelurosauria, Theropoda, Saurischia

CORYTHOSAURUS (ko-RITH-uh-sawr-us) "Helmet Lizard" (Greek *korythos* = helmet + *sauros* = lizard, referring to the shape of its crest.)

A LAMBEOSAURINE HADROSAUR. This Late Cretaceous dinosaur measured 30 feet (9 m) from the tip of its duck-like bill to the end of its long, heavy tail. It weighed 2 to 3 tons (1.8 to 2.7 metric tons). A hollow, helmet-shaped crest adorned its long, narrow head, and hundreds of teeth

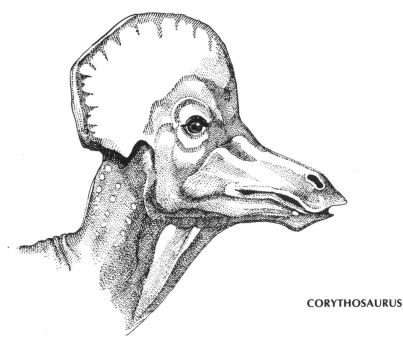

CORYTHOSAURUS

89

lined its jaws. Its SKIN had a pebbly surface, similar to the texture of a football. Three rows of larger bumps, or tubercles, covered the belly.

Corythosaurus was a BIPEDAL land dweller and probably a fast runner. It ate twigs, leaves, and pine needles. A nearly complete skeleton has been found in Alberta, Canada.

Classification: Hadrosauridae, Ornithopoda, Ornithischia

crests

Some dinosaurs and PTEROSAURS had bony crests on their heads. The purpose of these crests is not known.

The best known crested dinosaurs are the HADROSAURS (the duckbills), but not all hadrosaurs had crests. Among those that did, the crests varied greatly in size and shape. Some were only a small hump, while others were larger and hatchet-shaped, and still others were very long tubes. Some hadrosaur crests were of solid bone while others were hollow.

It was once thought that hollow crests served as snorkels, allowing the animals to hide or travel underwater. But it is now known that they could not have been used for this purpose—there were no openings in the top of them. The nostrils of LAMBEOSAURINES (hollow-crested hadrosaurs) were on the tip of their snouts, just as they were in all other duckbills.

It has also been suggested that the hollow crests were air storage spaces, but the crests were much too small to hold enough air for the lung capacity of these large animals.

More recent theories suggest that the crests were resonating chambers that made the hadrosaurs' voices louder. Or they may have improved the animals' sense of smell.

In some lambeosaurines, air passages ran from the nostrils up into the hollow crest before it descended down into the throat. Some scientists suggest these crests may have been an adaptation that allowed these hadrosaurs to breathe and eat at the same time. Since these animals probably ate almost continuously, this would have been very useful.

Solid crests may simply have marked different species, as the horns of antelope do today. Or they may have been sex characteristics—males having larger crests than females.

DILOPHOSAURUS, a large meat-eating dinosaur, had a double crest. It is the only known THEROPOD with a crest. This crest consisted of two large, blade-like ridges that ran lengthwise along the top of its head.

PTERANODON, a pterosaur, had a long crest on the back of its head. This flying reptile's crest may have been used as a brake when the creature landed, or it may have acted as a rudder. It might have been a sexual characteristic, since some did not have crests.

Cretaceous (kreh-TAY-shus) **Period** (From Latin *cretaceus* = chalk, referring to the chalk deposits of southeast England, which are of this age.)

The last of the three periods of the MESOZOIC ERA. It began about 135 million years ago and ended 65 million years ago. At the end of this geological time interval, the dinosaurs became EXTINCT.

Little is known about the dinosaurs of the first half of the Cretaceous Period. Not many exposed outcroppings of Early Cretaceous rocks containing fossils have been found. It is in the Late Cretaceous deposits that the most dinosaurs have been found.

crocodilians or **Crocodilia** (crok-o-DIL-ee-ah) (From Greek *krokodelos* = crocodile.)

Not dinosaurs, but an order of ARCHOSAURS. This is the

order to which modern alligators, crocodiles, and gavials belong. They first appeared in very late Triassic or early Jurassic times and have continued to live successfully to the present day. The crocodilians were close cousins of dinosaurs. They EVOLVED from the same branch of reptiles, the THECODONTS. ORNITHISCHIANS and SAURISCHIANS were no more closely related to one another than they were to crocodilians.

cycad or **Cycada** (SYE-kad-ah)

An order of plants which was the dominant plant of the MESOZOIC ERA. It had palm-like crowns from which stems of fern-like leaves grew. They flourished from the Triassic to the Cretaceous Periods, and one species exists in subtropical areas of the world today. Cycad plants were probably an important part of the diet of some plant-eating dinosaurs.

D

DACENTRURUS (day-sen-TROO-rus) "Very Spiny Lizard" (Greek *da* = very + *kentron* = spiny + *sauros* = lizard, referring to the spines on its back.) Also called OMOSAURUS.

A Jurassic STEGOSAUR. It was quite similar to STEGOSAURUS, but it had two rows of huge spikes running along its back and tail instead of plates, and its forelegs were somewhat longer than those of *Stegosaurus. Dacentrurus* was also smaller than *Stegosaurus;* it was only 15 feet (4.5 m) long.

This four-legged plant-eater is known from a nearly complete skeleton found in England. It has also been found in France and Portugal. Dinosaur EGGS found in Portugal are thought to be those of this dinosaur.

Classification: Stegosauridae, Stegosauria, Ornithischia

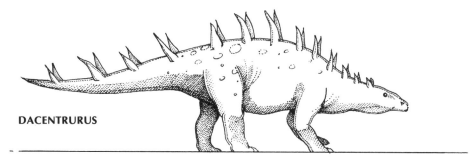

DACENTRURUS

DASPLETOSAURUS (dass-PLEE-tuh-sawr-us) "Frightful Lizard" (Greek *daspletos* = frightful + *sauros* = lizard, because of its fearsome teeth.)

A large Late Cretaceous CARNOSAUR. This two-legged,

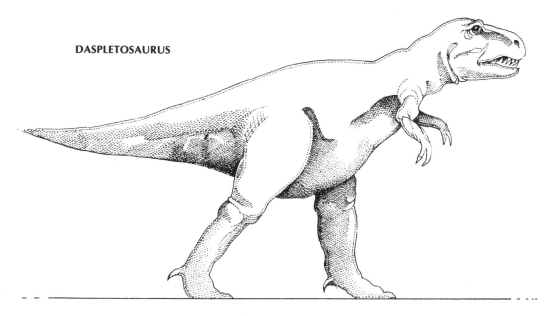

DASPLETOSAURUS

heavy-bodied dinosaur was a close relative of TYRAN-NOSAURUS, but was not as large. It measured 30 feet (9 m) long and may have weighed 7,000 pounds (3,175 kg). Like *Tyrannosaurus,* it had very short arms and two-fingered hands. A skeleton of this meat-eater, lacking only the hind limbs, was found in Alberta, Canada.

Classification: Carnosauria, Theropoda, Saurischia

defense

Dinosaurs defended themselves in many ways. The necks of CERATOPSIANS were covered with heavy shields, or frills, and enormous horns grew on the brows or snouts. Few predators would have dared to attack them. The spike-like thumbs of IGUANODON may have been defense weapons—perhaps they were used to gouge out the eyes of a CARNOSAUR. The ANKYLOSAURS developed the most effective method of protection. Their bodies were encased in bony plates and spines from head to tail—only their bellies were bare. When threatened, they simply flattened to the ground. They were so huge that it would have been impossible for a predator to turn them over. In addition, some had long spikes on their sides, while others had mace-like clubs or spikes on the ends of their tails. The tails of other dinosaurs were also effective defense weapons. STEGOSAURS's tails were armed with long spikes; and the long, whip-like tails of some SAUROPODS could have been very useful in warding off an attacker.

HERDING was probably the most important means of defense for unarmed plant-eating dinosaurs. Herding, along with speed, keen eyesight and hearing, and an excellent sense of smell, were the only means of defense of the ORNITHOPODS. (See SENSORY PERCEPTION.) Size may have been a means of defense for the sauropods.

The THEROPODS probably depended upon speed, good eyesight, superior "intelligence," and, in some, enormous size to protect them from enemies such as larger carnosaurs, PHYTOSAURS, or crocodiles.

deinocheirids or **Deinocheiridae** (dye-no-KYE-rih-dee) "Terrible Hands" (Named after DEINOCHEIRUS.)

A family of THEROPODS. Deinocheirids have been found only in Cretaceous deposits of Mongolia. These theropods had very long arms and huge claws on their fingers. They are sometimes listed as a family of CARNOSAURS and sometimes as COELUROSAURS. Only two kinds are known, DEINOCHEIRUS and THERIZINOSAURUS. No one knows how large these dinosaurs were, but they may have been as large or even larger than TYRANNOSAURUS. Some scientists think this group should be a separate infraorder of theropods, because they are so different from all other theropods.

DEINOCHEIRUS (dye-nuh-KYE-rus) "Terrible Hand" (Greek *deinos* = terrible + *cheir* = hand, because its hands were huge and had vicious claws.)

A gigantic Late Cretaceous CARNIVORE with arms and hands 9 feet (3 m) long. The hands alone were 2 feet (60 cm) long, and each had three enormous fingers capable of grasping and holding prey. We know that *Deinocheirus*

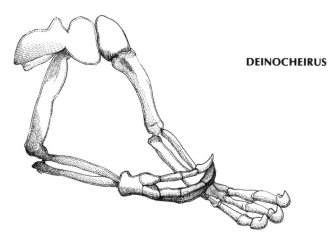

DEINOCHEIRUS

95

was BIPEDAL, because its forelimbs could not have been used for walking. Each finger was armed with a terrible, 8- to 12-inch (20- to 30-cm) hook-like claw. *Deinocheirus* was perhaps the most dangerous animal of Late Cretaceous times. Only the arms, hands, shoulders, and a few rib fragments of this giant creature have been found. These are similar to those of STRUTHIOMIMUS, but were more than three times as large! If the rest of the animal matched its hands, this meat-eater may have been 25 feet (7.5 m) tall and more than 45 feet (13.5 m) long. It may even have been larger than TYRANNOSAURUS. Its fossils were found in the Gobi Desert of Mongolia.

Classification: Carnosauria or Coelurosauria, Theropoda, Saurischia

DEINODON (DYE-no-don) "Terror Tooth" (Greek *deinos* = terrible + *odon* = tooth, because it had very long fangs.)

Name given to a jaw and twelve enormous curved and serrated teeth found in Montana in 1856. This CARNOSAUR may have been a species of ALBERTOSAURUS. It lived in Late Jurassic times.

Classification: Carnosauria, Theropoda, Saurischia

deinodonts or **Deinondontidae** (dye-no-DON-tih-dee) "Terror Teeth" (Named after DEINODON.)

A name sometimes used for the important CARNOSAURS of Late Cretaceous times, including ALBERTOSAURUS, DASPLETOSAURUS, TARBOSAURUS, and TYRANNOSAURUS. Most deinodonts were large, but one was no larger than a large dog.

deinonychosaurs or **Deinonychosauria** (dyne-ON-ik-o-sawr-ee-ah) "Terrible Claw Lizards" (Named after DEINONYCHUS + Greek *sauros* = lizard.)

A proposed new infraorder of THEROPODS. Some scientists believe that DROMAEOSAURS do not fit under either the

CARNOSAURS or COELUROSAURS. In these dinosaurs the hind legs and skulls were highly specialized for speed and savage attack. Their feet were equipped with sickle-like claws, and their tails were carried rigidly out behind, strengthened by bundles of bony rods that lay along the vertebrae. This infraorder would include all of the DROMAEOSAURIDAE family: CHIROSTENOTES, DEINONYCHUS, DROMAEOSAURUS, and VELOCIRAPTOR. These dinosaurs lived only in Cretaceous times. Not all scientists agree that this new classification is needed.

DEINONYCHUS (dyne-ON-ik-us) "Terrible Claw" (Greek *deinos* = terrible + *onychos* = claw, referring to the lethal claws on its feet.)

A vicious Early Cretaceous THEROPOD. This lightly built, fleet-footed BIPED was 9 feet (2.7 m) long, 5 feet (1.5 m) tall and weighed about 175 pounds (80 kg). Its long tail was held rigidly out behind by a bundle of bony rods running along the vertebrae. *Deinonychus* had a short neck, a large head, excellent eyesight, and sharp, serrated teeth. Its forelegs were half as long, as its hind. It had long, powerful, grasping hands; each hand had three fingers equipped with long sharp claws. The second toe of each foot was equipped with a powerful, 5-inch (13-cm) sickle-

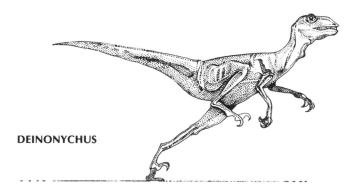

DEINONYCHUS

shaped claw that *Deinonychus* probably used to slash open the bellies of its prey.

Deinonychus probably hunted in packs and attacked animals much larger than itself. Like all theropods, it was probably ENDOTHERMIC (warm-blooded). The fossils of this formidable dinosaur were found in Montana. It is classified as a DROMAEOSAURIDAE, but some think it should be in a group of its own, the DEINONYCHOSAURIA. Its hips were OPISTHOPUBIC instead of lizard-like.

Classification: Coelurosauria, Theropoda, Saurischia

DESMATOSUCHUS (dez-mat-uh-SOOK-us)
See AETOSAURS.

diapsid or **Diapsida** (dye-APS-ih-dah)   "Two Arches" (Greek *di* = two + *apsid* = arches, referring to two openings in the skull.)

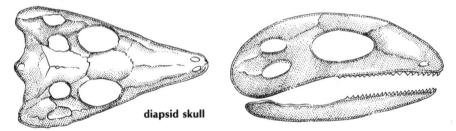

diapsid skull

A subclass of REPTILIA. Members of this group have two openings in the skull behind each eye socket. There are two kinds of diapsids: snakes and lizards form one group, and the ARCHOSAURS—crocodiles, DINOSAURS, PTEROSAURS, and THECODONTS—form the other. Many suggest that dinosaurs were not true reptiles, but partly because they had diapsid skulls, dinosaurs are still classed as reptiles.

Dicraeosaurinae (dye-CREE-sawr-ih-nee)   "Forked Lizards" (Named after DICRAEOSAURUS.)

A former subfamily of TITANOSAURIDAE SAUROPODS.

These were quite similar to the DIPLODOCINAE, but were smaller and their vertebrae were nearly solid instead of having hollow spaces. DICRAEOSAURUS is the only known member of this subfamily. Under a new reorganization of sauropods, this subfamily has been placed under the DIPLODOCIDAE.

DICRAEOSAURUS (dye-CREE-uh-sawr-us) "Forked Lizard" (Greek *dikros* = forked + *sauros* = lizard, referring to the forked spines on its vertebrae.)

A SAUROPOD of Late Jurassic Tanzania and Egypt. This four-legged dinosaur was similar to DIPLODOCUS, but was smaller—it was 40 feet (12 m) long, 10 feet (3 m) tall, and weighed about 6 tons (about 5.5 metric tons). *Dicraeosaurus* was a peaceful plant-eater. It had a moderately long neck and a very long tail with forked vertebral spines like those of DIPLODOCUS, but in *Dicraeosaurus* the vertebrae were nearly solid. This dinosaur is known from very incomplete material.

Classification: Sauropoda, Sauropodomorpha, Saurischia

diet

Scientists can tell what kind of food dinosaurs ate by the kind of teeth they had. Dinosaurs with sharp, serrated teeth ate meat. Those with peg-like or flat grinding teeth ate plants.

Of all the dinosaurs, only the THEROPODS were meat-eaters (with the possible exception of TROÖDON and some PROSAUROPODS). The carnosaurs could swallow huge hunks of meat whole. *Tyrannosaurus* probably preferred to prey on the peaceful HADROSAURS, which were quite plentiful when *Tyrannosaurus* lived. We know that ALLOSAURUS ate SAUROPODS, because scientists have found APATOSAURUS bones with *Allosaurus* tooth marks on them. Smaller theropods probably fed on any animal smaller than themselves. The smallest probably ate small lizards, insects, and reptile or dinosaur EGGS. The ORNITHOMIMIDS may have eaten both meat and plant food.

All other dinosaurs were plant-eaters. From fossilized stomach contents, we know that hadrosaurs ate leaves, twigs, pine needles, seeds, and fruit. No water plants were found in their stomachs. Other ORNITHOPODS probably ate similar diets.

The huge sauropods ate twigs and needles from the tops of tall pine, fir, and sequoia trees. One of the big mysteries about sauropods is how they could eat enough to stay alive. Elephants eat 300 to 600 pounds (135 to 270 kg) of food every day. They spend up to 18 hours a day just foraging and eating. The largest sauropod was 15 times as large as an Africa elephant. Did it eat 15 times as much? We don't know, but probably not.

Prosauropods foraged on smaller trees, while STEGO-SAURS, CERATOPSIANS, and ANKYLOSAURS ate low ground plants, and probably cycad and fern fronds.

DILOPHOSAURUS   (dye-LO-fuh-sawr-us) "Two-crested Lizard" (Greek *di* = two + *lophos* = crest, because it had two crests.)

A Late Triassic or Early Jurassic THEROPOD with two high crests running lengthwise along the top of its large

DILOPHOSAURUS

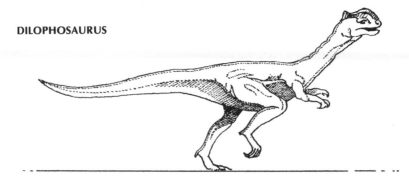

head. *Dilophosaurus* was a medium-sized dinosaur—it was about 20 feet (6 m) long. This BIPEDAL meat-eater had short arms and powerful legs built for speed. There were three fingers on its hands and four toes on its feet (however, only three toes reached the ground). Its fingers and toes were armed with sharp claws. The fossils of this dinosaur were found in Arizona. It is known from a nearly complete skeleton. Although this dinosaur was originally classed as a CARNOSAUR, it is now thought to be a large COELUROSAUR.

Classification: Coelurosauria, Theropoda, Saurischia

DIMETRODON (dye-MET-ruh-don) "Two-measure Teeth" (Greek *di* = two + *metron* = measure + *odon* = tooth, referring to the fact that it had teeth of two different sizes.)

Not a dinosaur, but a PELYCOSAUR, an ancestor of the mammal-like reptiles. *Dimetrodon* had a great sail 2 to 3 feet (60 to 90 cm) high along its back. This sail may have helped regulate its body temperature. *Dimetrodon* was 10 feet (3 m) long and was a four-legged CARNIVORE. It is the largest known meat-eater of the PERMIAN PERIOD. It had become EXTINCT by the beginning of the MESOZOIC ERA. Its fossils have been found in Texas.

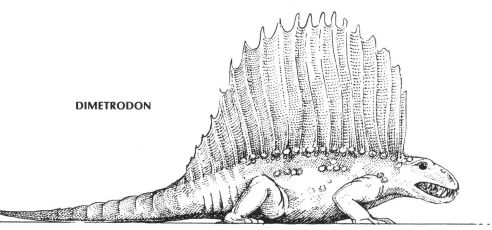

DIMETRODON

DIMORPHODON (dye-MORF-uh-don) "Two-form Teeth"
(Greek *di* = two + *morphe* = shape + *odon* = tooth,
referring to the fact that it had teeth of two different
shapes.)

Not a dinosaur, but one of the earliest flying reptiles—
a very primitive PTEROSAUR. It was a member of the RHAM-
PHORHYNCOID family, and had an enormous head and a
long naked tail. The fourth finger of each hand was
greatly lengthened and supported the wing. *Dimorphodon* was about 3 feet (90 cm) long. Fossils of this pterosaur
have been found in England. It lived from Early to Late
Jurassic times.

dinosaurs or **Dinosauria** (DYE-no-sawr-ee-ah) "Terrible
Lizards" (Greek *deinos* = terrible + *sauros* = lizard, because of their giant size and because at first these animals
were thought to be lizard-like.)

The name given to two separate kinds of EXTINCT animals—the SAURISCHIA and the ORNITHISCHIA—both orders
of the ARCHOSAURIA, a subclass of REPTILIA. These two
kinds of animals were no more closely related to one another than they were to crocodiles. However, they both
were scaly, egg-laying animals that walked erect, like
mammals, instead of sprawling like modern reptiles.
Some may even have taken care of their YOUNG. They
were possibly warm-blooded (ENDOTHERMIC), and many
were capable of moving very rapidly. These characteristics are not typical of reptiles, and some scientists suggest
that dinosaurs should be removed from the reptilian class
and placed in a separate class. However, they are still
classified as reptiles because of their very reptilian skulls.
(See DIAPSID.)

Dinosaurs lived from Middle Triassic times to the end
of the Cretaceous Period. As a group, they existed for
about 140 million years.

diplodocids or **Diplodocidae** (dih-pluh-DOE-kih-dee) "Double Beamed" (Named after DIPLODOCUS.)

A family of SAUROPODS that had peg-like teeth. It includes all those having "double-beamed" or "Y" shaped spines on their tail vertebrae similar to those found in *Diplodocus.* These bones may have provided extra protection for major blood vessels along the tail or extra muscle attachment. These four-legged plant-eaters were from 40 feet (12 m) to 90 feet (27 m) long.

Diplodocids lived during Late Jurassic times in North America, Europe, Asia, and Africa, but some also lived during the Cretaceous Period. APATOSAURUS, DIPLODOCUS, BAROSAURUS, CETIOSAURISCUS, DICRAEOSAURUS, MAMENCHISAURUS, and NEMEGTOSAURUS belong in this family based on a new study and reorganization of the sauropods.

Diplodocinae (dih-pluh-DOE-kih-nee) "Double Beamed" (Named after DIPLODOCUS.)

One of the subfamily groups of the TITANOSAURIDAE SAUROPODS. This group had only five vertebrae in the pelvic area. ALAMOSAURUS, ANTARCTOSAURUS, BAROSAURUS, and DIPLODOCUS were members of this group.

This subfamily has recently been restudied and reorganized. Many of the dinosaurs formerly included in this subfamily are now placed in a new family, the DIPLODOCIDAE. However, some scientists continue to use this old system.

DIPLODOCUS (dih-PLOD-uh-kus) "Double Beam" (Greek *diplos* = double + *dokos* = beam, referring to the double-beamed or "Y" shaped structure of spines on the tail vertebrae.)

A Late Jurassic SAUROPOD with a long snaky neck, a long whip-like tail, and front legs shorter than the hind legs. A complete skeleton of this dinosaur has been found. It is the longest dinosaur skeleton ever found. It is 90 feet (27 m) long, and has a 26-foot (8-m) neck and a 45-foot (3.5-m) tail. This *Diplodocus* stood 13 feet (4 m) tall at the hips, and probably weighed 25 tons (25.5 metric tons) when it was alive.

DIPLODOCUS

The elephant-like feet and legs of this four-legged plant-eater indicate that it was a land or swamp dweller. Because its nostrils were on top of its head, scientists once thought that it lived on the bottom of lakes with only the top of its head above water. It is now known that it could not have breathed in such deep water, because the pressure of the water would have been too great.

Diplodocus may have used its tail as a weapon. The "Y" shaped spines on the tail vertebrae could have provided extra places of attachment for muscles which made it possible to move the tail from side to side. Its long neck enabled the animal to lift its head to see an approaching enemy from a long distance. Many nearly complete skeletons and several partial ones have been found in the Rocky Mountain states of North America. *Diplodocus* may have lived into Early Cretaceous times.

Classification: Sauropoda, Sauropodomorpha, Saurischia

dome-headed dinosaurs
See PACHYCEPHALOSAURS.

DRACOPELTA (dra-ko-PEL-tah) "Fabulous Lizard with Shield" (Greek *drakon* = fabulous lizard-like animal + *pelta* = shield.)

An European ANKYLOSAUR from the Jurassic Period. This recently discovered armored dinosaur was a NODOSAURID. It had five different types of armor. Like all ankylosaurs, it was a four-legged plant-eater.

Classification: Nodosauridae, Ankylosauria, Ornithischia

DRAVIDOSAURUS (dra-VID-uh-sawr-us) "Dravid Lizard" (Named for the Dravidanadu peninsula of India, where it was found + Greek *sauros* = lizard.)

The only known STEGOSAUR from Middle Cretaceous Period. This plated ORNITHISCHIAN was found in southern India. It is known from a partial skull, a tooth, ten armor plates, a spike, and several other bones. It resembled STEGOSAURUS more than other stegosaurs, but was smaller. Like *Stegosaurus,* it was a four-legged plant-eater. Its back plates were thin and triangular-shaped. They ranged from 2 inches (5 cm) to 10 inches (25 cm) in height. The spike is 6 inches (15 cm) long and slightly curved.

Classification: Stegosauridae, Stegosauria, Ornithischia

dromaeosaurids or **Dromaeosauridae** (droh-mee-o-SAWR-ih-dee) "Swift Lizards" (Named after DROMAEOSAURUS.) Also called dromaeosaurs.

A family of advanced COELUROSAURS, sometimes called "emu lizards." These agile meat-eaters had large brains, huge eyes, and sickle-like claws on their inner toes. They were small, fierce, BIPEDAL predators, and were the most "intelligent" of the dinosaurs. (See BRAINS.) They lived in

North America, Asia, and South America from Early to Late Cretaceous times. CHIROSTENOTES, DEINONYCHUS, DROMAEOSAURUS, SAURORNITHOIDES, SAURORNITHOLESTES, STENONYCHOSAURUS, and VELOCIRAPTOR were dromaeosaurs.

Some scientists propose that this family be moved to a new infraorder of THEROPODS—the DEINONYCHOSAURIA.

dromaeosaurs (DROM-ee-uh-sawrz)
See DROMAEOSAURIDS.

DROMAEOSAURUS (drom-ee-uh-SAWR-us) "Swift Lizard" (Greek *dramaios* = swift-running + *sauros* = lizard, because it was a fast runner.)

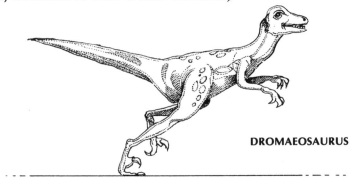

DROMAEOSAURUS

An advanced Late Cretaceous COELUROSAUR. This very fleet-footed dinosaur was about the size of a man; it weighed only 100 pounds (45 kg). It was a BIPEDAL meat-eater and was a vicious killer—it had razor-sharp teeth and a 3-inch (8-cm) eagle-like claw on the inner toe of each foot. The neck of this fearsome dinosaur was rather long, but thick and powerful. *Dromaeosaurus* had a broad head; its braincase (see BRAINS) was large and its eyes were huge. Fossils of this THEROPOD have been found in Alberta, Canada.

Classification: Coelurosauria, Theropoda, Saurischia

DROMICEIOMIMUS   (dro-miss-ee-o-MY-mus) "Emu Mimic" (Latin *Dromiceius* = genus name for emu + Latin *mimus* = mimic, because it resembled a big bird.)

A Late Cretaceous ORNITHOMIMID (ostrich dinosaur) about the size of an ostrich. It was closely related to ORNITHOMIMUS and STRUTHIOMIMUS and, like them, looked like an ostrich with a long tail. It had a long, slender neck; a bird-like beak; long slender legs; and huge eyes. But *Dromiceiomimus* had arms with three-fingered hands instead of wings. *Dromiceiomimus* was probably one of the most "intelligent" animals of the Cretaceous Period; its BRAIN was larger than that of an ostrich. This dinosaur was a swift runner that preyed on small animals. Its fossils have been found in Alberta, Canada; the partial skeletons of several individuals make up most of the parts of a whole animal.

Classification: Coelurosauria, Theropoda, Saurischia

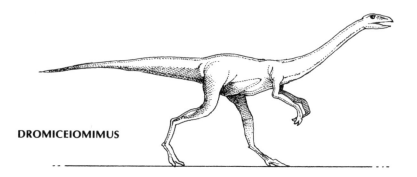

DROMICEIOMIMUS

DROMICOSAURUS (druh-MIK-o-sawr-us) "Fleet Lizard" (Greek *dromikos* = swift; fleet + *sauros* = lizard, because its long legs indicate it was a good runner.)

A very early PROSAUROPOD from South Africa. It lived in the Late Triassic Period. This long-necked, long-tailed dinosaur is known only from the hind legs, fragments of the forelimbs, a few vertebrae, and a few other bones. It is thought to be closely related to THECODONTOSAURUS and possibly resembled that dinosaur. *Dromicosaurus* walked on four legs, and ate plants.

Classification: Prosauropoda, Sauropodomorpha, Saurischia

DRYOSAURUS (DRY-o-sawr-us) "Oak Lizard" (Greek *dryos* = oak + *sauros* = lizard, because the top of the teeth were shaped somewhat like oak leaves.)

A small, graceful ORNITHOPOD of the HYPSILOPHODONT family. It was 12 feet (3.5 m) long, 4 feet (1.2 m) tall, and weighed 170 pounds (77 kg). Its small head had a slim, beak-like snout. *Dryosaurus* had five-fingered hands and walked on long, slender legs, carrying its body horizontally. It probably could run swiftly. Like all ornithopods, it was a peaceful plant-eater. *Dryosaurus* lived in western North America, in Europe, and in east Africa from Late Jurassic to Early Cretaceous times. It is known from a nearly complete skeleton found in Utah. DYSALOTOSAURUS is considered to be a species of this dinosaur.

Classification: Hypsilophodontidae, Ornithopoda, Ornithischia

DRYOSAURUS

DRYPTOSAURUS (DRIP-tuh-sawr-us) "Tearing Lizard" (Greek *dryptos* = to tear + *sauros* = lizard, referring to its fearsome teeth and claws.) Originally named LAELAPS.

A CARNOSAUR whose remains were found in New Jersey —the only known Late Cretaceous carnosaur from eastern North America. It probably resembled MEGALOSAURUS. Its exact size is unknown, because a complete skeleton hasn't been found, but the bones that have been found suggest it may have been 20 feet (6 m) long. This formidable BIPEDAL meat-eater had dagger-like teeth and 8-inch (20-cm), talon-like foot claws.

Classification: Carnosauria, Theropoda, Saurischia

DRYPTOSAURUS

duck-billed dinosaurs or **duckbills**

See HADROSAURS.

DYOPLOSAURUS (dye-OP-luh-sawr-us) "Double-armed Lizard" (Greek *dyo* = double + *oplos* = armed + *sauros* = lizard, referring to its two forms of defense—its armor and its clubbed tail.)

Name given to Late Cretaceous ANKYLOSAUR bones found in Mongolia and Alberta, Canada. *Dyoplosaurus* is now considered to be the same as EUOPLOCEPHALUS.

Classification: Ankylosauridae, Ankylosauria, Ornithischia

DYSALOTOSAURUS (dye-suh-LO-tuh-sawr-us) "Unconquerable Lizard" (Greek *dys* = un + *aloto* = hard to catch + *sauros* = lizard, referring to its supposed speed.)

Name given to a complete skeleton of a small HYPSILOPHODONT that was found in Late Jurassic rocks in Tanzania. This dinosaur is now considered by some to be a species of DRYOSAURUS.

Classification: Hypsilophodontidae, Ornithopoda, Ornithischia

E

ECHINODON (eh-KYE-nuh-don) "Spiny Tooth" (Greek *echinos* = spiny + *odon* = tooth, referring to the spines on its teeth.)

This name has been changed to SAURECHINODON, because another animal had already been given this name.

Classification: Fabrosauridae, Ornithopoda, Ornithischia

ectotherm (EK-toe-therm) "Outside Heat" (Greek *ektos* = outside + *therme* = heat.)

A cold-blooded animal; one that gets its body heat from the sun or something else in its environment. Ectotherms control their body temperature by moving into or out of the shade. Snakes, turtles, alligators, and lizards are ectotherms. It has long been thought that the dinosaurs were ectotherms, but now some scientists think that at least some dinosaurs were ENDOTHERMS. Compare: HOMOIOTHERM.

ectothermic

See ECTOTHERM.

EDMONTONIA (ed-mon-TOE-nee-uh) (Named for the Edmonton rock formation, where it was found.)

A Late Cretaceous ANKYLOSAUR whose nearly complete skeleton was found in Alberta, Canada. Some scientists think that *Edmontonia* was a species of PANOPLOSAURUS. Others do not agree; however, if it is not, they were very similar.

Classification: Nodosauridae, Ankylosauria, Ornithischia

EDMONTOSAURUS   (ed-MON-tuh-sawr-us) "Edmonton Lizard" (Named for the Edmonton rock formation, where it was found + Greek *sauros* = lizard.)

A HADROSAUR of Late Cretaceous Alberta, Canada. This duck-billed dinosaur was related to ANATOSAURUS and was a member of the HADROSAURINES. It had a heavy body; long, strong legs; short, slender forelimbs; a crestless head with a long slender nose; and a broad, spoon-shaped beak. Its jaws were packed with hundreds of teeth. *Edmontosaurus* was one of the largest hadrosaurs—it weighed 3 to 4 tons (2.7 to 3.6 metric tons) and was 32 feet (9.8 m) long. Like all hadrosaurs, it walked on two legs, carrying its body horizontally. It ate tree leaves and pine needles. Many specimens of this dinosaur have been found. *Edmontosaurus* was one of the most abundant animals of its time.

Classification:
Hadrosauridae,
Ornithopoda,
Ornithischia

EDMONTOSAURUS

EFRAASIA (eh-FRAH-see-ah)   (Named in honor of E. Fraas, an early German fossil collector.)

A PROSAUROPOD recently discovered in late Triassic of Germany. This plant-eating dinosaur resembled AN-CHISAURUS. It had a long neck and tail and was capable of walking on either two legs or all four.

Classification: Prosauropoda, Sauropodomorpha, Saurischia

eggs

Although it is possible that some dinosaurs gave birth to their YOUNG alive, most of them certainly reproduced by laying eggs. Scientists' knowledge of dinosaur eggs is based on abundant finds of pieces, and occasionally, of whole eggs; sometimes they have even found complete NESTS of dinosaur eggs. Scientists think that dinosaur eggs probably had brittle shells similar to those of modern crocodiles.

Huge dinosaurs such as SAUROPODS did *not* lay gigantic eggs. If they had done so, the shells would have been too thick to allow air to pass through to the baby dinosaurs inside—nor could the baby dinosaurs have succeeded in breaking out. Eggs believed to be those of the sauropod HYPSELOSAURUS were discovered in France. These were laid in crater-like dirt nests in clutches of five. The eggs were roundish in shape and about 10 inches (25 cm) long —twice the size of an ostrich egg. They had a rough sand-papery surface. These are the largest dinosaur eggs that are known up to this time.

The pig-sized PROTOCERATOPS laid its eggs in sand nests, arranging the eggs in three circles, one within another. There were as many as 18 potato-shaped eggs in some nests. These eggs were about 6 inches (15 cm) long and had rough, wrinkled shells. Another *Protoceratops* nest recently found in Mongolia had an even greater number of eggs in it. Scientists think that many females may have shared the same nest. They think it is unlikely one could have laid that many eggs. The total volume of the eggs was greater than the body of an adult.

Other dinosaur eggs have been found, but scientists are not sure which dinosaur laid them, because they were not found with dinosaur bones. However, tiny teeth and jaw fragments were recently found in Montana with 40 eggs from 30 different nesting spots. The teeth were similar to those of meat-eating dinosaurs. This could mean that the eggs were laid by a CARNIVORE, possibly TROÖDON. That would make them the first eggs of a carnivorous dinosaur ever found. These eggs are 6 inches (15 cm) by 4 inches (10 cm) and have black, pebbled shells.

A clutch of 16 eggs was recently found in China. A footprint believed to have been made by the dinosaur that laid them was impressed upon three of the eggs. These eggs are elongated and nearly pointed on each end.

ELAPHROSAURUS (eh-LOFF-ruh-sawr-us) "Lightweight Lizard" (Greek *elaphros* = lightweight + *sauros* = lizard, referring to its hollow bones.)

A slender, medium-size, hollow-boned COELUROSAUR—possibly the ancestor of the ORNITHOMIMIDS. This short-legged BIPED was about three times the size of ORNITHOLESTES—larger than most coelurosaurs. It measured 19 feet (5.8 m) from its snout to the tip of its tail. It was probably a scavenger, feeding on carcasses of dead animals left by large CARNOSAURS. Many fossils of *Elaphrosaurus,* including one nearly complete skeleton, have been found in Tanzania and Israel. It lived during Middle and Late Jurassic times.

Classification: Coelurosauria, Theropoda, Saurischia

ELASMOSAURUS (ee-LAZ-muh-sawr-us) "Thin-plated Lizard" (Greek *elasmos* = thin plate + *sauros* = lizard, referring to the plate-like bones of its pelvic girdle.)

113

Not a dinosaur, but a long-necked PLESIOSAUR. This marine reptile was 43 feet (13 m) long. About half of its length was its head and neck. The neck had 76 vertebrae. *Elasmosaurus* was not built for speed; it moved slowly through the Late Cretaceous oceans propelled by narrow, paddle-like flippers. Fossils of these fish-eaters have been found in North America.

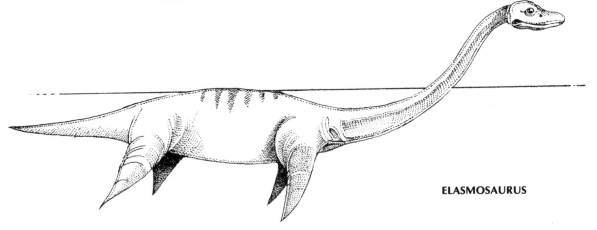

ELASMOSAURUS

ELMISAURUS (EL-mih-sawr-us) "Foot Lizard" (Mongolian *elmi* = foot + Greek *sauros* = lizard, referring to the foot, which had fused bones.)

A small COELUROSAUR found in Early Cretaceous sediments of Mongolia. It is known only from a foot and a hand. Based on the size of the foot, its height has been estimated to be about 3 feet (90 cm) at the hips. This little dinosaur was closely related to MACROPHALANGIA and CHIROSTENOTES and probably resembled them. It was a BIPEDAL meat-eater.

Classification: Coelurosauria, Theropoda, Saurischia

endotherm (EN-doe-therm) "Inner Heat" (Greek *endon* = within + *therme* = heat.)

A warm-blooded animal; one whose body temperature does not change with the temperature of its environment. Endotherms generate their own heat internally. They have developed ways of regulating their body temperature—such as perspiring or panting to cool off and shivering to warm up. In this way, they maintain a high and uniform temperature even when the temperature of their environment is very low or very high. (See HOMOIOTHERM.)

For a long time scientists thought dinosaurs were ECTOTHERMIC (cold-blooded), like modern reptiles. But now some scientists believe that at least some dinosaurs—particularly the THEROPODS—may have been endotherms, like birds and mammals. The great size of SAUROPODS may have been their means of controlling body temperature. The plates on the back of STEGOSAURS, and fins, such as those of SPINOSAURUS, may have been cooling mechanisms. A few dinosaurs may even have had insulating body covering such as fur or feathers like modern mammals and birds have.

There are many reasons to think that dinosaurs may have been endothermic. Dinosaurs had erect posture—that is, they walked with their legs vertical, or nearly so; they did not sprawl like alligators or crocodiles. Many BIPEDAL dinosaurs were swift runners, and they were highly active and very agile animals. The bone tissue of some dinosaurs was similar to that of mammals. And there is evidence that some dinosaurs lived in HERDS, and took some care of their YOUNG. Among modern animals, only endothermic ones have these characteristics.

endothermic
See ENDOTHERM.

EOCERATOPS (EE-o-sair-uh-tops) "Early Horned Face" (Greek *eos* = early + *keratops* = horned face, because it appears to be one of the earlier CERATOPSIANS.)

A ceratopsian similar to MONOCLONIUS. It is known only from a half skull and lower jaw fragments found in Alberta, Canada. The skull is over 3 feet (90 cm) long. *Eoceratops* had a short, slightly forward curved horn on its snout and small rounded horns on its brow that curved slightly toward the back. This four-legged plant-eater lived during the early part of Late Cretaceous times.

Classification: Ceratopsidae, Ceratopsia, Ornithischia

EOCERATOPS

EODELPHIS (ee-o-DEL-fiss) "Early Opossum" (Greek *eos* = early + *delphis* = opossum.)

Not a dinosaur, but a Late Cretaceous marsupial mammal. It was about two-thirds as large as the common modern opossum. Though small, it was a relatively large mammal compared with other mammals living at that time, and it is the largest known marsupial of Late Cretaceous times. This neighbor of the dinosaur is known only from jaw fragments and teeth found in Alberta, Canada, and Montana.

EODELPHIS

eosuchians or **Eosuchia** (ee-o-SOOK-ee-ah) "Early Crocodiles" (Greek *eos* = early + *souchos* = crocodile, because
they resembled modern crocodiles.)

Not dinosaurs, but an order of DIAPSID reptiles that
resembled modern gavials or crocodiles, but were more
closely related to lizards. They are thought to be the
ancestors of snakes and lizards. Eosuchians lived from
the PERMIAN PERIOD to the TERTIARY PERIOD and lived in
many parts of the world. They were meat-eaters and
probably preyed on insects and smaller dinosaurs. They
ranged in size from 4 feet (1.2 m) to 8 feet (2 m). They
walked on all fours with a sprawling gait, as modern
crocodiles do. CHAMPSOSAURUS and MALERISAURUS were
eosuchians.

ERECTOPUS (ee-REK-tuh-pus) "Upright Foot" (Latin *erec-
tus* = upright + Greek *pous* = foot, because the animal
apparently walked upright.)

Name given to a few fossil bones of a large Early Cretaceous CARNOSAUR. *Erectopus* was probably closely related
to MEGALOSAURUS. Like all carnosaurs, it was a two-legged
meat-eater. Its fossils were found in northern France.

Classification: Carnosauria, Theropoda, Saurischia

ERLIKOSAURUS (er-LIK-uh-sawr-us) "Erlik's Lizard"
(Named after Erlik, legendary Lamaist king of the dead
+ Greek *sauros* = lizard. Lamaism is a kind of Buddhist
religion found in Mongolia.)

An unusual kind of Late Cretaceous dinosaur recently
found in Mongolia. Its skull is unlike that of any other
known dinosaur. It had a long, slender, toothless beak, but
sharp teeth lined the sides of its jaws. This meat-eater
had a long neck and tail. It may have been partially QUAD-
RUPEDAL. Its four-toed feet were short and massive with
long narrow claws. *Erlikosaurus* closely resembled SEG-
NOSAURUS and belonged to the same family, the SEG-

NOSAURIDAE, but it was smaller. *Erlikosaurus* is currently classed as a SAURISCHIAN THEROPOD, but some paleontologists suspect it might prove to be an ORNITHOPOD. It is known from a skull and an incomplete skeleton.

Classification: Carnosauria, Theropoda, Saurischia?

ERYOPS (ER-ee-ops) "Drawn-out Face" (Greek *eryein* = to draw out + *ops* = face, because most of its skull was in front of its eyes.)

Not a dinosaur, but an Early PERMIAN amphibian whose fossils were found in Texas. Amphibians are born in the water, but often live much of their adult lives on land. Toads and frogs are modern amphibians. *Eryops* lived in and near streams and ponds. It ate fish. This long-faced creature was EXTINCT before the dinosaurs appeared.

ERYOPS

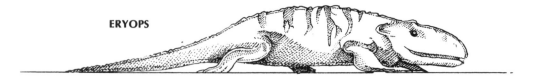

EUBRONTES (you-BRON-teez) "Like Thunder" (Greek *eu* = like + *brontos* = thunder, because it was thought that the footsteps of this large animal would surely be thunderous.)

Name given to three-toed dinosaur TRACKS found in Dinosaur State Park in Connecticut and also in Glen Canyon, Arizona. They provide evidence that large THEROPODS lived in North America during very late Triassic and early Jurassic times. It is speculated that the animal that made the tracks was 20 feet (6 m) long and was a heavy-bodied CARNOSAUR similar to MEGALOSAURUS. Similar tracks have been found in Germany, but no bones of the animal that made them have ever been found.

Some of the Connecticut tracks appear to have bee
made while the dinosaur was floating in water. Only th
tips of the toes made impressions in the mud as the ani·
mal pushed itself along. This seems to indicate that some
carnosaurs could swim. Before the discovery of these
tracks, it was assumed that carnosaurs did not swim.

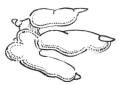

EUBRONTES TRACKS

Euhelopodinae (you-heh-lo-PO-dih-nee)   "Like Marsh Feet"
(Named for EUHELOPUS.)

A subfamily of BRACHIOSAURID SAUROPODS. They were
similar to the CAMARASAURINAE in some ways; their forelimbs were as long as the hind legs and they had short
skulls. But Euhelopodinae had relatively longer legs and
very long necks. Some may have carried their short tails
high off the ground. They ranged between 40 to 60 feet (12
to 18 m) in length. This group of four-legged plant-eaters
has only been found in China and Mongolia. They lived
throughout the Cretaceous Period. EUHELOPUS, OMEISAU-
RUS, OPISTHOCOELICAUDIA, and TIENSHANOSAURUS are members of this family.

EUHELOPUS (you-heh-LO-pus)   "Like Marsh Feet" (Greek
eu = like + *helos* = marsh + *pous* = foot, probably
because it was assumed that this dinosaur lived in
marshy areas.) A new name for HELOPUS. It was renamed
because that name was taken.

An Early Cretaceous SAUROPOD 45 feet (13.5 m) long. Two

partial skeletons of this long-necked SAURISCHIAN were found in China; together, they provide most of the parts of a whole animal. Its skull was similar to that of CAMARASAURUS, and its forelimbs were as long as its hind. But the neck of *Euhelopus* was much longer than the neck of *Camarasaurus*. Like all sauropods, *Euhelopus* was a QUADRUPEDAL plant-eater.

Classification: Sauropoda, Sauropodomorpha, Saurischia

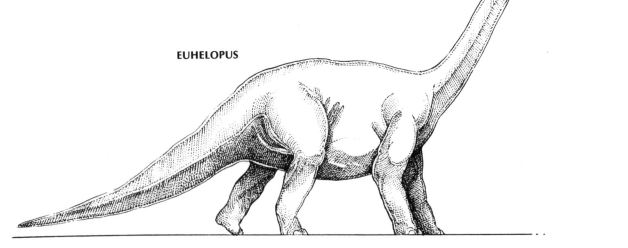

EUHELOPUS

EUOPLOCEPHALUS   (you-op-luh-SEF-uh-lus) "Well-protected Head" (Greek *euoplo* = well-protected + *kephale* = head, referring to the armor on its head.)

A Late Cretaceous ANKYLOSAUR (armored dinosaur). The upper part of its body—from the nose to the tail—was covered with bony plates studded with rows of horny spikes 4 to 6 inches (10 to 15 cm) long. The tail was short and fat, and ended in a bony club armed with two spikes. This plant-eater was about 20 feet (6 m) long and 8 feet (2.5 m) wide, and it weighed 3.5 tons (3.2 metric tons). It walked on four short, stout legs with hoofed feet. Its snout ended in a horny beak. The fossils of *Euoplocephalus* have been found in Alberta, Canada.

ANODONTOSAURUS, DYOPLOSAURUS, and SCOLOSAURUS are other names given to fossil remains that are now considered to be the same as *Euoplocephalus*. It was once thought that *Euoplocephalus* was the same as ANKYLOSAURUS, but scientists now believe they were two different animals.

Classification: Ankylosauridae, Ankylosauria, Ornithischia

EUOPLOCEPHALUS

EUPARKERIA (you-park-AIR-ee-ah)   (Named in honor of W. K. Parker, English scientist.)

Not a dinosaur, but a PSEUDOSUCHIAN (an advanced THECODONT). Some scientists think it may be an ancestor of the ORNITHISCHIAN dinosaurs; others suggest it was an ancestor of the SAURISCHIANS. It was a relatively small animal—5 feet (1.5 m) long and weighed 40 pounds (18 kg). It

EUPARKERIA

had a long tail. Armor plates covered its back. It probably walked on all fours most of the time, but it may have run on two legs, like modern lizards do. This meat-eater lived in South Africa during Triassic times.

EUSKELOSAURUS (you-SKEL-uh-sawr-us) "Primitive Leg Lizard" (Greek *eu* = primitive + *skelos* = leg + *sauros* = lizard, because it was an early dinosaur.)

A Late Triassic PROSAUROPOD similar to PLATEOSAURUS. It is known from fragmentary material of several individuals. This dinosaur had a long neck and tail. It was capable of walking either on four legs or two, and ate plants.

Classification: Prosauropoda, Sauropodomorpha, Saurischia

EUSTREPTOSPONDYLUS (you-strep-tuh-SPON-dih-lus) "Well-curved Vertebrae" (Greek *eustreptos* = well-curved + *spondylos* = vertebrae, because its vertebrae were more curved than those of most MEGALOSAURS.)

A CARNOSAUR that was very similar to MEGALOSAURUS. It lived about the same time and was about the same size. *Eustreptospondylus* was a meat-eater and walked on two powerful hind legs. Its forelimbs were very short. Its head was large, and its long jaws were lined with sharp, serrated teeth. Fossils of *Eustreptospondylus* have been found in Middle Jurassic rock in England and Madagascar, and in Late Jurassic rock in Europe and South America. It is known from most of the parts of a skeleton.

Classification: Carnosauria, Theropoda, Saurischia

evolve (ih-VOLV) (From Latin *evolvere* = to unroll.)

To change or development by slow stages. When a plant or animal evolves, it gradually develops new features and adaptations, from one generation to another, that make it better suited to its environment. This usually takes many centuries.

extinction (ek-STINK-shun)

By the end of the MESOZOIC ERA all of the dinosaurs had died out, along with PLESIOSAURS, AMMONITES, certain kinds of plankton, PTEROSAURS, and many kinds of plants. Their extinction appears to have been relatively sudden. Some scientists think it took just a few years. Others think it took thousands of years, or even millions of years. But in terms of geological time, even that is rather sudden.

Extinction is a natural process. It happens all of the time. There have even been other periods of earth's history in which large numbers of animals died out at one time. Also during the Mesozoic Era individual species of dinosaurs were dying out from time to time. Even whole families, like the STEGOSAURS, vanished. But never had there been such a massive dying out of so many kinds of plants and animals without leaving any descendants. Only the COELUROSAURS, of all the dinosaurs, left descendants (in the form of birds), and these were only descendants of very early coelurosaurs. There were no large land animals left after the dinosaurs and their contemporaries became extinct.

What caused them all to disappear is not known. Many scientists have studied the problem. Many theories have been proposed.

Some modern PALEONTOLOGISTS believe that excessive radiation plus a cooling of the environment are the most likely reasons for the extinction at the end of the Cretaceous. Some scientists believe that a supernova exploded near the earth and flooded the earth with excessive radiation for several decades. Others suggest that volcanic activity temporarily destroyed the earth's ozone layer, allowing too much deadly ultraviolet radiation from the sun to reach the earth's surface. Still others suggest that there was a reversal of the earth's magnetic poles. Scientists know that the magnetic poles have reversed a number of times in the history of the earth. While a reversal is occurring, the earth's magnetic field is weak. When its magnetic field is weak, the earth is exposed to large doses of radiation.

Other experts believe that sudden, severe cold weather caused the exterminations. Dinosaurs may have been warm-blooded, but they lacked insulative coverings such as hair or feathers. If temperatures dropped a great deal, they wouldn't have been able to retain enough body heat and would have perished. One theory suggests that sea-floor spreading and the breakup of the supercontinents, LAURASIA and GONDWANALAND, caused changes in the climate. Another suggests that a spillover of water from an arctic ocean reduced the salinity of the world's oceans and affected the climate.

A recently proposed theory suggests that an asteroid from our own solar system collided with the earth. This theory is based on discoveries of unusually high levels of iridium (a metallic element) in clay sediments that mark the very end of the Cretaceous Period. Scientists proposing this theory suggest that the asteroid collision caused a cloud of dust to circle the earth for several years, blocking the sunlight and causing the death of both plants and animals. This is the only theory with solid evidence to back it up, but it still does not explain why some kinds of animals became extinct, while others (such as turtles, crocodiles, mammals, and birds) survived. Perhaps the real answer will be found in a combination of these theories.

eyesight

Scientists can tell how large a dinosaur's eyes were from the size of the eye sockets in the skull. In general, the larger the eyes, the better the vision. Eyes placed in front of the skull provide better vision than those on the sides of the skull, and widely spaced eyes enable an animal to judge distances more accurately.

Most plant-eating dinosaurs had fairly large eyes. One of their best DEFENSES was their very good vision. Only the STEGOSAURS and ANKYLOSAURS had quite small eyes in comparison to their body size. Of the plant-eaters, the ORNITHOPODS had the largest eyes. They undoubtedly could see very well. When they saw danger approaching from a distance, they fled. SAUROPODS, too, had rather good vision and had the advantage of an extraordinarily long neck, which gave them a much larger range of vision.

Predatory dinosaurs also had large eyes and keen eyesight. Of all the dinosaurs, the DROMAEOSAURS had the largest eyes compared to body size. We know that DEINONYCHUS had to have good eye-and-foot coordination to use its sickle-like claw to kill prey. Such coordination requires good vision. STENONYCHOSAURUS probably had the best eyesight of all. Its eyes were forward-directed and spaced far apart, like those of humans. It probably could judge distances very accurately, and probably had good night vision as well. In modern animals, the largest eyes are found in nocturnal animals.

F

fabrosaurids or **Fabrosauridae** (fab-ruh-SAWR-ih-dee) "Fabre's Lizards" (Named after FABROSAURUS.) Also called fabrosaurs.

A primitive family of Triassic ORNITHOPODS, all resembling FABROSAURUS or LESOTHOSAURUS. They had lightweight bones and no muscular cheeks. A single row of teeth lined the jaws to the tip of the snout. In other groups, the teeth only lined the side jaws. Fabrosaurs did not have canine teeth like those found in the HETERODONTOSAURS. Fabrosaurs were quite small—3 to 4 feet (90 to 120 cm) long. Their forelimbs were much smaller than the hind, but were strong, indicating that they could walk either on two feet or on all four. Fabrosaurs first appeared in Late Triassic times. They have been found in Africa and North America. FABROSAURUS, LESOTHOSAURUS, and SCUTEL-LOSAURUS were fabrosaurs. Some scientists also include SAURECHINODON in this family. It was found in Late Jurassic sediments in England.

FABROSAURUS (FAB-ruh-sawr-us) "Fabre's Lizard" (Named in honor of Jean Henri Fabre, French entymologist + Greek *sauros* = lizard.)

An ORNITHOPOD known only from an incomplete lower right jaw that was found in Triassic sediments of South Africa. It is generally described as a small, 3-foot (90-cm) plant-eater with a small head, a horny beak-like jaw with teeth, short front limbs, five-fingered hands, long slender back legs, and long feet. This description was based on other fossil material that was once believed to be a species of *Fabrosaurus*. It has now been decided that this other material belonged to a different GENUS and has been named LESOTHOSAURUS. The two are very closely related and probably resembled one another.

Classification: Fabrosauridae, Ornithopoda, Ornithischia

feet

Dinosaur feet came in many shapes and sizes. However, all members of the same group of dinosaurs had similar feet. THEROPODS had bird-like feet usually with three forward-pointing toes and a dewclaw pointing inward or backward. Their toes were equipped with talon-like claws, like all predators. SAUROPODS had broad, padded, elephant-like feet. The hind feet were equipped with three or more claws, but the front had only one, or none. These were the feet of land animals. PROSAUROPODS had four forward-pointing toes on the hind feet with strong claws on the two middle toes. The forefeet were smaller, but strong, and had two clawed fingers and a thumb.

Nearly all of the ORNITHISCHIANS had blunt, hoof-like claws on both fore and hind feet. ORNITHOPODS had three or four toes on their hind feet and four or five fingers on their forefeet. The hind feet of STEGOSAURS were also three-toed, while the forefeet had five toes, all ending in hoof-like nails. ANKYLOSAURS and CERATOPSIANS had broad feet with hoofed toes, four toes on the hind feet and five on the forefeet.

fins

See SPINES.

flying reptiles

See PTEROSAURS.

footprints

See TRACKS and TRACKWAYS.

fossil (FOS-il)   (From Latin *fossilis* = dug up.)

A piece or trace of a once living thing—plant or animal —that has been preserved in stone by the replacement of once living tissues with minerals dissolved in water. Fossils of dinosaurs may be actual remains—teeth, bones, stomach contents—or they may be footprints or skin impressions.

Fossils were formed when an animal's body was covered by deep layers of mud or sand soon after it died. It takes millions of years for fossils to form. We know that dinosaurs existed, because scientists have found their fossilized bones. Scientists can tell by the shape of a fossil bone or tooth what kind of animal it belonged to. By studying a dinosaur's bones, they can determine what kind of dinosaur it was. Fossils tell scientists nearly everything about a dinosaur's appearance except its color.

By piecing together entire fossil skeletons, scientists have learned how large the creatures were and how many fingers or toes they had. Scientists know how and where muscles were fastened to the bones, so that they can determine how the animal looked when it was alive. Fossilized SKIN impressions tell them what the skin of that dinosaur looked like. Fossilized TRACKS give information about the habits of the dinosaur. Fossilized EGGS tell how they reproduced. On rare occasions, scientists have even found fossilized stomach contents; these show what some dinosaurs ate.

frills

Bony shields, or frills, covered the necks of CERATOPSIANS. These frills protected the necks, but their primary purpose was to provide a place of attachment for the strong neck and jaw muscles required to support the weight of the animals' huge heads and HORNS. As the size of the skulls and horns increased, the frills became larger to support them. PROTOCERATOPSIANS had relatively small heads and only suggestions of horns. Their frills were very small. Long-frilled ceratopsians had huge heads and very long brow horns. They had enormous shields that extended back over their shoulders. The frills of the short-frilled ceratopsians were about halfway between these two. Their heads were smaller than those of the long-frilled group, and their brow horns were either very short or non-existent. Their shields did not even reach to their shoulders. The frills of protoceratopsians and short-frilled ceratopsians were solid or had small holes through the bone, while the enormous frills of long-frilled ceratopsians had large openings in the bone to lighten their weight.

TOROSAURUS had the longest frill. Its skull and frill together measured 8.5 feet (2.6 m) long—one third of its total body length! The frill was 5.5 feet (1.5 m) wide.

G

GALLIMIMUS (gall-ih-MY-mus) "Rooster Mimic" (Latin *gallus* = rooster + *mimus* = mimic, because it resembled a big bird.)

The largest of the ORNITHOMIMIDS ("ostrich dinosaurs"). From the tip of its snout to the end of its tail, *Gallimimus* was 20 feet (6 m) long. With its small head; long, toothless, beak-like jaws; and long slender neck, it resembled a huge ostrich. Like an ostrich, it was BIPEDAL and could run swiftly. It had long, strong legs and three-toed feet; the

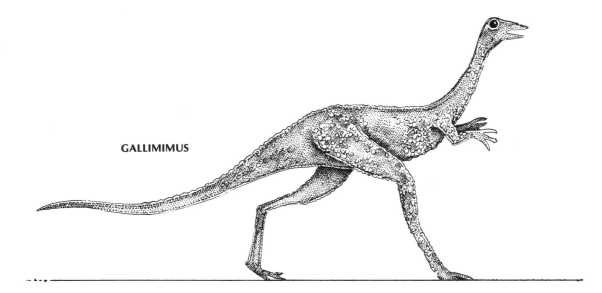

GALLIMIMUS

toes were armed with sharp claws. The arms were short, and they had three-fingered hands. *Gallimimus* probably ate small animals, eggs, and plants. It is known from several complete skeletons found in Late Cretaceous deposits in Mongolia.

Classification: Coelurosauria, Theropoda, Saurischia

GARUDIMIMUS (gah-RUE-dye-me-mus) "Garudi Mimic" (Named for a fierce mythological bird of Hindu and east Asian literature + Latin *mimus* = mimic.)

A very primitive ORNITHOMIMID ("ostrich dinosaur"). It was similar to ORNITHOMIMUS, but was more primitive. *Garudimimus* is known from most of a skull and a fragmentary skeleton—a pelvis, an incomplete hind leg, and one foot—found in Middle and Late Cretaceous deposits in Mongolia. The skull is 1 foot (30 cm) long. The total length of this fierce meat-eater is estimated to be about 14 feet (4 m). It walked on two legs.

Classification: Coelurosauria, Theropoda, Saurischia

gastroliths (GAS-tro-liths) "Stomach Stones" (Greek *gastros* = stomach + *lith* = stone.)

Small, rounded stones used to grind food in the gizzards or stomachs of some animals. (Modern birds swallow gravel for this purpose.) Gastroliths found near SAUROPOD fossils have led scientists to speculate that these dinosaurs swallowed vegetation whole and ground it with gastroliths. (Sauropods had no molars.) This adaptation would have made it possible for sauropods to eat almost continuously and thus generate enough energy to sustain their huge bodies.

Gastroliths have also been found in the fossilized stomachs of PLESIOSAURS.

genera (JEN-er-uh)
Plural of GENUS.

genus (JEE-nus) (Latin meaning "race" or "kind.")

A unit of classification for plants and animals; a group of similar and closely related SPECIES. Some species within a genus can interbreed to produce hybrids (like the mule). Species of different genera cannot. Canis (the group to which dogs belong) is a genus. There are many species of Canis—dogs, wolves, foxes, coyotes, jackals. The same is true of dinosaurs. *Triceratops* is a genus name. There were many species of *Triceratops.* Dinosaurs are known by their genera names. As a rule, only scientists are familiar with the species names of the different dinosaur genera. *Tyrannosaurus rex* is one of the few that is well known by its species name. *Rex* is the species name.

GENYODECTES (jen-ee-o-DEK-teez) "Biting Jaw" (Greek *genyos* = jaw + *dektes* = biting, because they were the jaws of a meat-eater.)

A late Cretaceous CARNOSAUR. A partial skull including the jaws is all that is known of this dinosaur. The skull is similar to that of TYRANNOSAURUS, and *Genyodectes* may be a member of the TYRANNOSAURIDS. The fossils of this large two-legged meat-eater were found in Argentina.

Classification: Carnosauria, Theropoda, Saurischia

GEOSAURUS (JEE-uh-sawr-us) "Earth Lizard" (Greek *ge* = earth + *sauros* = lizard. It is no longer known why this animal was given this name.)

Not a dinosaur, but an ocean-dwelling Early Jurassic crocodile. It had a long snout and paddle-like arms and legs. It was 15 feet (4.5 m) long, and its tail was broad and flat. *Geosaurus* went ashore only to lay EGGS. Its fossils have been found in Belgium and Argentina.

GERANOSAURUS (jer-AN-uh-sawr-us) "Crane Lizard" (Greek *geranodes* = crane-like + *sauros* = lizard, referring to its long, slender legs.)

The first Triassic ORNITHISCHIAN ever discovered and one of the three earliest known. Only PISANOSAURUS and HETERODONTOSAURUS are older in age. *Geranosaurus* was an ORNITHOPOD—a two-legged plant-eater. It resembled *Heterodontosaurus,* and had long, slender legs; a horny beak-like snout; and canine teeth. It is known only from a broken skull, lower jaws, a couple of leg bones, and part of a foot. These were found in Late Triassic deposits in South Africa.

Classification: Heterodontosauridae, Ornithopoda, Ornithischia

GIGANDIPUS (jih-GAN-dih-pus) "Giant Biped" (Greek *gigantos* = giant + *dipous* = two-footed, because only large hind footprints are known.)

Name given to TRACKS made by a large, three-toed BIPEDAL dinosaur in Late Triassic or very early Jurassic mud in what is now the Connecticut River Valley. Scientists believe these tracks were made by a large CARNOSAUR, possibly a North American species of the European carnosaur TERATOSAURUS. So far, no bones of the animal that made the tracks have been found.

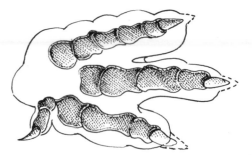

GIGANDIPUS TRACK

GILMOREOSAURUS (gil-MOR-o-sawr-us) "Gilmore's Lizard" (Named in honor of Charles W. Gilmore, American paleontologist + Greek *sauros* = lizard.) Formerly considered a species of MANDSCHUROSAURUS.

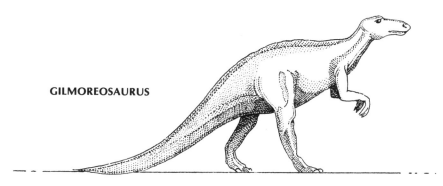

GILMOREOSAURUS

The earliest known HADROSAURINE (flat-headed HADROSAUR). This primitive duckbill had many IGUANODONT features, and was rather small for a hadrosaur. Like all hadrosaurs, it walked on two legs and ate plants. It is known from an incomplete skeleton found in Middle Cretaceous sediments in Asia.

Classification: Hadrosauridae, Ornithopoda, Ornithischia

Gondwanaland (gond-WAH-nuh-land) (Named for the land of the Gonds, an ancient kingdom of central India.)

The name given to the southern supercontinent that was formed when PANGAEA broke up about 180 million years ago. It was made up of what are now South America, Africa, Arabia, India, Madagascar, Australia, New Zealand, and Antarctica.

GORGOSAURUS (GOR-guh-sawr-us) "Terrible Lizard" (Greek *gorgos* = terrible + *sauros* = lizard, referring to its enormous mouth and teeth.)

133

See ALBERTOSAURUS. These two dinosaurs are now considered to be the same animal, though *Gorgosaurus* may be a somewhat smaller species. The name *Albertosaurus* is the older name and therefore is the preferred one, even though the name *Gorgosaurus* was given to a nearly complete skeleton found in Alberta, Canada, whereas the name *Albertosaurus* was given to very fragmentary remains. Fossils assigned to *Gorgosaurus* have also been found in Baja California.

Classification: Carnosauria, Theropoda, Saurischia

GRALLATOR (GRAL-uh-tor) "Stilt Walker" (Greek *grallator* = one who walks on stilts, referring to the length of the strides.)

Name given to three-toed dinosaur footprints that resemble those of long-legged wading birds. These TRACKS have been found in Late Triassic or Early Jurassic rock in the eastern and southwestern United States, and in Germany. The animal that made them was a small, two-legged, bird-like dinosaur that probably resembled COELOPHYSIS. It is possible that they were made by that dinosaur or a very close relative.

GRALLATOR TRACK

GRAVITHOLUS (GRAV-eh-tho-lus) "Heavy Dome" (Latin *gravis* = heavy + *tholus* = dome, referring to its thickened skull.)

A new GENUS of PACHYCEPHALOSAUR (dome-headed dinosaur). This Late Cretaceous creature is known only from a skull found in Alberta, Canada. Its skull roof was very wide and was thicker than that of STEGOCERAS, though its BRAIN was about the same size as that of *Stegoceras*. Instead of knobs and spikes such as are found on some pachycephalosaur skulls, the skull of *Gravitholus* had a large depression and many smaller pits.

Like all pachycephalosaurs, *Gravitholus* was a BIPEDAL plant-eater. It was probably about the same size as *Stegoceras*.

Classification: Pachycephalosauridae, Ornithopoda or Pachycephalosauria, Ornithischia

H

HADROSAURICHNUS (HAD-ruh-sawr-ik-nus) "Bulky Lizard Footprint" (Greek *hadros* = bulky + *sauros* = lizard + *ichnus* = footprint.)

Name given to ORNITHOPOD footprints that were found in Late Cretaceous sediments in northern Argentina. These TRACKS resemble those of duck-billed dinosaurs (HADROSAURS) and are thought to have been made by one of them.

hadrosaurines or **Hadrosaurinae** (had-ruh-SAWR-ih-nee) "Bulky Lizards" (Named after HADROSAURUS.)

One of the two groups or subfamilies of HADROSAURS (duck-billed dinosaurs). Members of this group had long, slender limbs and low spines on their pelvic vertebrae. Their duck-like bills flared only slightly at the end, and in some curled up a little along the edges making them rather spoon-shaped. Some had crests of solid bone; others had no crests at all. These HERBIVORES lived in North America, Europe, and Asia during Late Cretaceous times. ANATOSAURUS, BRACHYLOPHOSAURUS, CLAOSAURUS, EDMONTOSAURUS, GILMOREOSAURUS, HADROSAURUS, LOPHORHOTHON, PROSAUROLOPHUS, and SAUROLOPHUS were hadrosaurines.

hadrosaurids or **Hadrosauridae** (had-ruh-SAWR-ih-dee) "Duck-billed Lizards" (Named after HADROSAURUS.) Commonly called hadrosaurs.

The family of ORNITHOPODS called "duckbills" because their long, flat snouts were covered by horny material like the beak of a duck. They walked on two legs with their bodies horizontal and their tails extended for balance. They may have browsed on all fours. Hadrosaurs had strong, heavy legs; three-toed feet; medium-length arms; and webbed, four-fingered hands. The toes were hoofed. The SKIN had a pebbly surface, and some hadrosaurs were covered with small, scaly, knob-like bumps. There were no teeth in the front of the jaws, but the sides of the jaws were lined with hundreds of teeth arranged in several very complicated rows. Hadrosaurs ranged in size from 10 to 40 feet (3 to 12 m) long.

Because of their webbed hands, it was once thought that hadrosaurs were water dwellers that ate soft water plants. Scientists now believe that hadrosaurs lived in upland regions. They probably went into water only to escape predators such as ALBERTOSAURUS or TYRANNOSAURUS. Fossilized stomach contents show that they ate leaves, twigs, pine needles, seed, and fruit—food of land animals.

Hadrosaurs seem to have evolved from an Asian IGUANODONT, PROBACTROSAURUS. They have been found in Late Cretaceous sediments in North America, South America, Europe, and Asia. Two kinds of hadrosaurs are known: HADROSAURINES, which were crestless or had solid skull crests—ANATOSAURUS, BRACHYLOPHOSAURUS, and SAUROLOPHUS—belonged to this group; and LAMBEOSAURINES, which had hollow crests. CORYTHOSAURUS, LAMBEOSAURUS, and PARASAUROLOPHUS were members of this group. Because of differences in their body skeletons, scientists can tell which group a hadrosaur belongs to even if they have not found its skull.

hadrosaurs (HAD-ruh-sawrz)
  See HADROSAURIDS.

HADROSAURUS   (HAD-ruh-sawr-us) "Bulky Lizard"
(Greek *hadros* = bulky + *sauros* = lizard, because it was
a large animal.)

The first dinosaur discovered in North America that
has been recorded. The fossils of this Late Cretaceous
HADROSAUR were first found in New Jersey, but remains
have since been found in Montana and Alberta, Canada,
as well. Although the top of its skull has not been found,
Hadrosaurus is considered to be a HADROSAURINE because
of its body structure. *Hadrosaurus* was 30 feet (9 m) long,
10 feet (3 m) tall at the hips, and weighed 3 tons (2.7 metric
tons). It walked on two legs and ate plants.

Some scientists consider *Hadrosaurus* and KRITOSAURUS
to be the same. Others think that although these two hadrosaurs were quite similar, they were different GENERA.

Classification: Hadrosauridae, Ornithopoda, Ornithischia

HADROSAURUS

HALLOPUS (hal-LO-pus) "Different Foot" (Greek *hallos* =
different + *pous* = foot, because its foot was unlike those
of dinosaurs.)

Not a dinosaur, although at first it was thought to be. Further study of additional remains of this creature have led some scientists to think it was a THECODONT. Others believe it was a CROCODILIAN. It was about the size of a rooster and had four fingers and three toes. Its fossils have been found in Colorado. It lived during Late Triassic and very early Jurassic times. It is known from a partial skeleton and a few other fragmentary bits.

HALTICOSAURUS (HALT-ih-kuh-sawr-us) "Holding Lizard" (Greek *haltos* = hold + *sauros* = lizard, referring to its grasping hands.)

A very primitive Late Triassic COELUROSAUR. This meat-eating BIPED is one of the earliest known THEROPODS. It was small, agile, and lightly built, with feet similar to those of the PROSAUROPODS. It was probably an early ancestor of PROCOMPSOGNATHUS and COELOPHYSIS. It is known from a fragmentary skeleton found in Germany.

Classification: Coelurosauria, Theropoda, Saurischia

hands

The forefeet of BIPEDAL dinosaurs are frequently called "hands." Each dinosaur group had distinctive hands, and scientists can tell by looking at a fossil hand which dinosaur group it belonged to. Five-fingered hands, arranged somewhat like those of human hands with four short fingers and a shorter thumb, were the most common among the ORNITHOPODS. In all groups the fingers were tipped with hoof-like nails. The earliest ornithopod families—the FABROSAURS and the HYPSILOPHODONTS—had hands that appear to be capable of grasping, quite similar to those of THEROPODS. However, the fingers were shorter. It is not known what they may have held. In some IGUANODONTS, the thumb was a bony spike, which was probably used as a defense weapon. The HADROSAURS had only four fingers on their hands, which were connected with webbing.

The number of fingers on the hands of theropods ranged from two to five. Most COELUROSAURS had strong, three-fingered grasping hands. The fingers were long and could have been used to catch and hold large prey. Some CARNOSAURS may have had five-fingered hands, but most had only three, and the TYRANNOSAURS had only two. The fingers in both coelurosaurs and carnosaurs ended in long, sharp claws—up to 6 inches (15 cm) long.

HAPLOCANTHOSAURUS   (hap-luh-KANTH-uh-sawr-us)
"Single-spined Lizard" (Greek *haplos* = single + *akantha* = spine + *sauros* = lizard, referring to its single-spined vertebrae as opposed to the double spine on some SAUROPOD vertebrae.)

An early North American sauropod—the most primitive known from this continent. This 72-foot (22-m) QUADRUPEDAL plant-eater resembled CETIOSAURUS. It had long forelegs, a long body, and a relatively short neck and tail, but the bones in its vertebrae were nearly solid instead of

HAPLOCANTHOSAURUS

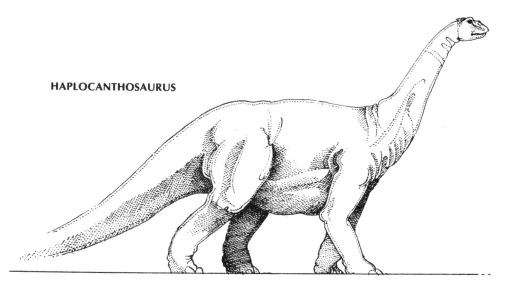

spongy. A nearly complete skeleton of *Haplocanthosaurus* was found in Late Jurassic deposits in Colorado.

Classification: Sauropoda, Sauropodomorpha, Saurischia

hearing
See SENSORY PERCEPTION.

HELOPUS (he-LOP-us)
See EUHELOPUS.

herbivore (HER-bi-vor) "Plant-eater" (Latin *herba* = plant + *vorare* = to devour.)

Any animal that eats mainly plants, such as modern cows or horses. There were many more plant-eating (herbivorous) dinosaurs than meat-eaters. All of the ORNITHISCHIAN dinosaurs (with the possible exception of TROÖDON) and all of the SAUROPODOMORPHS were herbivores. Compare CARNIVORE; OMNIVORE.

herbivorous (her-BIV-or-us)
See HERBIVORE.

herds, herding

Many modern animals herd together for protection. Scientists think that many dinosaurs herded for the same reason. They have found evidence to support this theory. At Dinosaur State Park in Connecticut, thousands of dinosaur footprints have been uncovered. Some of these are parallel, suggesting herd movement. At Holyoke, Massachusetts, the TRACKWAYS of 19 BIPEDAL dinosaurs lead in a westerly direction. According to scientists, this is clearly evidence of herding. Near Glen Rose, Texas, a long line of huge tracks records the passage of a herd of SAUROPODS. These fossil footprints seem to show an elephant-like herd structure, with YOUNG in the center surrounded by adults.

Tracks are not the only evidence that dinosaurs herded. In Belgium, scientists discovered the skeletons of 31 adult IGUANODONS that had met simultaneous death. The bones of adult and juvenile ALLOSAURUS have been found together in Utah; entire families of COELOPHYSIS (from very young to adult) have been found in New Mexico; and great numbers of skeletons of PROTOCERATOPS (from hatchlings to adults) have been found together in Mongolia.

Herding is generally associated only with warm-blooded animals. Thus, herding behavior in dinosaurs is a strong argument for those scientists who believe dinosaurs were ENDOTHERMIC (warm-blooded).

herrerasaurids or **Herrerasauridae** (her-ray-rah-SAWR-ih-dee) "Herrera's Lizards" (Named after HERRERASAURUS.)

The most primitive family of PROSAUROPODS. Some scientists think that this group may have included the ancestors of all the SAURISCHIAN dinosaurs. The herrerasaurids lived during Middle Triassic times and have been found in Argentina. They were smaller than later groups and were capable of walking on two or four legs. They had blade-like teeth, perhaps for eating meat, as well as teeth adapted for eating plants. *Herrerasaurus* and ISCHISAURUS were members of this family. They are the oldest known saurischian dinosaurs.

Some scientists suggest that this family should be placed in a suborder called PALEOPODA.

HERRERASAURUS (her-RAY-rah-sawr-us) "Herrera's Lizard" (Named in honor of a friend of the discoverer + Greek *sauros* = lizard.)

A primitive PROSAUROPOD, and one of the earliest known dinosaurs. It was closely related to the ancestors of all SAURISCHIAN dinosaurs. *Herrerasaurus* resembled AN-

CHISAURUS, but was smaller and more primitive. It normally walked on all four legs, but could possibly walk on two. It may have eaten both plants and meat. *Herrerasaurus* is known from the incomplete remains of five individuals found in Argentina. It lived in Middle Triassic times.

Classification: Prosauropoda, Sauropodomorpha, Saurischia

HERRERASAURUS

HESPERORNIS (hes-per-ORN-iss) "Western Bird" (Greek *hesperios* = western + *ornis* = bird, referring to the area where it was found.)

HESPERORNIS

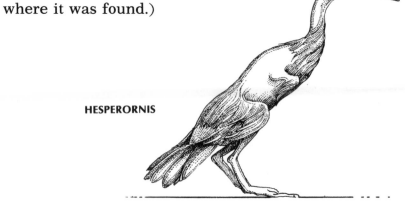

Not a dinosaur, but a 4-foot (1.2-m) primitive, flightless bird resembling a modern loon or grebe. Although this bird could not fly, it was a good swimmer and diver. It lived on the surface of the NIOBRARA SEA. Sharp teeth lined the beak of this fish-eater. Its fossils were found in Late Cretaceous deposits in Kansas and Alberta, Canada.

HESPEROSUCHUS (hes-per-uh-SOOK-us) "Western Crocodile" (Greek *hesperios* = western + *souchus* = crocodile, because it was discovered in western regions.)

Not a dinosaur, but a small PSEUDOSUCHIAN of Late Triassic western North America. It had sharp teeth and grasping hands. This agile meat-eater was 4 feet (1.2 m) long, about the size of a modern fox. It walked on four legs, but probably ran on two. Dinosaurs are thought to have EVOLVED from a similar, but earlier, type of THECODONT.

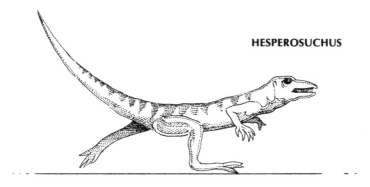

HESPEROSUCHUS

heterodontosaurids or **Heterodontosauridae** (het-er-uh-don-tuh-SAWR-ih-dee) "Different-toothed Lizards" (Named after HETERODONTOSAURUS.) Also commonly called heterodontosaurs.

A family of primitive ORNITHOPODS. Members of this family had unusual teeth for ORNITHISCHIANS. They had canine teeth in both upper and lower jaws; biting teeth in the front upper jaw that bit against a horny, toothless beak on the lower jaw; and flat-topped molars in the back part of the jaws. These BIPEDAL plant-eaters were quite small—about the size of a turkey. They have been found in Late Triassic sediments in South Africa. GERANOSAURUS, HETERODONTOSAURUS, and LYCORHINUS were members of this family.

HETERODONTOSAURUS   (het-er-uh-DON-tuh-sawr-us)
"Different-toothed Lizard" (Greek *hetero* = different + *odon* = tooth + *sauros* = lizard, referring to its three different kinds of teeth.)

A very primitive ORNITHOPOD; the first Triassic ORNITHISCHIAN known from a nearly complete skeleton. It was found in South Africa. The bones were fastened together so that scientists could tell exactly how they looked when the animal died. This BIPEDAL plant-eater had a turkey-sized body. It was built for speed and had grasping hands. Unlike most HERBIVOROUS dinosaurs, which had only one kind of teeth, *Heterodontosaurus* had three kinds. The front uppers, which were designed for biting and nipping, bit against a horny, toothless beak at the front of the lower jaw. There were molars in the back and sides of the jaws for chewing, and there were a pair of canines in both the upper and lower jaws (in mammals, canines are used for tearing meat or for defense). *Heterodontosaurus* probably used its canines as weapons. Its teeth, small size, and light build suggest that *Heterodontosaurus* was ENDOTHERMIC (warm-blooded).

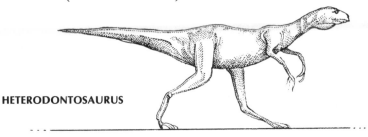

HETERODONTOSAURUS

Classification: Heterodontosauridae, Ornithopoda, Ornithischia

HIEROSAURUS (HAIR-uh-sawr-us) "Powerful Lizard" (Latin *hieros* = powerful + Greek *sauros* = lizard, the reason for its name is unknown.)

A Late Cretaceous ANKYLOSAUR found in the NIOBRARA SEA formation in Kansas. *Hierosaurus* was probably washed into the sea by a flood. It is believed by some authorities that this dinosaur is the same as NODOSAURUS.

Classification: Nodosauridae, Ankylosauria, Ornithischia

HOMALOCEPHALE (ho-mah-luh-SEF-uh-lee) "Level Head" (Greek *homalos* = level + *kephale* = head, referring to its dome.)

A Late Cretaceous PACHYCEPHALOSAUR (dome-headed dinosaur). It is known only from a partial skull found in Mongolia. Its head was large and flat. The dome was only slightly developed and was decorated with nodes along the back like the dome of PACHYCEPHALOSAURUS. It has been suggested that *Homalocephale* might have been a female pachycephalosaur, but others doubt this. Like all pachycephalosaurs, *Homalocephale* was BIPEDAL and ate plants. It had short forelegs, and was probably about the size of a goat.

Classification: Pachycephalosauridae, Ornithopoda or Pachycephalosauria, Ornithischia

homoiotherm (HO-moy-o-therm) "Uniform Heat" (Greek *homoios* = uniform + *therme* = heat.)

An animal whose body temperature remains very nearly the same all the time. Usually homoiotherms are ENDOTHERMIC (warm-blooded), but large-bodied ECTOTHERMS (cold-blooded animals) may also achieve a uniform temperature. The larger an ectotherm's body, the slower the rate of heat absorption and heat loss.

Some scientists suggest that the very large dinosaurs, such as the SAUROPODS, were homoiotherms (but not necessarily endotherms). They believe that these dinosaurs could have maintained a nearly uniform body temperature in the mild MESOZOIC climate without being warm-blooded, simply because they were so large.

homoiothermic

See HOMOIOTHERM.

HOPLITOSAURUS (hop-LEE-tuh-sawr-us) "Armed Lizard" (Greek *hoplites* = armed + *sauros* = lizard, referring to the plates on its back.)

An ANKYLOSAUR of Early Cretaceous South Dakota. This armored dinosaur was similar to SAUROPELTA, and some think it may be the same as that dinosaur. Its back was covered with rows of flattened, horny plates like those of an armadillo. *Hoplitosaurus* walked on four legs and ate plants. It is known only from incomplete material.

Classification: Nodosauridae, Ankylosauria, Ornithischia

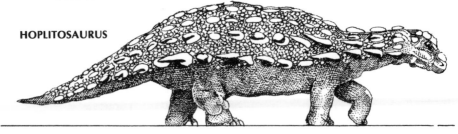

HOPLITOSAURUS

horned dinosaurs

See CERATOPSIANS.

horns

The best-known of the horned dinosaurs are the CERA-TOPSIANS. Their horns were used as defense weapons, and male ceratopsians may have used their horns as dueling weapons in fighting for mates or territories, as modern-day mountain goats do. Both male and female ceratopsians had horns; babies, however, were hornless until they were half-grown. Some ceratopsians had small stubby horns on their brows and a long nose-horn— STYRACOSAURUS had a nose-horn 2 feet (60 cm) long! Others had a short nose-horn and very long brow horns— TRICERATOPS had enormous 40-inch (102-cm) brow horns.

CERATOSAURUS had a horn-like growth on its nose. It is the only known THEROPOD with such a growth. MAIASAURA, a HADROSAUR, had a horn-like CREST, but this was not a true horn.

HYLAEOSAURUS (hy-LAY-ee-uh-sawr-us) "Wood Lizard" (Greek *hyle* = wood + *sauros* = lizard, referring to the place where it was found.)

A primitive ANKYLOSAUR whose fossils were found in England. It was one of the first three dinosaurs to be named. *Hylaeosaurus* was similar to ACANTHOPHOLIS. Two rows of spines ran down its back, and two rows of triangular bony plates protected its clubless tail. A solid shield of bone covered the hips of this 15-foot (4.5-m) long NODO-

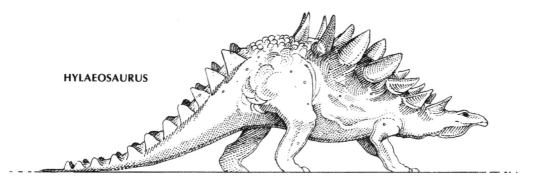

HYLAEOSAURUS

SAUR. Like all ankylosaurs, *Hylaeosaurus* was a QUAD-
RUPEDAL plant-eater. It lived during Early Cretaceous
times, and is known from a skull and most of a skeleton.
POLACANTHUS is now considered to be the same as this
dinosaur.

Classification: Nodosauridae, Ankylosauria, Ornithischia

HYPACROSAURUS (hi-PAK-ruh-sawr-us) "Very High-
ridged Lizard" (Greek *hy* = very
+ *akros* = high + *sauros*
= lizard, referring to the
high spines on its
vertebrae.)

HYPACROSAURUS

A large, hollow-crested HADROSAUR. This duck-billed dinosaur resembled CORYTHOSAURUS, but had a larger and
less rounded crest. Long spines on its vertebrae gave it a
high ridge down its back. This 30-foot (9-m) LAMBEOSAU-
RINE was a fast-running, BIPEDAL plant-eater, and was one
of the most abundant animals of Late Cretaceous Baja
California. Its fossils have also been found in Alberta,
Canada.

Classification: Hadrosauridae, Ornithopoda, Ornithischia

HYPSELOSAURUS (HIP-sih-luh-sawr-us) "High Lizard" (Greek *hypselos* = high + *sauros* = lizard, referring to its high back.)

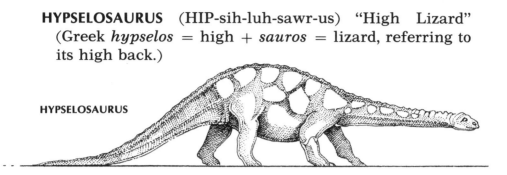

HYPSELOSAURUS

A small SAUROPOD of Late Cretaceous Europe. This four-legged plant-eater resembled TITANOSAURUS. It was only 35 feet (10.5 m) long and weighed about 10 tons (9 metric tons). *Hypselosaurus* is best known for EGGS, which were found in France. Scientists think the eggs were laid by *Hypselosaurus.* These fossil eggs are twice the size of ostrich eggs and are nearly round; they have rough sand-papery surfaces. They had been laid in crater-like NESTS in clutches of five, and are the largest dinosaur eggs ever found.

Classification: Sauropoda, Sauropodomorpha, Saurischia

HYPSILOPHODON (hip-sih-LO-fuh-don) "High-crested Tooth" (Greek *hypselos* = high + *lophos* = crest + *odon* = tooth, referring to the high, crest-like growths on the teeth.)

A small, primitive ORNITHOPOD whose fossils were first found on the Isle of Wight. This agile, long-legged, plant-eating BIPED was probably the swiftest of the ORNITHISCHI-ANS.

Hypsilophodon was 5 feet (1.5 m) long, 2 feet (60 cm) tall, and weighed about 140 pounds (63.5 kg). Half of its length was a rigid tail that it used for balancing. A few teeth lined the front of its beak-like jaws. Although *Hyp-*

silophodon was once thought to be a tree climber, it is now known that it could not have been. It had grasping hands, but the fingers were too short to hold tree branches, and the feet were not equipped for climbing. The four toes all pointed forward and could not have gripped branches.

Hypsilophodon lived from Early to Late Cretaceous times. It is known from 20 complete or partial skeletons. Fragments of this dinosaur have also been found in South Dakota, as well as on the Isle of Wight.

Classification: Hypsilophontidae, Ornithopoda, Ornithischia

HYPSILOPHODON

hypsilophodonts or **Hypsilophodontidae** (hip-sih-lo-fuh-DON-tih-dee) "High-crested Tooths" (Named after HYPSILO-PHODON.)

A family of small to medium-sized ORNITHOPODS ranging from 2.5 to 7 feet (76 to 200 cm) long. All were BIPEDAL plant-eaters with small heads, short beak-like snouts, large eyes, long legs, and medium-length arms. The teeth were set in a single row, and there were no large canines. Hypsilophodonts had five fingers and four toes. They lived from Late Triassic through Cretaceous times and have been found in North America, South America, Europe, and Africa. Some scientists suggest that the ancestors of the PACHYCEPHALOSAURS were hypsilophodonts. DRYOSAURUS, HYPSILOPHODON, OTHNIELIA, PARKSOSAURUS, and PISANOSAURUS were hypsilophodonts.

I

ICHTHYORNIS (ik-thee-ORN-iss) "Fish Bird" (Greek *ichthys* = fish + *ornis* = bird, referring to its diet.)

Not a dinosaur, but a primitive bird similar to a seagull. This bird was 8 inches (20 cm) tall. It had long wings, a flat beak, and teeth. It is the oldest known bird that could fly well. *Ichthyornis* was a fish-eater. Its fossils have been found in Kansas. It lived during Late Cretaceous times.

ichthyosaurs or **Ichthyosauria** (ik-thee-uh-SAWR-ih-ah) "Fish Lizards" (Greek *ichthys* = fish + *sauros* = lizard, because they resembled fish.)

Not dinosaurs, but MESOZOIC marine reptiles with vertical tail fins and long, streamlined heads. These 15 to 30 feet (4.5 to 9 m) long flesh-eaters gave birth to live YOUNG. We know this because scientists have found skeletons of adult ichthyosaurs that contained baby ichthyosaurs within the abdominal cavity. These animals could not leave the water to lay their EGGS as sea turtles do. Scientists think that ichthyosaurs retained the eggs in their body cavities until they hatched. Ichthyosaurs appeared in the middle of the Triassic Period and lived to Cretaceous times. They have been found in North America, South America, and Europe.

IGUANODON (ig-WAN-oh-don) "Iguana-tooth" (Iguana + Greek *odon* = tooth, because its teeth resembled those of the modern iguana lizard.)

An Early Cretaceous ORNITHOPOD. The largest known specimens were 25 feet (7.5 m) long, 15 feet (4.5 m) tall, and weighed 5 tons (4.5 metric tons). This BIPEDAL, plant-eating dinosaur had three-toed feet; its five-fingered hands had unique spike-like thumbs that grew at right angles to the other four fingers.

IGUANODON

Traces of *Iguanodon* have been found on every continent except Antarctica. It was the second dinosaur named, and perhaps the first ever found. Several dozen adult specimens were found buried together in Belgium, which suggests that these animals traveled in HERDS.

Classification: Iguanodontidae, Ornithopoda, Ornithischia

iguanodont or **Iguanodontidae** (ig-wan-uh-DON-tih-dee) "Iguana-toothed" (Named after IGUANODON.)

A family of large ORNITHOPODS with medium-sized to

large heads, long toes, and teeth arranged in a single row. These BIPEDAL plant-eaters ranged in size from 15 to 20 feet (4.5 to 6 m) long. They probably lived all over the world from Late Jurassic through Late Cretaceous times. IGUANODON, OURANOSAURUS, PROBACTROSAURUS, and TENONTOSAURUS were iguanodonts. (*Probactrosaurus* is thought to be the ancestor of the HADROSAURS.)

INDOSAURUS (in-doe-SAWR-us) "Indian Lizard" (Named for India, where it was found + Greek *sauros* = lizard.)

A Late Cretaceous CARNOSAUR; it was probably similar to ALLOSAURUS, but was more specialized. It had a broad head, and, like all carnosaurs, it walked on two legs and ate meat. *Indosaurus* belonged to the family MEGALOSAURIDAE. It is known only from a partial skull found in India.

Classification: Carnosauria, Theropoda, Saurischia

INDOSUCHUS (in-doe-SOOK-us) "Indian Crocodile" (Named for India, where it was found + Greek *souchus* = crocodile. The reason for this name is unknown. Perhaps it was first thought to be a crocodile.)

A CARNOSAUR of Late Cretaceous India. The head of this BIPEDAL meat-eater resembled that of TYRANNOSAURUS, but was smaller and less advanced. Its teeth were sharply tapered and serrated. *Indosuchus* is known only from a partial skull.

Classification: Carnosauria, Theropoda, Saurischia

INGENIA (in-JEN-ee-ah) (Etymology unknown, perhaps from the Latin *ingenus* = native, noble.)

A recently discovered OVIRAPTORID THEROPOD from Late Cretaceous deposits in southwest Mongolia. This little BIPED was closely related to OVIRAPTOR, but was smaller. From the end of its toothless snout to the tip of its long tail, it was perhaps 4.5 feet (1.4 m) long. Like *Oviraptor,* it probably ate EGGS of other dinosaurs, insects, and possibly dead animals.

Classification: Coelurosauria, Theropoda, Saurischia

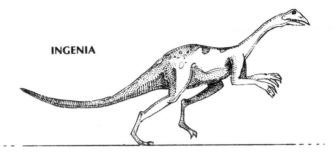

INGENIA

intelligence

Dinosaurs are usually considered to have been dim-witted, because most of them had very small BRAINS in proportion to the size of their bodies. However, recent studies have caused scientists to think that perhaps dinosaurs were not as stupid as was formerly thought. They have discovered evidence that many kinds of dinosaurs— COELUROSAURS, ORNITHOPODS, CERATOPSIANS, PROSAUROPODS, and even SAUROPODS (which had tiny brains in comparison to their body size)—HERDED together and apparently protected their YOUNG. These are considered rather intelligent things to do. Also, most THEROPODS had relatively large brains. Those of CARNOSAURS were huge; the brain of TYRANNOSAURUS was even larger than human brains. Of course, carnosaurs were much larger than humans, but even so, their brains were a quite respectable size. Large brains in comparison to body size is associated with superior intelligence in modern animals. ANKYLOSAURS and STEGOSAURS had very small brains, but if nothing else they managed to live 50 million years or more, and that is not bad for an animal such as STEGOSAURUS with a golf-ball-sized brain. The most intelligent of all the dinosaurs probably was STENONYCHOSAURUS. It probably was at least as smart as an ostrich, which is smarter than any reptile living today.

ISCHISAURUS (ISH-ee-sawr-us) "Ischigualasto Lizard" (Named for the Ischigualasto rock formation, where it was found + Greek *sauros* = lizard.)

A PROSAUROPOD of Middle Triassic Argentina—one of the earliest known dinosaurs. This plant-eater was related to PLATEOSAURUS, but was much more primitive than that dinosaur. Like all prosauropods, it had a long neck and tail, and its head was small. It probably walked on all fours, but could run on two. It is known only from skull fragments, parts of legs and pelvis, and some vertebrae.

Classification: Prosauropoda, Sauropodomorpha, Saurischia

ITEMIRUS (eye-TIM-ih-rus) "Itemir Lizard" (Named for the Itemir site in Russia, where it was found.)

A small CARNOSAUR unlike any other known. It is known from an extremely well-preserved braincase recently found in Russia. This little meat-eater was somewhat similar to the TYRANNOSAURIDAE, but was much smaller and lived earlier in the Late Cretaceous Period. It probably shared a close ancestor with TYRANNOSAURUS. The earliest known of the Cretaceous carnosaurs, it has been placed in a family of its own—the Itemiridae.

Classification: Carnosauria, Theropoda, Saurischia

J

JAXARTOSAURUS (jax-AR-tuh-sawr-us) "Jaxartes Lizard" (Named for the Jaxartes River in Russia near which it was found + Greek *sauros* = lizard.)

A primitive LAMBEOSAURINE HADROSAUR. This BIPEDAL plant-eater is known only from fragments and a partial skull found in Late Cretaceous rock in Russia. The skull had a dome-like crest. Its discovery is important because it showed that hadrosaurs lived in many areas of Asia.

Classification: Hadrosauridae, Ornithopoda, Ornithischia

Jurassic (jer-ASS-ik) **Period** (Named for the Jura Mountains of France and Switzerland, because the rocks of those mountains are of that age.)

The middle period of the MESOZOIC ERA. This geological period began 190 million years ago and ended 135 million years ago.

Very little is known about the dinosaurs of Early Jurassic times because most rock formations of that age (that we know about) are marine sediments and dinosaurs were land animals. However, exciting new dinosaur discoveries that are of Early Jurassic age have been made in India. We may soon know much more about the dinosaurs of this age.

Many fossils of Late Jurassic dinosaurs have been found. The largest of the dinosaurs (and the largest known land animals) lived during this period.

K

KENTROSAURUS (KEN-truh-sawr-us) "Spiked Lizard" (Greek *kentros* = spiked + *sauros* = lizard, referring to the spikes on its back.)

A Late Jurassic STEGOSAUR. A double row of plates ran down the neck of this dinosaur and halfway down its back, then there were eight pairs of spikes running from there to the tip of the tail. Another pair of spikes projected from the hips. The tail ended in double spikes. This plant-eater was 16 feet (4.8 m) long and weighed 2 tons (1.8 metric tons) or more. It walked on four legs and had hoof-like claws on its toes. A nearly complete skeleton was found in Tanzania.

Classification: Stegosauridae, Stegosauria, Ornithischia

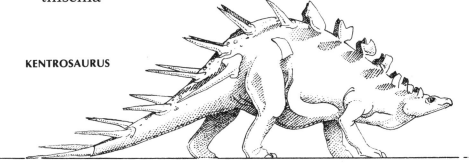

KENTROSAURUS

KRITOSAURUS (KRIT-uh-sawr-us) "Noble Lizard" (Greek *kritos* = excellent; noble + *sauros* = lizard, because of its "Roman Nose.")

A Late Cretaceous HADROSAUR with a flat, broad head and a low ridge of bone in front of its eyes, giving it a humped nose. Some scientists think this duckbill was identical to HADROSAURUS, but others think they are different GENERA. *Kritosaurus* was a BIPEDAL plant-eater. Its remains have been found in New Mexico and Baja California, and it is known from a nearly complete skeleton. It was about 30 feet (9 m) long and 15 feet (4.5 m) tall, and probably weighed about 3 tons (2.7 metric tons).

Classification: Hadrosauridae, Ornithopoda, Ornithischia

KRITOSAURUS

KRONOSAURUS   (KRO-nuh-sawr-us) "Crown Lizard" (Greek *krona* = crown + *sauros* = lizard, because its skull was the largest reptile skull known.)

Not a dinosaur, but a short-necked, large-headed PLESIOSAUR. This marine reptile was 40 feet (12 m) long, and its

KRONOSAURUS

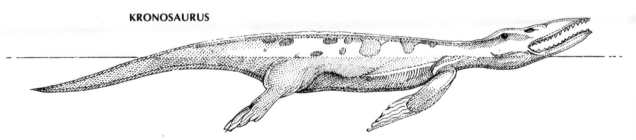

head was 12 feet (3.5 m) long. It propelled itself through Early Cretaceous oceans with long flippers. Fossils of this fish-eater have been found in Australia.

L

LABOCANIA (lab-o-KAY-nee-uh) (Named for the LaBocana Rojo rock formation, where it was found.)

A large CARNOSAUR whose fossils were found in Baja California. *Labocania* was related to TYRANNOSAURUS, but

LABOCANIA

it was only two thirds as large as *Tyrannosaurus*, and had a larger head and a more massive body. Only a few bones of this BIPEDAL meat-eater have been found. It lived during very early Late Cretaceous times.

Classification: Carnosauria, Theropoda, Saurischia

LAELAPS (LYE-laps) "Terrible Leaper" (Named after a creature in Greek mythology that turned to stone while leaping.)

Same as DRYPTOSAURUS. *Laelaps* was the first name given to this large CARNOSAUR, but the name was changed because another fossil animal had already been named *Laelaps*.

Classification: Carnosauria, Theropoda, Saurischia

LAGOSUCHUS (lah-go-SOOK-us) "Rabbit Crocodile" (Greek *lagos* = hare + *souchos* = crocodile, referring to its size.)

Not a dinosaur, but a primitive PSEUDOSUCHIAN THECODONT. This rabbit-sized creature was lightly built and had a small head. Like all early pseudosuchians, it probably held its body partially upright, rather than sprawling. Its hind legs were strong, and its hands could grasp small prey. Scientists think that one of its relatives may have been an ancestor of the THEROPOD dinosaurs. *Lagosuchus* lived during Late Triassic times. Its fossils have been found in Argentina.

lambeosaurine or **Lambeosaurinae** (lam-be-uh-SAWR-ih-nee) "Lambe's Lizards" (Named after LAMBEOSAURUS.)

One of the two groups of HADROSAURS; these were the hollow-crested duck-billed dinosaurs. Members of this group had robust limbs, high spines on their pelvic vertebrae, and broad, blunt beaks. The lower jaws curved downward. These HERBIVORES ranged in size from 13 to 40 feet (4 to 12 m) long. They lived during Late Cretaceous times and have been found in North America and Asia. CORYTHOSAURUS, HYPACROSAURUS, LAMBEOSAURUS, PARASAUROLOPHUS, and TSINTAOSAURUS were lambeosaurines. Compare HADROSAURINES.

LAMBEOSAURUS (LAM-be-uh-sawr-us) "Lambe's Lizard" (Named in honor of Lawrence Lambe, Canadian vertebrate paleontologist + Greek *sauros* = lizard.)

A Late Cretaceous, hollow-crested HADROSAUR (a LAMBEOSAURINE). This duck-billed dinosaur may have been the longest ORNITHISCHIAN dinosaur. The largest known specimen was 40 feet (12 m) or more in length.

Lambeosaurus had a large, hatchet-shaped crest with a backward-pointing spike. Its nose was narrow and ended in a broad, blunt beak. Its SKIN was pebbly, like that of CORYTHOSAURUS, but lacked the bumps on the stomach. Pine needles and twigs or leaves of flowering trees were its favorite food. This BIPED lived in upland regions. It is known from complete skeletons found in Alberta, Canada, and Baja California. It was almost as abundant as HYPACROSAURUS.

Classification: Hadrosauridae, Ornithopoda, Ornithischia

LAMBEOSAURUS

LAOSAURUS (LAY-uh-sawr-us) "Fossil Lizard" (Greek *laos* = stone; fossil + *sauros* = lizard, because the bones had turned to stone.)

Name given to several Late Jurassic fossils found in the

western United States. They were long-legged ORNITHO-
PODS of the HYPSILOPHODONT line. The name *Laosaurus* has
also been given to an ornithopod found in Late Cretaceous
rock in Wyoming. The Cretaceous animal was medium-
sized—possibly 7.5 feet (2.3 m) long—and was very similar
to HYPSILOPHODON. The Jurassic specimens varied greatly
in size. A turkey-sized specimen has been reclassified and
named *Othnielia rex.* (See OTHNIELIA.) Other Jurassic fossils called *Laosaurus* need further study.

Classification: Hypsilophodontidae, Ornithopoda, Ornithischia

LAPLATASAURUS (lah-PLAH-tuh-sawr-us) "La Plata Lizard" (Named for La Plata, Argentina, where it was found
+ Greek *sauros* = lizard.)

A medium-sized Late Cretaceous SAUROPOD similar in
appearance to DIPLODOCUS, but more closely related to
TITANOSAURUS. *Laplatasaurus* was a slender-limbed
sauropod about 70 feet (21.5 m) long, and like *Titanosaurus,* may have had bony plates, or scutes, embedded in its
SKIN. This long-necked, four-legged HERBIVORE is known
only from incomplete skeletons. Its fossils have been
found in Argentina, Uruguay, India, Madagascar, and
Nigeria. Some scientists think that its discovery in so
many different regions might indicate that there was a
land connection between South America and Africa during the Late Cretaceous Period. Others think that some of
the fossil remains now thought to be those of *Laplatasaurus* may actually belong to a different sauropod.
Some of the specimens are so fragmentary that it is difficult to make a positive identification at this time.

Classification: Sauropoda, Sauropodomorpha, Saurischia

Laurasia (lor-AY-shah) (Named for the Laurentian Mountains of Quebec, Canada, and Asia.)

Name given to the northern supercontinent that was formed when PANGAEA broke apart about 180 million years ago. It was made up of what is now North America, Greenland, Iceland, Europe, and Asia.

LEPTOCERATOPS (lep-toe-SAIR-uh-tops) "Slender Horned Face" (Greek *leptos* = slender + *keratops* = horned face, referring to its slender build.)

A small, primitive CERATOPSIAN. It had a large head with a short, solid frill, and a parrot-like beak, but no horns. This plant-eater was only 6 feet (1.8 m) long and 2.5 feet (76 cm) tall at the hips. It was basically QUADRUPEDAL, but may have been capable of walking on two legs. Its forelegs were shorter than its hind legs. *Leptoceratops* is known from very complete material found in Alberta, Canada, in sediments that were formed during the late part of the Late Cretaceous Period.

Classification: Protoceratopsidae, Ceratopsia, Ornithischia

LEPTOCERATOPS

LESOTHOSAURUS (leh-SOTH-uh-sawr-us) "Lesotho Lizard" (Named for Lesotho, the country in Africa, where it was found + Greek *sauros* = lizard.)

A primitive ORNITHOPOD of the FABROSAURID family. This BIPEDAL plant-eater was only 3 feet (90 cm) long and was similar in build to HETERODONTOSAURUS, but it had a flatter, more primitive skull, and no canine teeth. Its small head had a horny beak-like jaw lined with small serrated teeth. *Lesothosaurus* had short front legs and five-fingered hands. The hind legs were long and slender; the feet were also long and had hoof-like claws. *Lesothosaurus* probably grazed on all fours, but ran on two legs. This Late Triassic dinosaur is one of the earliest known ORNITHISCHIANS. It is known from most of the skeleton and a skull found in southern Africa. It was originally considered a SPECIES of FABROSAURUS and most descriptions of that dinosaur were based on the fossils that are now known as *Lesothosaurus*.

Classification: Fabrosauridae, Ornithopoda, Ornithischia

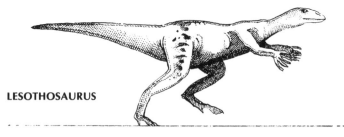

LESOTHOSAURUS

LEXOVISAURUS (lex-OH-vuh-sawr-us) "Lexovix Lizard" (Named for an ancient Gallic people, who lived in the area near Lyons, France + Greek *sauros* = lizard.)

A STEGOSAUR of Middle Jurassic England and France. This four-legged plant-eater was related to KENTROSAURUS, but lived earlier. It is known only from incomplete material, but we do know that its plates and spikes were more varied than those of *Kentrosaurus*.

Classification: Stegosauridae, Stegosauria, Ornithischia

lizard-hipped dinosaurs
See SAURISCHIANS.

long-frilled ceratopsians

See CERATOPSIANS.

LOPHORHOTHON (lo-for-HO-thon) "Crested Nose" (Greek *lophos* = crest + *rhothon* = nose, because it had a crest on its nose.)

A Late Cretaceous, solid-crested HADROSAUR whose fossils have been found in Alabama and North Carolina. This duck-billed dinosaur was a member of the HADROSAURINE group and, like KRITOSAURUS, it had a solid bony hump on its nose. It is known only from a partial skeleton, which appears to be that of a juvenile. It is estimated that this specimen was 12 to 15 feet (3.5 to 4.5 m) long. If the animal had lived to be adult, it would have grown to be much larger. Like all hadrosaurs, *Lophorhothon* was a BIPEDAL plant-eater.

Classification: Hadrosauridae, Ornithopoda, Ornithischia

LUFENGOSAURUS (loo-FEN-guh-sawr-us) "Lufeng Lizard" (Named for the Lufeng rock formation, where it was found + Greek *sauros* = lizard.)

A Late Triassic PROSAUROPOD similar to PLATEOSAURUS and about the same size as that dinosaur. *Lufengosaurus* was basically QUADRUPEDAL, but could stand on two legs. It had a small head and a long neck and tail. A nearly complete skeleton of this plant-eater was found in western China.

Classification: Prosauropoda, Sauropodomorpha, Saurischia

LUKOUSAURUS (LOO-kow-sawr-us) "Lukou Lizard" (Named for the place in Yunnan, China, where it was found + Greek *sauros* = lizard.)

Name given to a partial skull and jaws of a small COELUROSAUR found in Late Triassic deposits in China. This little BIPEDAL meat-eater was probably closely related to PROCOMPSOGNATHUS.

Classification: Coelurosauria, Theropoda, Saurischia

LYCORHINUS (ly-kuh-RYE-nus) "Wolf Nose" (Greek *lykos* = wolf + *rhinos* = nose, referring to its mammal-like snout.)

A small Late Triassic ORNITHOPOD. It was closely related to HETERODONTOSAURUS, but was somewhat more primitive. This plant-eater had large canines in both its upper and lower jaws and had cheek teeth, but no teeth in the front of its jaws. Its canines may have been used for defense. *Lycorhinus* was BIPEDAL. It is known only from a jaw and several teeth found in South Africa.

Classification: Heterodontosauridae, Ornithopoda, Ornithischia

M

MACROPHALANGIA (mak-ruh-fuh-LAN-jee-uh) "Long Toe" (Greek *makros* = long + *phalanges* = toe bone, because the toes were very long.)

Name given to the right foot of a COELUROSAUR found in Late Cretaceous rock in Alberta, Canada. This dinosaur was BIPEDAL, like all coelurosaurs, but we don't know what it ate. The foot was similar to that of ORNITHOMIMUS, and *Macrophalangia* probably resembled that dinosaur. It, too, may have been OMNIVOROUS, subsisting on fruit, insects, and eggs of other dinosaurs.

Classification: Coelurosauria, Theropoda, Saurischia

MACRUROSAURUS (mak-ROO-ruh-sawr-us) "Long Tailed Lizard" (Greek *makros* = long + *ouros* = tail + *sauros* = lizard, because of the great length of the tail.)

Name given to 40 tail vertebrae of an Early Cretaceous SAUROPOD. This four-legged plant-eater was closely related to TITANOSAURUS, but probably resembled DIPLODOCUS. The vertebrae were found in England. No other fossils of this dinosaur are known.

Classification: Sauropoda, Sauropodomorpha, Saurischia

MAIASAURA (mah-ee-ah-SAWR-uh) "Good Mother Lizard" (Greek *maia* = good mother + *saura* = lizard, feminine—because it was found near a nest of young.)

A primitive Late Cretaceous HADROSAUR. This two-legged duck-billed dinosaur was found in Montana near a NEST of 15 babies. It is estimated that the adult, which is known only from a skull, was 30 feet (9 m) long and 15 feet (4.5 m) tall. It had a tiny, solid, horn-shaped crest above and between its eyes. The jaws were shallow like those of the HADROSAURINES, and it belonged to that group, however, its bill was short and wide, similar to those of LAMBEOSAURINES.

The babies were a little over 3 feet (1 m) long and 12 inches (30 cm) tall. They were perhaps about a month old. Apparently they had either been taken to graze on

MAIASAURA

167

coarse plant food, or food had been brought to them in the nest, because their teeth show considerable wear. Fossils of hatchlings and "adolescent" *Maiasaura* have also been found. The hatchlings were 18 inches (46 cm) long and the half-grown juveniles were about 15 feet (4.5 m) long.

The nest found in Montana was a hollowed out, bowl-shaped structure that had been dug on a small mud mound. It was about 7 feet (2 m) in diameter, and 30 inches (76 cm) deep. There were many other such nests in the same area, suggesting a dinosaur "nursery" (or crèche). The discovery of this hadrosaur family provides some evidence that hadrosaurs cared for their YOUNG.

Classification: Hadrosauridae, Ornithopoda, Ornithischia

MAJUNGASAURUS (mah-JUNG-ah-sawr-us) "Majunga Lizard" (Named for the Majunga District of Madagascar, where it was found + Greek *sauros* = lizard.)

A medium-sized CARNOSAUR of Late Cretaceous Madagascar. This BIPEDAL meat-eater was a member of the MEGALOSAUR family. It is known from an incomplete jaw, some teeth, and numerous other skeletal remains.

Classification: Carnosauria, Theropoda, Saurischia

MAJUNGATHOLUS (mah-JUNG-ah-tho-lus) "Majunga Dome" (Named for the Majunga District of Madagascar, where it was found + Latin *tholus* = dome, because it had a domed skull.)

The first PACHYCEPHALOSAUR to be found in GONDWANA-LAND sediments. It is known only from a partial skull found in Madagascar. Unlike the skulls of most pachycephalosaurs, which have divided domes on the back of the skull and small fenestrae (holes) in the temples, the skull of *Majungatholus* has a single dome on the front portion and large fenestrae at the temples. The sides of the skull are decorated with nodes or small bumps and grooves. This Late Cretaceous dinosaur was larger than most pachycephalosaurs. The only larger "dome-head" was PACHYCEPHALOSAURUS. Like other pachycephalosaurs, *Majungatholus* was BIPEDAL and ate plants.

Classification: Pachycephalosauridae, Ornithopoda or Pachycephalosauria, Ornithischia

MALERISAURUS (MAL-er-ee-sawr-us) "Maleri Lizard" (Named for the Maleri rock formation, where it was found + Greek *sauros* = lizard.)

Not a dinosaur, but an EOSUCHIAN, a possible ancestor of lizards. This 4-foot (1.2-m) insect-eater lived during the Early Jurassic period. It was probably BIPEDAL—its hind limbs were large and almost twice as long as its forelimbs. Two complete skeletons were found in India inside the rib cages of two PARASUCHUS. *Parasuchus,* a crocodile-like reptile, obviously preyed on *Malerisaurus.*

MAMENCHISAURUS (mah-MEN-chee-sawr-us) "Mamenchi Lizard" (Named for Mamenchi, the area of China where it was found + Greek *sauros* = lizard.)

A Late Jurassic or Lower Cretaceous SAUROPOD. This huge four-legged plant-eater resembled DIPLODOCUS. It had short legs and a very long, 33-foot (10-m) neck that had 19 vertebrae—longer than the neck of any other dinosaur known. *Mamenchisaurus* was about 80 feet (25 m)

MAMENCHISAURUS

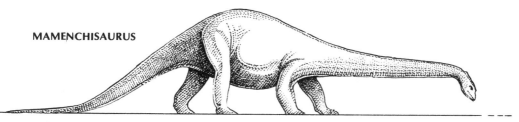

long and weighed approximately 30 tons (27 metric tons). It is known from a skeleton that is complete except for the end of the tail.

Classification: Sauropoda, Sauropodomorpha, Saurischia

MANDASUCHUS (man-dah-SOOK-us) "Manda Crocodile" (Named for Manda, Tanzania, where it was found + Greek *souchos* = crocodile.)

Not a dinosaur, but a PSEUDOSUCHIAN THECODONT. Some scientists think it may have been an ancestor of the PROSAUROPODS. This four-legged reptile looked like a crocodile. It was about the same size as a crocodile—8 feet (2.5 m) in length—but it had a shorter snout, and it probably lived only on dry land. Its fossils have been found in Triassic rock in Tanzania; they are over 200 million years old.

MANDSCHUROSAURUS (mand-CHUR-uh-sawr-us) "Manchurian Lizard" (Named for Manchuria, where it was found + Greek *sauros* = lizard.)

A flat-headed HADROSAUR found in Late Cretaceous rock in Manchuria. This HADROSAURINE is known from very incomplete skeletal material. It seems to be closely related to NIPPONOSAURUS. *Mandschurosaurus* was a BIPEDAL plant-eater.

Classification: Hadrosauridae, Ornithopoda, Ornithischia

MARSHOSAURUS (MARSH-uh-sawr-us) "Marsh's Lizard" (Named in honor of Othniel Charles Marsh, North American paleontologist + Greek *sauros* = lizard.)

A medium-sized Late Jurassic CARNOSAUR. It is estimated that this BIPEDAL meat-eater was 6 feet (1.8 m) tall,

17 feet (5.2 m) long, and weighed about 1,000 pounds (450 kg). It had long heavy legs, a large head, and serrated teeth. It is known from an incomplete skeleton found in Utah.

Classification: Carnosauria, Theropoda, Saurischia

MASSOSPONDYLUS (mass-o-SPON-dih-lus) "Bulky Vertebrae" (Greek *massa* = bulky + *spondylos* = vertebra, because its vertebrae were large.)

A lightly built, 12- to 20-foot (4- to 6-m) PROSAUROPOD. It was a close relative of THECODONTOSAURUS and resembled that dinosaur. *Massospondylus* was probably at least partially BIPEDAL. It may have eaten both meat and plants. Its jaws were lined with both powerful serrated teeth suitable for tearing meat, and weak flat teeth suitable only for eating plants. This dinosaur was a slender animal with a long neck and tail. It is known from an incomplete skeleton found in Late Triassic rock in South Africa.

Classification: Prosauropoda, Sauropodomorpha, Saurischia

MASSOSPONDYLUS

MASTODONSAURUS (MAS-tuh-don-sawr-us) "Mast-toothed Lizard" (Greek *mastos* = breast + *odon* = tooth

+ *sauros* = lizard, referring to the nipple-shaped projections on its molars.)

Not a dinosaur, but the largest amphibian that ever lived. This contemporary of the dinosaur is known from 15 complete and very well-preserved skulls and a skeleton recently discovered in Middle Triassic rock in Germany. The skulls are about 4.5 feet (1.4 m) long. The skeleton has not yet been assembled. These animals apparently were frequent prey of CARNIVOROUS THECODONTS. Many of their bones bear thecodont tooth marks. *Mastodonsaurus* in turn preyed on smaller amphibians. Many small amphibian bones have been found with mastodonsaur tooth marks on them.

megalosaurids or **Megalosauridae** (meg-uh-lo-SAWR-ih-dee) "Big Lizards" (Named after MEGALOSAURUS.) Also commonly called megalosaurs.

A family of THEROPODS. This family includes a large number of dinosaurs that are so poorly known they cannot be specifically placed in one of the other family groups. Megalosaurs probably averaged 25 to 30 feet (7.5 to 9 m) in length. They had massive skulls; long jaws; sharp serrated teeth; medium-length arms; three or more fingers; powerful hind legs; and large, sharp, curved claws. Some had elongated spines on their neck vertebrae to help support the heavy muscles needed to hold up their enormous heads. These BIPEDAL meat-eaters lived in Europe, Asia, Africa, North America, South America, Australia, and Madagascar. They flourished from Early Jurassic through Cretaceous times. ALTISPINAX, DRYPTOSAURUS, MEGALOSAURUS, and TORVOSAURUS were megalosaurs.

megalosaurs (MEG-uh-lo-sawrz) See MEGALOSAURIDS.

MEGALOSAURUS (MEG-uh-lo-sawr-us) "Big Lizard" (Greek *megalo* = big + *sauros* = lizard, because it was such a large animal.)

A large CARNOSAUR closely related to ALLOSAURUS. This meat-eater had a large head, knife-like teeth, short arms, and strong hind legs. It was 30 feet (9 m) long and 12 feet (3.5 m) tall when standing erect, and weighed 2 tons (1.8 metric tons). It was BIPEDAL; it probably walked with its body held horizontally and its tail outstretched, to balance its huge head.

Megalosaurus was the first dinosaur on record to be discovered and named. An IGUANODON bone had been found earlier, but it was not identified or named. *Megalosaurus* lived throughout Jurassic and Early Cretaceous times. Fossil bones have been found in Europe, Africa, and Asia, but a complete skeleton of this vicious predator has never been discovered. However, many of its TRACKS have been found. Scientists have learned nearly as much from the tracks as they have from the fossil bones.

Classification: Carnosauria, Theropoda, Saurischia

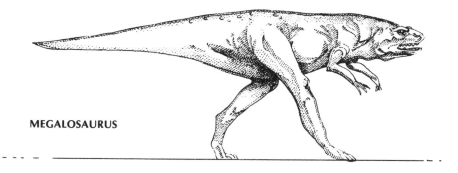

MEGALOSAURUS

melanorosaurids or **Melanorosauridae** (mel-an-or-uh-SAWR-ih-dee) "Black Mountain Lizards" (Named for MELANOROSAURUS.)

A family of PROSAUROPODS. Members of this family were

the largest and latest of the prosauropods. They ranged from 20 to 40 feet (6 to 12 m) in length, and they lived in Africa and Argentina during Late Triassic times. The melanorosaurids were completely QUADRUPEDAL. They had massive limbs and heavy bodies. Unlike earlier prosauropods, their bones were long and solid. Their heads were small, and their legs were elephant-like. In general, they looked very much like small sauropods. They ate only plants. MELANOROSAURUS and RIOJASAURUS were melanorosaurids. VULCANODON is also sometimes classed as a melanorosaurid. It lived during Early Jurassic times, but some authorities think *Vulcanodon* was a primitive SAUROPOD rather than a prosauropod.

MELANOROSAURUS   (mel-AN-or-uh-sawr-us) "Black Mountain Lizard" (Greek *melas* = black + *oros* = mountain + *sauros* = lizard.)

The largest of the PROSAUROPODS. It was about 40 feet (12 m) long. In general, it resembled the later SAUROPODS. It had a small head, massive legs, elephant-like feet, a long neck and tail, and solid bones to support its greater body weight. An incomplete skeleton of this four-legged plant-eater was found in South Africa.

Classification: Prosauropoda, Sauropodomorpha, Saurischia

Mesozoic (mez-uh-ZO-ik) **Era** "Middle Life" (Greek *mesos* = middle + *zoikos* = life.)

The "age of reptiles"—the geological period that followed the PALEOZOIC ERA and came before the CENOZOIC ERA. The Mesozoic began 225 million years ago and ended 65 million years ago. This was the era when the dinosaurs ruled the earth. The Mesozoic is divided into three periods: the TRIASSIC, the JURASSIC, and the CRETACEOUS.

METRICANTHOSAURUS   (met-rih-KANTH-uh-sawr-us)
"Moderate-spined Lizard" (Greek *metrios* = moderate + *akantha* = spine + *sauros* = lizard, referring to the vertebral spines.)

A large CARNOSAUR of Late Jurassic England. It had 10-inch (25-cm) spines on its vertebrae, but otherwise was similar to MEGALOSAURUS, and was a member of the MEGALOSAURIDAE. *Metricanthosaurus* was a BIPEDAL meat-eater. It is known from a pelvis, right femur, and vertebral column.

Classification: Carnosauria, Theropoda, Saurischia

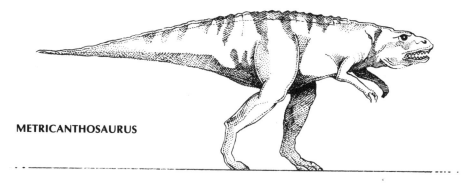

METRICANTHOSAURUS

MICROCERATOPS (my-kro-SAIR-uh-tops) "Tiny Horned Face" (Greek *mikros* = tiny; small + *keratops* = horned face, referring to its overall size.)

A primitive PROTOCERATOPSIAN of Late Cretaceous Mongolia. This tiny plant-eater was only 30 inches (76 cm) long. It was closely related to PROTOCERATOPS, and had a

MICROCERATOPS

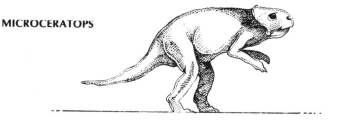

horny beak and a small frill. It may have run on its two long, slender hind legs, but probably grazed on all fours. It is known only from fragments.

Classification: Protoceratopsidae, Ceratopsia, Ornithischia

MICROPACHYCEPHALOSAURUS (my-kro-pak-ee-SEF-uh-lo-sawr-us) "Small Thick-headed Lizard" (Greek *mikros* = small + *pachys* = thick + *kephale* = head + *sauros* = lizard, because it was a small dome-headed dinosaur.)

A small PACHYCEPHALOSAUR. *Micropachycephalosaurus* was closely related to HOMALOCEPHALE and resembled that dinosaur. It had a flat dome. This BIPEDAL plant-eater is known only from a partial skull recently discovered in Late Cretaceous rocks in China.

Classification: Pachycephalosauridae, Ornithopoda or Pachycephalosauria, Ornithischia

MICROVENATOR (my-kro-ven-AY-tor) "Small Hunter" (Greek *mikros* = small + *venator* = hunter, because it was a small predator.)

A turkey-sized Early Cretaceous COELUROSAUR of western North America. This hollow-boned dinosaur was a BIPEDAL meat-eater. Counting the tail, it was 4 feet (1.2 m) long. It was 30 inches (76 cm) tall and weighed about 14 pounds (6.4 kg). It was very bird-like, and had a small head, a long neck, short arms with three long fingers, strong hind legs, and a long tail. It probably was a swift

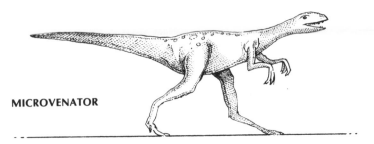

MICROVENATOR

runner. It is known from a partial skeleton found in Montana.

Classification: Coelurosauria, Theropoda, Saurischia

MINMI (MIN-mee) (Named for the Minmi rock formation in which it was discovered.)

A peculiar ANKYLOSAUR recently found in Queensland, Australia. This armored dinosaur was a NODOSAUR about the size of STRUTHIOSAURUS—5 to 6 feet (1.5 to 1.8 m) long. This dinosaur is different from all other known ankylosaurs. It had a unique spinal structure called paravertebrae. These were little horizontal plates of bone that ran along each side of the spine on its back vertebrae. The purpose of these little plates is not known. Paravertebrae are not found in any other known vertebrate animal. Because of its paravertebrae, this dinosaur's species name is "paravertebra"; its full name is *Minmi paravertebra.* *Minmi paravertebra* was discovered in Cretaceous marine deposits. It had apparently drifted out to sea and sank to the bottom upside down, and was buried in that position, preserving the paravertebrae in place.

Minmi was a four-legged plant-eater. It is known only from the trunk portion immediately in front of the pelvis, one foot, a fragment of the pelvis, and some armor.

Classification: Nodosauridae, Ankylosauria, Ornithischia

MONGOLOSAURUS (mon-go-luh-SAWR-us) "Mongolian Lizard" (Named for Mongolia, where it was found + Greek *sauros* = lizard.)

One of the last of the SAUROPODS. This four-legged plant-eater lived in Mongolia during Late Cretaceous times. It was related to TITANOSAURUS and probably resembled that dinosaur. It is known only from very fragmentary material.

Classification: Sauropoda, Sauropodomorpha, Saurischia

MONOCLONIUS (mon-uh-CLO-nee-us) "Single Stem" (Greek *mono* = single + *clonius* = stem, referring to the single horn on its nose.)

One of the first true CERATOPSIANS of western North America. Its frill was short, but its huge head was 6 feet (1.8 m) long from the tip of its beak-like snout to the end of its frill. A single, long horn grew on its nose, but only knobs appeared on the brow. The nose-horn curved slightly upward. *Monoclonius* was QUADRUPEDAL and had hoofed toes. It carried its huge head close to the ground and fed on low ground plants. *Monoclonius* was 20 feet (6 m) long. Its fossils have been found in Late Cretaceous deposits in Alberta, Canada, and it is known from several complete skulls and other skeletal material.

Classification: Ceratopsidae, Ceratopsia, Ornithischia

MONOCLONIUS

MONTANACERATOPS (mon-TAN-uh-sair-uh-tops) "Montana Horned Face" (For the state where it was found + Greek *keratops* = horned face.)

A very early PROTOCERATOPSIAN. It was a close relative of both PROTOCERATOPS and LEPTOCERATOPS, but was more advanced than either. The bony frill was longer than that of

Protoceratops, and a small horn grew on its nose. Its head was smaller than that of *Leptoceratops,* and its forelegs were longer. This small dinosaur is known from a nearly complete skeleton found in Late Cretaceous rocks in Montana.

Classification: Protoceratopsidae, Ceratopsia, Ornithischia

MONTANACERATOPS

MOROSAURUS (MORE-uh-sawr-us) "Foolish Lizard" (Greek *moros* = foolish + *sauros* = lizard, because it had a small head and was presumed to be stupid.)

Name given to a small SAUROPOD found in Wyoming. This dinosaur is now considered to be a young CAMARASAURUS.

Classification: Sauropoda, Sauropodomorpha, Saurischia

mosasaurs or **Mosasauridae** (mo-zuh-SAWR-ih-dee) "Meuse Lizards" (Named after MOSASAURUS.)

Not dinosaurs, but a group of large Late Cretaceous marine lizards related to modern monitor lizards. Mosasaurs were 50 feet (15 m) or more long. They had large heads; short legs with flipper-like hands and feet; and long, slim bodies. The nostrils were rather far back on the top of the skull. Mosasaurs were meat-eaters. They probably hunted various kinds of sea animals. AMMONITE shells have been found that clearly show mosasaur tooth marks. Mosasaurs swam close to the surface of oceans all over the world, and have been found in marine deposits in many places. MOSASAURUS and TYLOSAURUS were mosasaurs.

MOSASAURUS (MO-zuh-sawr-us) "Meuse Lizard" (Named after the Meuse River in Holland, where it was first found + Greek *sauros* = lizard.)

Not a dinosaur, a Late Cretaceous MOSASAUR—the first of its kind found. It is known only from a huge head with enormous 4-foot (1.2-m) long jaws filled with sharp teeth. This giant marine lizard is estimated to have been 20 to 26 feet (6 to 8 m) long. It was found in Holland, and was one of the very first MESOZOIC fossils ever discovered.

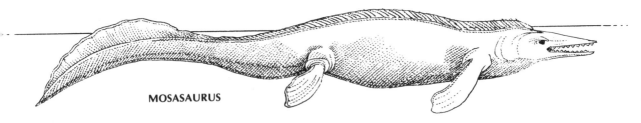

MOSASAURUS

MOSCHOPS (MOSS-kops) "Calf Face" (Greek *moschos* = calf + *ops* = face, because its skull resembled that of a calf.)

Not a dinosaur, but a THERAPSID. (Therapsids were the mammal-like reptiles from which mammals arose). *Mos-*

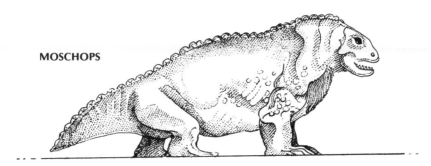

MOSCHOPS

chops lived during the PERMIAN PERIOD; it was already extinct by the beginning of the MESOZOIC ERA. It was 8 feet (2.5 m) long and 5 feet (1.5 m) tall at the shoulders. The shoulders of this QUADRUPED were much higher than the hips, so that the back sloped sharply backward. Its bulky body, heavy limbs, and broad feet gave *Moschops* a rather clumsy look. Its weak jaws and peg-like teeth indicate that it was a plant-eater. Its remains have been found in South Africa and Russia.

MUSSAURUS (moose-SAWR-us) "Mouse Lizard" (Latin *mus* = mouse + Greek *sauros* = lizard, referring to the very small size of the specimen.)

The smallest dinosaur ever found. It appears to be a newly hatched baby PROSAUROPOD, but was very close to being a primitive SAUROPOD. *Mussaurus* was about the size of a robin. The skull of this tiny four-legged SAURIS-CHIAN was only 1.25 inches (3.2 cm) long. It was very much like the skulls of sauropods. A nearly complete *Mussaurus* skeleton (lacking only the tail and rib cage) was found in a NEST that contained remains of four more individuals and several large eggshell fragments. *Mussaurus* and the nest were found in Argentina. The rock in which it was found is either very late Triassic or very early Jurassic.

Classification: Prosauropoda, Sauropodomorpha, Saurischia

MUTTABURRASAURUS (mut-tah-BUR-rah-sawr-us) "Muttaburra Lizard" (Named for Muttaburra, Queensland, Australia, the locality where it was found + Greek *sauros* = lizard.)

An Early Cretaceous IGUANODONTID ORNITHOPOD from Australia. This animal is known from a nearly complete skeleton and several partial skeletons. It is one of the best-known of all Australian dinosaurs. *Muttaburrasaurus* was a BIPEDAL plant-eater that probably foraged on low shrubs. It closely resembled IGUANODON, and was about the same size. It even had the same kind of spiked thumbs that *Iguanodon* had.

Classification: Iguanodontidae, Ornithopoda, Ornithischia

N

NANOSAURUS (NAN-uh-sawr-us) "Dwarf Lizard" (Greek *nanus* = dwarf + *sauros* = lizard, referring to its overall size.)

A very small Jurassic ORNITHOPOD of the HYPSILO-PHODONT family. It closely resembled HYPSILOPHODON. It ranged from 2 to 4 feet (60 to 120 cm) long and 12 to 18 inches (30 to 46 cm) tall at the hips. This little BIPEDAL plant-eater is known from most of a skeleton (minus the skull) recently found in Utah, and from fragments found in Colorado.

Classification: Hypsilophodontidae, Ornithopoda, Ornithischia

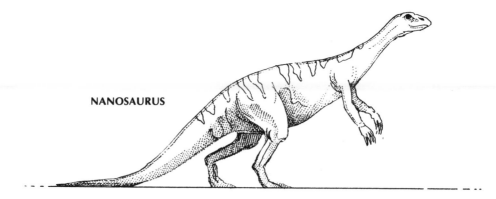

NANOSAURUS

NANSHIUNGOSAURUS (nan-SHOONG-uh-sawr-us) "Nan-shiung Lizard" (Named for Nanshiung, China, where it was found + Greek *sauros* = lizard.)

An unusual new SAUROPOD recently found in China. It is currently classed as a TITANOSAURID, but it does not resemble other titanosaurids or any other sauropod. When scientists have had time to study it further, it may be placed in a family of its own. It lived during the Cretaceous Period. Like all sauropods, it was QUADRUPEDAL and ate plants.

Classification: Sauropoda, Sauropodomorpha, Saurischia

NAVAHOPUS (nah-vah-HO-pus) "Navaho Foot" (Named for the formation in which it was discovered and the Navaho Indian Reservation + Greek *pous* = foot.)

Name given to a TRACKWAY made in Arizona by an Early Jurassic PROSAUROPOD. The trackway consists of a trail of six prints of the hind feet and six prints of the forefeet. The hind feet had four toes with strong claws on the middle toes—they were quite similar to the hind feet of AMMOSAURUS. The forefeet are unique. They were small and rather hoof-like, with two short, clawed fingers and a sickle-like claw on the thumb. The dinosaur that made the tracks was basically QUADRUPEDAL, but was able to walk on two legs. It was about four-fifths the size of a specimen of *Ammosaurus* found in the same area.

NEMEGTOSAURUS (NEH-meh-tuh-sawr-us) "Nemegt Lizard" (Named for the Nemegt rock beds, where it was found + Greek *sauros* = lizard.)

A Late Cretaceous SAUROPOD related to DIPLODOCUS; it probably resembled that dinosaur. This four-legged plant-eater lived later than most DIPLODOCIDAE. It was a long-necked beast and probably cropped the tops of tall trees. It is known from a skull and much of a skeleton found in Mongolia.

Classification: Sauropoda, Sauropodomorpha, Saurischia

NEMEGTOSAURUS

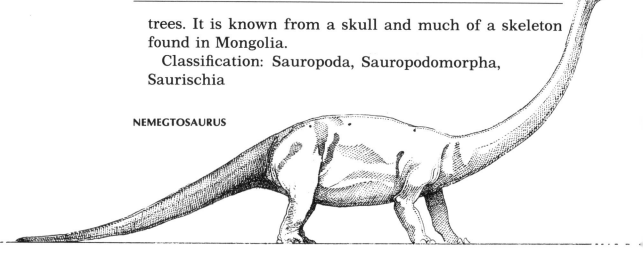

nests

We know that at least some dinosaurs laid EGGS in nests. Dinosaur nests are quite similar to those of modern crocodiles and marine turtles. They were crater-like pits dug in sand or mud. The eggs were usually laid in concentric circles arranged in tiers. The smallest circle being at the bottom of the pit, the next larger circle a tier above it, and the largest at the top. The eggs were separated by and covered with sand.

Although the best-known dinosaur nests, and the first discovered, are those of PROTOCERATOPS in Mongolia, nests of at least four other kinds of dinosaurs have been found. In most cases, many nests belonging to the same kind of dinosaur seem to be grouped together in a single area. Such a grouping is called a "crèche." In one site in Montana, more than 30 CARNIVORE nests were found. (These nests may have been made by TROÖDON.) However, at a site in Argentina, only a single nest has been found to date. This nest contained five tiny PROSAUROPOD hatchlings, which have been named MUSSAURUS.

The size of dinosaurs' nests varied according to the size of the dinosaur that made them. A nest found in France is 15 feet (4.5 m) in diameter. Scientists believe this nest was made by the SAUROPOD, HYPSELOSAURUS. The bowl-shaped nest of MAIASAURUS (a HADROSAUR) is 7 feet (2 m) in diameter and 2.5 feet (76 cm) deep; it was found in Montana.

Some scientists think that, at least in the case of *Protoceratops,* more than one female may have shared a single nest. They think it unlikely that one could have laid as many eggs as have been found in some nests.

Niobrara (nye-o-BRAR-ah) **Sea** (Named for the Niobrara River in northern Nebraska and Wyoming.)

Name given to the shallow sea that extended across central North America from the Gulf of Mexico to the Arctic Ocean, splitting the continent in half, during Late Cretaceous times. The Niobrara Sea was 1,000 miles (1,600 km) wide. Inhabitants of this sea tended to be large. Even oysters were huge, some as much as 18 inches (46 cm) in diameter, and some PLESIOSAURS were 43 feet (13 m) long.

NIPPONOSAURUS (nip-on-uh-SAWR-us) "Japanese Lizard" (Japanese *Nippon* = Japan, where it was found + Greek *sauros.*)

A small, Late Cretaceous HADROSAUR with a small dome-like crest on its skull. This HADROSAURINE is known from an incomplete skeleton found in Japan. It may be the same as GILMOREOSAURUS.

Classification: Hadrosauridae, Ornithopoda, Ornithischia

NOASAURUS (NO-uh-sawr-us) "Northwestern Argentina Lizard" (NOA = Spanish abbreviation for Northwestern Argentina + Greek *sauros* = lizard.)

A Late Cretaceous COELUROSAUR found in Argentina. It resembled the DROMAEOSAURIDS, but the sickle-like claw on its foot was of a different shape, and *Noasaurus* was probably smaller. This small THEROPOD may have been 6 feet (1.8 m) long. It is known from a jaw, limb bones, a few pieces of skull, and vertebrae.

Classification: Coelurosauria, Theropoda, Saurischia

nodosaurids or **Nodosauridae** (no-doe-SAWR-ih-dee) "Toothless Lizards" (Named after NODOSAURUS.)

One of the two families of ANKYLOSAURS. These were the most primitive of the armored dinosaurs; they had clubless tails, large spikes on their sides, pear-shaped heads, and thick bony plates, or scutes, on their backs, heads, and tails. Their legs were more slender and not as massive as those of the ANKYLOSAURIDAE. The smallest nodosaurid was 5 feet (1.5 m) long; the largest was 19 feet (5.8 m) long. These four-legged plant-eaters lived in Europe and North America throughout the Cretaceous Period. HYLA-EOSAURUS, NODOSAURUS, PANOPLOSAURUS, SAUROPELTA, and STRUTHIOSAURUS were Nodosauridae.

NODOSAURUS (no-doe-SAWR-us) "Toothless Lizard" (Greek *anodon* = toothless + *sauros* = lizard. Mis-named—it probably did have teeth.)

One of the earliest known ANKYLOSAURS (armored dino-saurs). This four-legged plant-eater was 17.5 feet (5.3 m) long and 6 feet (1.8 m) tall. It was a NODOSAURID. Shell-like, knobby plates covered its head, body, and clubless tail,

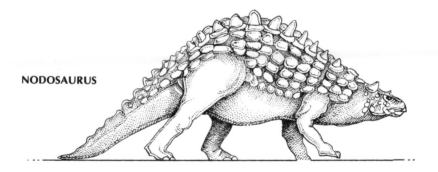

NODOSAURUS

and there were spikes on its sides. It is known from incomplete skeletal material. Fossils of *Nodosaurus* have been found in Early Cretaceous deposits in New Jersey, Alabama, Kansas, and Wyoming. STEGOPELTA is the same as this dinosaur and some authorities think HIEROSAURUS is also the same animal.

Classification: Nodosauridae, Ankylosauria, Ornithischia

nothosaurs or **Nothosauria** (no-tho-SAWR-ih-ah) "Spurious Lizards" (Greek *nothos* = spurious; false + *sauros* = lizard, because they no longer lived on land.)

Not dinosaurs, nor even related to dinosaurs, but Triassic reptiles that had returned to a life in the sea. These small, rather long-necked and long-tailed animals had small skulls and sharp teeth. They preyed on fish and other sea animals. They had paddle-like arms and legs with webbed hands and feet; only moderately changed for a life in the sea. They probably lived near shores, and may have been able to move about on land like the seals and walruses of today. Nothosaurs were the ancestors of PLESIOSAURS. The best-known nothosaur is NOTHOSAURUS, which was 10 feet (3 m) long. Its fossils have been found in Europe and Israel.

NOTHOSAURUS (no-tho-SAWR-us)
See NOTHOSAURS.

O

OHMDENOSAURUS (OHM-den-o-sawr-us) "Ohmden's Lizard" (Named in honor of a German scientist + Greek *sauros* = lizard.)

An Early Jurassic SAUROPOD—one of the earliest known. This dinosaur was related to CETIOSAURUS and probably resembled that dinosaur. It is known from very fragmentary material found in the Holzmaden Beds in southern West Germany. The discovery of this large four-legged plant-eater is important, because the study of its remains will help to fill in some of the gaps in our understanding of the EVOLUTION of all sauropods.

Classification: Sauropoda, Sauropodomorpha, Saurischia

OHMDENOSAURUS

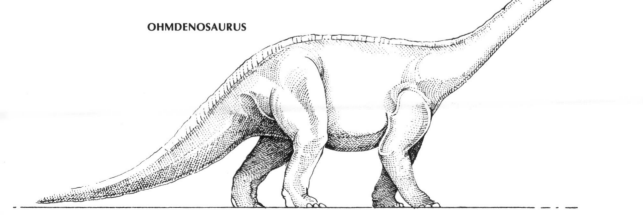

OMEISAURUS   (o-meh-ee-SAWR-us) "Omei Lizard" (Named for Omei, a city in China, near where it was found + Greek *sauros* = lizard.)

A large Late Jurassic SAUROPOD. It was similar to EUHELOPUS and, like that dinosaur, had forelegs and hind legs of nearly equal length. *Omeisaurus,* like all sauropods, was huge, had a long neck and tail, and walked on four legs. It was a plant-eater, and probably browsed on treetops. It is known from a partial skeleton found in central China.

Classification: Sauropoda, Sauropodomorpha, Saurischia

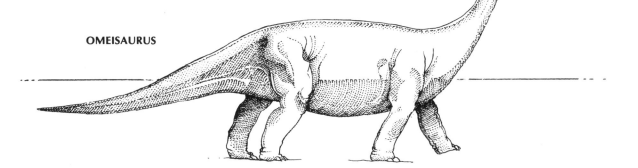

OMEISAURUS

omnivore (AHM-nih-vor) "All-eater" (Latin *omnis* = all + *vorare* = to devour.)

Any animal that eats both plants and other animals. The "ostrich dinosaurs" and the early PROSAUROPODS may have been omnivores. Coyotes and raccoons are modern omnivorous animals. Compare CARNIVORE; HERBIVORE.

omnivorous (ahm-NIV-or-us)
See OMNIVORE.

OMOSAURUS (O-mo-sawr-us) "Rough Lizard" (Greek *omos* = rough + *sauros* = lizard, referring to its spiny back.)

Same as DACENTRURUS. The name was changed because another animal had already been named *Omosaurus.*

Classification: Stegosauridae, Stegosauria, Ornithischia

OPISTHOCOELICAUDIA (o-piss-tho-SEE-luh-caw-dee-uh) "Backward Hollow Tail" (Greek *opisthen* = backward + *koelas* = hollow + Latin *cauda* = tail, referring to its tail vertebrae.)

A recently discovered Late Cretaceous SAUROPOD similar to EUHELOPUS. This ponderous QUADRUPED had forelegs and hind legs of nearly equal length. It had a short tail, which it held far off the ground. *Opisthocoelicaudia* was a plant-eater and probably ate almost continuously, nipping off the top branches of trees and swallowing them whole. It is known from a nearly complete skeleton (minus the neck and skull) that was found in Mongolia.

Classification: Sauropoda, Sauropodomorpha, Saurischia

OPISTHOCOELICAUDIA

opisthopubic (o-PISS-tho-pew-bic) **pelvis**
"Backward Pubis" (Greek *opisthen* =
backward + *pubic* = pubis bone.)

A type of dinosaur pelvis that is
unlike those of either the "bird-hipped"
ORNITHISCHIANS or the "lizard-hipped"
SAURISCHIANS. In this type of pelvis,
the ilium is broad and deep as in the
saurischians, but the pubis bone slants
toward the rear, as in the ornithischians,
rather than toward the front as is usual for
saurischians. This type of pelvis has been
found in DEINONYCHOSAURS and
SEGNOSAURS.

ilium

hip socket

ischium

pubis

opisthopubic pelvis

ornithischians or **Ornithischia** (or-nih-THISS-kee-ah)   "Bird-
hipped" (Greek *ornithos* = bird + *ischion* = hip, because their pelvises resembled those of modern birds.)

One of the two orders of animals called DINOSAURS. All
ornithischians had bird-like pelvises and hoofed toes, and
all (except possibly one) were plant-eaters. (A recent discovery not yet fully studied, but currently thought to be
TROÖDON, may prove to be the first known CARNIVOROUS
ORNITHISCHIAN.) All except the PACHYCEPHALOSAURS had
beaked mouths. Both two and four-legged kinds lived
world-wide from Middle Triassic times to the end of the
Cretaceous Period. Some were no larger than a cat, while
others were 40 feet (12 m) long. Ornithischians are generally divided into four suborders: the ORNITHOPODA, the
STEGOSAURIA, the ANKYLOSAURIA, and the CERATOPSIA. Some

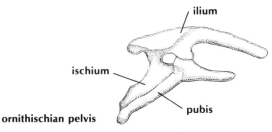

ilium

ischium

pubis

ornithischian pelvis

scientists add a fifth: the PACHYCEPHALOSAURIA. If the new discovery does turn out to be a carnivorous ornithischian, it will be a sixth suborder.

ORNITHOLESTES (or-nith-o-LESS-teez) "Bird Robber" (Greek *ornithos* = bird + *lestes* = robber, because it was imagined catching ARCHAEOPTERYX.)

A 6-foot (1.8-m), lightly built COELUROSAUR of Late Jurassic North America. This small-headed, long-tailed, BIPEDAL dinosaur ate lizards and other small game that it caught with its long-fingered, three-clawed hands. It is known from incomplete skeletal material found in Wyoming. *Ornitholestes* has long been considered to be the same as COELURUS, but new studies indicate that they were different GENERA.

Classification: Coelurosauria, Theropoda, Saurischia

ORNITHOLESTES

ornithomimids or **Ornithomimidae** (or-nith-o-MY-mih-dee) "Ostrich Imitator" (Named after ORNITHOMIMUS.) Also called "ostrich dinosaurs."

A family of COELUROSAURS resembling modern ostriches in size and shape. Ornithomimids had small heads, toothless beaks, enormous eyes, large brains, long necks, and long legs. Unlike ostriches, however, these dinosaurs had long tails and three-toed feet (ostriches have only two toes), and instead of wings they had medium-length arms with three-fingered hands. These swift little THEROPODS lived in Late Cretaceous North America, Africa, Israel, and Asia. They probably were OMNIVORES—that is, they may have eaten both meat and plants. DROMICEIOMIMUS, ELAPHROSAURUS, GALLIMIMUS, ORNITHOMIMUS, and STRUTHIOMIMUS were ornithomimids.

ORNITHOMIMUS (or-nith-uh-MY-mus) "Bird Imitator" (Greek *ornithos* = bird + *mimos* = imitator, because it resembled an ostrich.)

A Late Cretaceous ORNITHOMIMID ("ostrich dinosaur") that lived in Colorado, Wyoming, Montana, Mongolia, and Alberta, Canada. It is known from the incomplete skeletons of several different individuals. This BIPEDAL dinosaur so closely resembled STRUTHIOMIMUS that some scientists consider them to be the same. However, others are convinced that the two were different dinosaurs.

Ornithomimus was probably about 8 feet (2.5 m) tall and 15 feet (4.5 m) long. Most of its length was neck and tail. A horny beak covered its toothless jaws. Its diet may

ORNITHOMIMUS

have consisted of fruit, small reptiles, insects, and the eggs of other dinosaurs. *Ornithomimus* may have been ENDOTHERMIC (warm-blooded). It probably could run as swiftly as an ostrich—few other dinosaurs would have been faster. Although its head was small, it had a quite large braincase, and it is considered to be one of the most intelligent of the dinosaurs. Its intelligence and its speed were its best defenses against larger predators.

Classification: Coelurosauria, Theropoda, Saurischia

ornithopods or **Ornithopoda** (or-nith-uh-PO-dah) "Bird-footed" (Greek *ornithos* = bird + *podos* = foot, because the feet were thought to resemble those of birds, though they actually do not.)

One of the suborders of ORNITHISCHIAN dinosaurs. Ornithopods first appeared in Late Triassic times, and, as a group, they lasted through Late Cretaceous times. All were plant-eaters with horned beaks and were basically BIPEDAL (some may have grazed on all fours). They walked or ran with their bodies parallel to the ground and their tails outstretched for balance. Their feet had three or four toes, with hoof-like claws or nails. Ornithopod hands had either four or five fingers. The ornithopods included the HYPSILOPHODONTS, FABROSAURS, HETERODONTOSAURS, CAMP-TOSAURS, IGUANODONTS, and HADROSAURS. The PACHYCEPH-ALOSAURS have always been included in this suborder until recently. Now some scientists think pachyceph-alosaurs belong in a suborder of their own because they were quite different from other ornithopods.

Ornithosuchidae (or-nith-uh-SOOK-ih-dee) "Bird Croco-diles" (Named after ORNITHOSUCHUS.)

A family of very advanced PSEUDOSUCHIANS. These THECODONTS were so advanced some scientists think they may have been primitive dinosaurs. ORNITHOSUCHIANS lived in North America, South America, Europe, and Africa during Middle and Late Triassic times. These four-legged meat-eaters were 4 to 6 feet (1.2 to 1.8 m) long. They had sharp, dagger-like teeth, and five-fingered hands. HESPEROSUCHUS, ORNITHOSUCHUS, RIOJASUCHUS, and SAL-TOPOSUCHUS were members of this family.

ORNITHOSUCHUS (or-nith-uh-SOOK-us) "Bird Crocodile" (Greek *ornithos* = bird + *souchos* = crocodile, because it was lightly built and BIPEDAL, like a bird.)

Not a dinosaur, but possibly an ancestor of the THERO-PODS. A few think that *Ornithosuchus* was a very primitive dinosaur, but most scientists think it was an advanced PSEUDOSUCHIAN THECODONT. This meat-eater was 6 feet (1.8 m) long, weighed 110 pounds (50 kg), and had sharp, dagger-like teeth. Its skull was large and narrow, and its hands had five fingers. The remains of this creature were found in Middle and Late Triassic rocks in Scotland. Similar animals have been found in North America, Europe, Africa, and South America.

ORNITHOSUCHUS

"ostrich dinosaurs"
See ORNITHOMIMIDS.

OTHNIELIA (oth-NEEL-ee-ah) (Named in honor of Othniel Charles Marsh, American paleontologist.)

A small ORNITHOPOD of Late Jurassic North America. It was only 2.5 feet (80 cm) long. It had a small head and large eyes; its beak-like jaws were lined with teeth; and its hands had five fingers. This turkey-sized, BIPEDAL plant-eater was found in Utah, Wyoming and Colorado. It was once thought to be a species of LAOSAURUS, but is now considered a separate GENUS.

Classification: Hypsilophodontidae, Ornithopoda, Ornithischia

OTHNIELIA

OURANOSAURUS (our-AHN-uh-sawr-us) "Valiant Lizard" (Touareg, a Nigerian dialect, *ourane* = valiant; fearless + Greek *sauros* = lizard, because the natives use this word to describe fearless animals.)

An Early Cretaceous ORNITHOPOD. This BIPEDAL plant-eater was related to IGUANODON, and was about the same size—it measured 23 feet (7 m) long and 16.5 feet (5 m) tall. But unlike *Iguanodon, Ouranosaurus* had very high spines on its vertebrae that ran down the middle of its back and tail. These spines may have supported a sail or fin that helped keep *Ouranosaurus* from overheating. Two complete specimens of this animal were found in the Sahara Desert of Niger, Africa. *Ouranosaurus* is the only known ORNITHISCHIAN with a sail.

Although *Ouranosaurus* is classed as an IGUANODONT, it had several features like those of HADROSAURS. Its head was long and flat, and it had a duck-like bill. This dinosaur was probably related to the ancestors of the hadrosaurs.

Classification: Iguanodontidae, Ornithopoda, Ornithischia

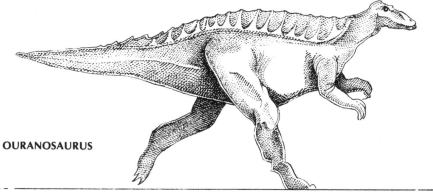

OURANOSAURUS

OVIRAPTOR (o-vee-RAP-tor) "Egg Stealer" (Latin *ovum* = egg + *raptor* = robber, because it was found near a nest of eggs.)

A small Late Cretaceous COELUROSAUR. This dinosaur was similar to ORNITHOMIMUS, but was much smaller—it was only 5 feet (1.5 m) long. With its lightly built skull, large brain, and powerful, toothless beak, *Oviraptor* resembled birds even more closely than *Ornithomimus*.

OVIRAPTOR

Its body may even have been insulated by feathers or something similar.

Oviraptor had huge hands with three long, slender fingers that were capable of holding prey. It walked on two long, slender legs. Parts of several skeletons of this little THEROPOD were found in Mongolia. One specimen was found near a NEST of PROTOCERATOPS EGGS. This has led scientists to assume that *Oviraptor* ate eggs. Its diet probably also included insects and berries, and it may have scavenged on carcasses of dead animals like crows of today.

Classification: Coelurosauria, Theropoda, Saurischia

oviraptorid or **Oviraptoridae** (o-vee-rap-TOR-ih-dee) "Egg Stealers" (Named after OVIRAPTOR.)

A family of small Late Cretaceous COELUROSAURS whose fossils were found in Mongolia. They had toothless beaks and were BIPEDAL, lightly built animals with hollow bones. Their skulls were unusually short and deep, with large BRAIN cavities. Oviraptorids were about five feet long, but their bodies were only about the size of a large turkey. Oviraptorids closely resembled birds. OVIRAPTOR is the best known of this family.

P

Pachycephalosauria (pak-ee-sef-uh-lo-SAWR-ee-ah) "Dome-headed Lizards" (Named after PACHYCEPH-ALOSAURUS.)

A proposed new suborder of Ornithischia. (See PACHYCEPHALOSAURS.)

pachycephalosaurs or **Pachycephalosauridae** (pak-ee-sef-uh-lo-SAWR-ih-dee) "Dome-headed Lizards" (Named after PACHYCEPHALOSAURUS.)

A specialized branch of small ORNITHISCHIAN dinosaurs that is usually included in the ORNITHOPODA suborder. However, some scientists now think this group should be in a separate suborder called the PACHYCEPHALOSAURIA because they are different from other ORNITHOPODS. The pachycephalosaurs had very thick skulls or "domes." The purpose of these domes is unknown, but males had thicker skulls than females. Perhaps pachycephalosaurs lived in HERDS, and the males competed for mates or territories by butting their heads together, like mountain goats. The domes might have been used as a means of defense, too. Perhaps males warded off attackers while the females and YOUNG fled. However, pachycephalosaurs seem to have had a very good sense of smell, which would have been their best defense against large CARNOSAURS.

Pachycephalosaurs probably derived from a line of HYPSILOPHODONTS. They were BIPEDAL plant-eaters. They walked with their bodies held horizontally, like birds, with their tails extended for balance. Unlike other ornithopods, pachycephalosaurs had no beaks. Their jaws were lined with short, sharp teeth.

Pachycephalosaurs ranged from turkey-sized to 15 feet (4.5 m) long. Their fossils have been found in Late Cretaceous deposits in North America, England, China, Madagascar, and Mongolia. GRAVITHOLUS, PACHYCEPHALOSAURUS, STEGOCERAS, TYLOCEPHALE, and YAVERLANDIA are pachycephalosaurs.

The GENERA in this family varied a great deal. Some had very thick, high-rising domes, while others had rather flat domes. In some the dome was divided, in others it was a single mass.

PACHYCEPHALOSAURUS (pak-ee-SEF-uh-lo-sawr-us) "Thick-headed Lizard" (Greek *pachys* = thick + *kephale* = head + *sauros* = lizard, because of its thick skull.)

A large Late Cretaceous PACHYCEPHALOSAUR. This dinosaur had a plate of bone 9 inches (23 cm) thick covering its BRAIN. Wart-like knobs and 5-inch (13-cm) spikes fringed this dome and decorated the dinosaur's small nose. This BIPEDAL plant-eater is known only from skulls found in Wyoming and Alberta, Canada. These skulls were 26 inches (66 cm) long—three times as large as the skull of STEGOCERAS. If the rest of *Pachycephalosaurus's* body was in proportion to its skull, it was 15 feet (4.5 m) long—the largest of the pachycephalosaurs.

Classification: Pachycephalosauridae, Ornithopoda or Pachycephalosauria, Ornithischia

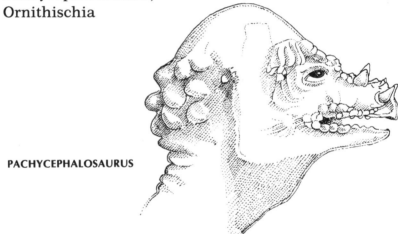

PACHYCEPHALOSAURUS

PACHYRHINOSAURUS (PAK-ee-rye-no-sawr-us) "Thick-nosed Lizard" (Greek *pachys* = thick + *rhinos* = nose + *sauros* = lizard, referring to the thick plate on its nose.)

A Late Cretaceous CERATOPSIAN. This unusual horned dinosaur had a large oval plate of bone on its nose instead of a horn. This plate measured 14 inches by 22 inches (36 cm by 56 cm), and was 5 inches (13 cm) thick. It was slightly cratered, like a volcano. Similar fist-sized knobs grew above the eyes, and spikes edged the short, wide frill. *Pachyrhinosaurus* had strong teeth and a beak-like snout. It was 20 feet (6 m) long and weighed 4 tons (3.6 metric tons). It walked on four strong legs; it carried its head near the ground, because its hind legs were longer than the forelegs. *Pachyrhinosaurus* probably ate very coarse ground plants. Its fossils have been found in Alberta, Canada.

Classification: Ceratopsidae, Ceratopsia, Ornithischia

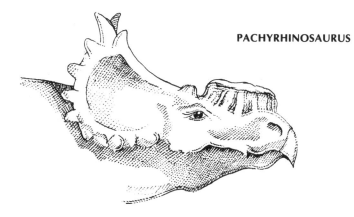

PACHYRHINOSAURUS

PALAEOSCINCUS (pay-lee-o-SKINK-us) "Ancient Lizard" (Greek *palaios* = ancient + *scincus* = GENUS name of modern lizards called skinks, because its tooth resembled that of a skink.)

An ANKYLOSAUR (armored dinosaur) of Late Cretaceous North America. It was once thought to be the same as PANOPLOSAURUS or EDMONTONIA; however, recent authorities believe that *Palaeoscincus,* which is known only from a single tooth found in Montana, is a different ankylosaur.

Classification: Nodosauridae, Ankylosauria, Ornithischia

paleontologist (pay-lee-on-TOL-o-jist) (From PALEONTO-
LOGY.)
  A person who learns about ancient life by studying fos-
sils; a specialist in paleontology.

paleontology (pay-lee-on-TOL-o-jee) (From Greek *palaios*
  = ancient + *onta* = being; living things.)
  The science of studying ancient life as it is revealed by
FOSSILS; a branch of biology and geology.
  Paleontology is an exciting field of study. One branch
deals only with fossil animals without backbones. This is
called invertebrate paleontology. Vertebrate paleontology deals only with fossil animals that had backbones.
Some paleontologists specialize in studying dinosaurs.
This is a branch of vertebrate paleontology. Some of them
go all over the world looking for new fossils. Others spend
their lives studying fossils that have already been col-
lected; still others do a little of both. Many thousands of
tons of fossils are stored in museums around the world,
waiting to be studied and identified. From these fossils,
scientists will gather many pieces of evidence that will
tell them what life on earth was like many millions of
years ago.

Paleopoda (pay-lee-uh-PO-dah) "Ancient Feet" (Greek
  palaios = ancient + *poda* = foot.)
  A name given to a suborder sometimes used for the very
early SAURISCHIANS. This suborder includes the
STAURIKOSAURIDS, the HERRERASAURIDS, the ANCHISAURIDS,
and the PLATEOSAURIDS.

Paleozoic (pay-lee-o-ZO-ik) **Era** "Ancient Life" (Greek
  palaios = ancient + *zoikos* = life.)
  The geological age preceding the MESOZOIC ERA. It

began 600 million years ago and ended 225 million years ago. This is the period during which fish, sea plants, amphibians, land plants, and reptiles developed.

Pangaea (pan-JEE-ah) "All Earth" (Greek *pan* = all + *gaia* = earth.)

Name given to the huge "supercontinent" that probably existed on earth during the PERMIAN and TRIASSIC Periods. Scientists believe that at that time, all of earth's land mass was clumped together into one single continent. According to the theory, Pangaea began to break up during the Late Triassic Period, forming two supercontinents, which are called LAURASIA and GONDWANALAND. Then, during Late CRETACEOUS times, these supercontinents also broke up and drifted apart, finally forming the continents as we know them today.

PANOPLOSAURUS (pan-OP-luh-sawr-us) "Armored Lizard" (Greek *panoplo* = armored + *sauros* = lizard, referring to the plates on its back.)

A Late Cretaceous ANKYLOSAUR of western North America. This four-legged plant-eater was the last of the North American NODOSAURIDS. Rows of thick bony plates covered its pear-shaped head and its neck, back, and tail. Long spikes protected its sides and shoulders, but its tail was clubless. *Panoplosaurus* grew to be at least 18 feet (5.5 m)

PANOPLOSAURUS

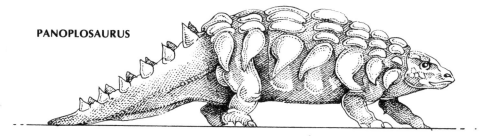

long and weighed about 3 tons (2.7 metric tons). It has been found in Alberta, Canada; Montana; and Texas. Although not everyone agrees, it is now generally believed that EDMONTONIA was a species of *Panoplosaurus.*

Classification: Nodosauridae, Ankylosauria, Ornithischia

PARASAUROLOPHUS   (par-ah-sawr-OL-uh-fus)   "Similar Crested Lizard" (Greek *para* = similar + SAUROLOPHUS, because this dinosaur also had a crest.)

A Late Cretaceous LAMBEOSAURINE HADROSAUR of western North America. The remarkable crest of this duck-billed dinosaur was a hollow tube 5 feet (1.5 m) long that extended back over the animal's shoulders. The purpose of this tube is not known. It was once thought to be a snorkel, but it has no opening at the end. It may have improved the dinosaur's sense of smell. All of the air *Parasaurolophus* breathed traveled from the nostrils at the tip of the snout, up to the tip of the crest, and then back down the crest before it went down the windpipe to the lungs.

Parasaurolophus was 30 feet (9 m) long and 16 feet (4.8 m) tall, and weighed 3 to 4 tons (2.7 to 3.6 metric tons). It was a BIPEDAL land dweller, and ate pine needles and oak

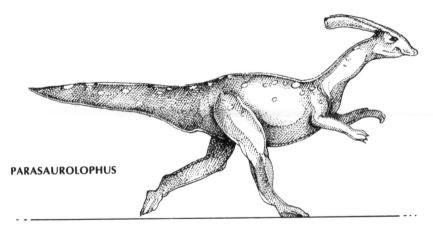

PARASAUROLOPHUS

or poplar leaves. Its hands were webbed, and its duck-like beak was spoon-shaped. It is known from a nearly complete skeleton found in Alberta, Canada. Its fossils have also been found in New Mexico.

Classification: Hadrosauridae, Ornithopoda, Ornithischia

PARASUCHUS (par-ah-SOOK-us) "Like a Crocodile" (Greek *para* = similar; like + *souchos* = crocodile, because it resembled crocodiles.)

Not a dinosaur, but a crocodile-like reptile that lived in India during the Early Jurassic Period. This four-legged meat-eater was about 20 feet (6 m) long. Two complete skeletons were found side by side on a flood plain. More remarkable still, discovered beneath the rib cage of each *Parasuchus* was a fossil skeleton of another reptile, MALERISAURUS. Apparently each *Parasuchus* had devoured one of these lizards for its last meal.

parental care

For a long time, scientists assumed that dinosaurs laid their EGGS and then left the babies to fend for themselves when they hatched (as some modern reptiles do). But now some scientists believe that at least some dinosaurs gave some kind of care to their YOUNG. This theory is supported by several pieces of evidence.

Many families of COELOPHYSIS (both juveniles and adults) have been found together in New Mexico, and two young DROMICEIOMIMUS were found with an adult in Alberta, Canada. Five young BRACHYCERATOPS were found near an adult in Montana, and many hatchling and juvenile HADROSAURS have been found with only one or two adults in several areas of Montana. More recently, the skull of an adult hadrosaur was found near a NEST of month-old babies in Montana. The teeth of the 15 MAIASAURA babies were worn, indicating that the babies had been eating coarse food. Scientists think this indicates that one or both parents were taking care of the young. The adults may have taken the young from the nest to graze during the day and returned them at night, or the adults could have brought food to the nest. Either way, the babies surely must have had some kind of adult supervision.

Perhaps the most convincing evidence of adult care of the young is supplied by a SAUROPOD TRACKWAY discovered in Texas. This trackway seems to show that sauropods traveled in HERDS with a ring of adults surrounding and protecting the young in the same way that modern elephants do.

Scientists suggest that some dinosaurs may have watched and protected the nests until the young hatched. Then, the babies that were too small to travel with the adults may have been placed in "nurseries" with one or more adults protecting them until they were large enough to join the herd. Modern giraffes care for their young in this way.

PARKSOSAURUS (PARKS-uh-sawr-us) "Parks's Lizard" (Named in honor of W. A. Parks, Canadian dinosaur collector and researcher + Greek *sauros* = lizard.)

A small Late Cretaceous ORNITHOPOD of western North America. It was 7 feet (2 m) long and weighed 150 pounds (68 kg). This dinosaur belonged to the HYPSILOPHODONT

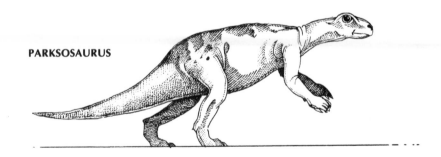

PARKSOSAURUS

family, and resembled HYPSILOPHODON. It had a long neck and a small head with a horny beak. Its forelimbs were short and strong; it ran on its long hind legs, but may have grazed on all fours in the bushy undergrowth of evergreen forests. *Parksosaurus* fossils have been found in Alberta, Canada, and in Montana.

Classification: Hypsilophodontidae, Ornithopoda, Ornithischia

PARROSAURUS (PAR-uh-sawr-us) "Parr's Lizard" (Named in honor of Albert Parr, American zoologist + Greek *sauros* = lizard.)

Name given to 13 vertebrae of a Late Cretaceous SAUROPOD found in southeastern Missouri. This four-legged plant-eater is believed to be a descendant of CAMARASAURUS; however, it probably resembled TITANOSAURUS. Like all sauropods, it had a small head and a long neck. Not enough material has been found to determine its size.

Classification: Sauropoda, Sauropodomorpha, Saurischia

PATAGOSAURUS (PAT-uh-go-sawr-us) "Patagonian Lizard" (Named for the area of Argentina, where it was found + Greek *sauros* = lizard.)

A SAUROPOD found in Middle Jurassic rock in Patagonia, Argentina. It is known from fossils of seven individuals, including one nearly complete skeleton (minus the skull). At one site, a "family" of four specimens of various sizes was found. This huge, four-legged plant-eater was a CETIOSAURID, and was about the same size and shape as CETIOSAURUS, but was more primitive. It was also more primitive than HAPLOCANTHOSAURUS, but was more advanced than AMYGDALODON.

Classification: Sauropoda, Sauropodomorpha, Saurischia

pelycosaurs or **Pelycosauria** (pel-ee-ko-SAWR-ee-ah) "Basin Lizards" (Greek *pelyco* = basin + *sauros* = lizard, referring to the shape of their hips.)

Not dinosaurs, nor even distant relatives of dinosaurs, but an order of primitive mammal-like reptiles. They lived during the PERMIAN PERIOD and were extinct before the beginning of the Triassic, millions of years before the dinosaurs lived. They were probably the ancestors of the THERAPSIDS, which in turn were the ancestors of mammals.

Some pelycosaurs were meat-eaters; others were plant-eaters. Some grew to be 10 feet (3 m) long. Many were semi-aquatic. All were QUADRUPEDAL. Some had sails on their backs which may have helped regulate their body temperature. DIMETRODON was a pelycosaur.

PENTACERATOPS (PEN-tah-sair-uh-tops) "Five-horned Face" (Greek *pente* = five + *keratops* = horned face, because it had five horns.)

A long-frilled CERATOPSIAN related to CHASMOSAURUS. It had two long brow horns, a shorter nose-horn, and two additional horn-like growths, one on each cheek. This four-legged plant-eater had an enormous neck shield or frill. Its head (including the frill) was 7.5 feet (2.3 m) long —more than one-third as long as its 20-foot (6-m) body.

PENTACERATOPS

Pentaceratops fossils have been found in Late Cretaceous rock in New Mexico and Alberta, Canada; it is known from a nearly complete skeleton.

Classification: Ceratopsidae, Ceratopsia, Ornithischia

Permian (PUR-mee-en) **Period** (Named for the old province of Perm in northeastern Russia, where rocks of this age were first described.)

The last period of the PALEOZOIC ERA; the geological time period that came just before the TRIASSIC PERIOD (the first period of the MESOZOIC ERA). The Permian Period began 290 million years ago and ended 225 million years ago.

PHOBOSUCHUS (fo-bo-SOOK-us) "Fear Crocodile" (Greek *phobos* = fear + *souchos* = crocodile, because it was the most fearsome of all CROCODILIANS.)

Not a dinosaur, but the largest crocodile that ever lived. This 50-foot (15-m) reptile lived in swamps in Late Cretaceous Texas and Montana. The skull of this meat-eater was 6 feet (1.9 m) long. *Phobosuchus* probably preyed on dinosaurs as well as anything else it could catch.

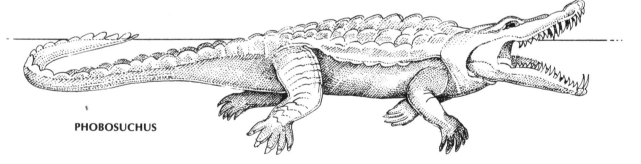

PHOBOSUCHUS

phytosaurs or **Phytosauria** (fye-toe-SAWR-ee-ah) "Plant Lizards" (Greek *phyton* = plant + *sauros* = lizard, because it was first thought that they were plant-eaters.)

Not dinosaurs, but a suborder of THECODONTS. They looked very much like crocodiles, but were not closely related to them. These reptiles grew to be 10 to 30 feet (3 to 9 m) long. They were the dominant animals of the Late Triassic Period. Phytosaurs lived in freshwater marshes, lakes, and streams, and ate fish, small amphibians, dinosaurs, or any other small animal they could catch. Their bodies were protected by heavy bony plates, or scutes. RUTIODON is the best-known phytosaur.

PIATNITZKYSAURUS   (pee-aht-NIT-skee-sawr-us) "Piatnitsky Lizard" (Named in honor of a friend of the finder + Greek *sauros* = lizard.)

PIATNITZKYSAURUS

A middle-sized CARNOSAUR. *Piatnitzkysaurus* was related to ALLOSAURUS, but was smaller and more primitive, and it had longer arms. It lived 15 million years earlier than *Allosaurus*. This vicious BIPEDAL meat-eater is known from most of a skeleton (minus feet and hands) that were found in Middle Jurassic rock in Patagonia, Argentina.

Classification: Carnosauria, Theropoda, Saurischia

PINACOSAURUS (pin-AH-kuh-sawr-us) "Board Lizard" (Greek *pinakos* = board + *sauros* = lizard, referring to its hard armored back.)

One of the earliest known ANKYLOSAURIDS. This armored dinosaur was related to ANKYLOSAURUS. It had sharp spikes along its back and sides; its tail ended in a flat bone with sharp edges (it looked somewhat like a double-edged stone ax). *Pinacosaurus* was lightly built and had short legs and slender feet. It grew to be about 12 feet (3.5 m) long. This QUADRUPED traveled arid uplands during Late Cretaceous times, seeking low ground plants to eat. An almost complete skeleton of a young adult was found in Mongolia. Its fossils have also been found in China. SYRMOSAURUS is now known to be the same as this dinosaur.

Classification: Ankylosauridae, Ankylosauria, Ornithischia

PINACOSAURUS

PISANOSAURUS (pee-SAN-uh-sawr-us) "Pisano's Lizard" (Named for a friend of the finder + Greek *sauros* = lizard.)

The earliest ORNITHISCHIAN known. This primitive ORNITHOPOD may have been an ancestor of HYPSILOPHODON. It was a small, BIPEDAL plant-eater and had long, slender feet. It probably was a good runner. Its skull and teeth resembled those of the PROSAUROPODS. *Pisanosaurus* is known from very incomplete material found in Argentina. It lived about the middle of the Triassic Period.

Classification: Hypsilophodontidae, Ornithopoda, Ornithischia

PIVETEAUSAURUS (PEEV-uh-toe-sawr-us) "Piveteau's Lizard" (Named in honor of Jean Piveteau, French paleontologist + Greek *sauros* = lizard.)

Name given to the skull of a Middle Jurassic CARNOSAUR that was found in Normandy, France. The cranium closely resembles that of ALLOSAURUS. This BIPEDAL meat-eater is classed as a MEGALOSAURIDAE. It was once considered to be a species of EUSTREPTOSPONDYLUS.

Classification: Carnosauria, Theropoda, Saurischia

plated dinosaurs

See STEGOSAURS.

plateosaurids or Plateosauridae (play-tee-uh-SAWR-ih-dee) "Flat Lizards" (Named after PLATEOSAURUS.)

An advanced family of PROSAUROPODS. They had larger and heavier bodies than earlier prosauropods. Their hands were fairly short and the fingers spread outward, indicating that they were used to support weight much of the time. Plateosaurids were probably more QUADRUPEDAL than BIPEDAL, and probably ate only plants. They did not have blade-like teeth such as ANCHISAURIDS had. Plateosaurids have been found on almost every continent. They lived during Late Triassic times. They ranged from 7 to 26 feet (3 to 8 m) long. AMMOSAURUS, LUFENGOSAURUS, and PLATEOSAURUS were plateosaurids.

PLATEOSAURUS (PLAY-tee-uh-sawr-us) "Flat Lizard" (Greek *plata* = flat + *sauros* = lizard, referring to its flat, plate-like teeth.)

One of the earliest and one of the largest SAURISCHIAN dinosaurs of the Triassic Period. *Plateosaurus* was a 26-foot (8-m) PROSAUROPOD that lived in Europe, South Africa, and Nova Scotia. It had a small head and a long neck and tail. This plant-eater was basically QUADRUPEDAL, but could stand on its hind legs to eat from the tops of trees. It probably lived in HERDS. A number of complete *Plateosaurus* skeletons have been found.

Classification: Prosauropoda, Sauropodomorpha, Saurischia

PLATEOSAURUS

plesiosauroids or **Plesiosauroidea** (plee-zee-uh-sawr-OY-dee-ah) "Near Lizards" (Named after PLESIOSAURUS.)

Not dinosaurs, but a suborder of PLESIOSAURS. They had small heads at the end of very long snaky necks. Their bodies were barrel-shaped. These sea-going reptiles probably swam close to the surface of the oceans, using their long necks to catch fish below the surface. They ranged in size from 7 to 45 feet (2 to 13.5 m) long. They lived during the Late Jurassic to the Late Cretaceous times and have been found in North America, Europe, and Australia. ELASMOSAURUS and PLESIOSAURUS were plesiosauroids.

plesiosaurs or **Plesiosauria** (plee-zee-uh-SAWR-ee-ah) "Near Lizards" (Named after PLESIOSAURUS.)

Not dinosaurs, but an order of marine reptiles that lived in the open oceans of MESOZOIC times. Plesiosaurs were not related to dinosaurs in any way, but they lived during the same time period. Some plesiosaurs swallowed small stones, either for ballast so that they could dive or to grind their food. Plesiosaurs were fish-eaters that propelled themselves through the water with flippers much the same way that modern marine turtles do. They may have been able to move about on land like modern walruses.

There were two kinds of plesiosaurs, the PLIOSAUROIDS and the PLESIOSAUROIDS. Plesiosauroids had long snaky necks, small heads, and barrel-shaped bodies. ELASMOSAURUS and PLESIOSAURUS belonged to this group. Pliosauroids were large animals and probably were comparable to modern whales. They were quite streamlined with large heads and short necks. KRONOSAURUS was a pliosauroid.

Plesiosaurs have been found in Cretaceous sediments on every continent, including Antarctica. They also lived in Jurassic times. They were the largest of the marine reptiles—some were only 8 feet (2.5 m) long, but the largest were 40 feet (12 m) long.

PLESIOSAURUS (PLEE-zee-uh-sawr-us) "Near Lizard" (Greek *plesios* = near + *sauros* = lizard, because it was once thought to be related to lizards.)

Not a dinosaur, but a long-necked PLESIOSAUR. This marine reptile was 10 feet (3 m) long. It had a long snaky neck, a barrel-shaped body, and a small head. *Plesiosaurus* swam close to the surface of oceans during Jurassic times, propelling itself along with its long paddle-like legs. It used its long neck to search for food below the surface. It ate small fish and other sea animals. *Plesiosaurus* remains have been found in England.

PLEUROCOELUS (ploor-uh-SEE-lus) "Hollow Side" (Greek *pleura* = side + *coelis* = hollow, referring to the hollows in the sides of its vertebrae.) Also called ASTRODON.

An Early Cretaceous SAUROPOD that lived in the eastern and western part of the United States and in Portugal and England. This four-legged plant-eater had long, narrow teeth and probably resembled APATOSAURUS in size and shape. Its hind feet had three claws, but its forefeet had no inner claw like those of *Apatosaurus* or DIPLODOCUS. A long line of huge sauropod TRACKS found in Texas near the Paluxy River may have been made by *Pleurocoelus*. The dinosaur that made the tracks also had three claws on its hind feet and none on its front feet.

An incomplete skeleton of a very young *Pleurocoelus,* estimated to have been 13.5 feet (about 4 m) long, was found in Maryland and the District of Columbia. Fossil bones found in Texas and Montana were much larger. These animals were probably adult *Pleurocoelus.*

The dinosaur named *Astrodon* turned out to be the same as the one named *Pleurocoelus.* Since the name *Pleurocoelus* was given first, it is the name used.

Classification: Sauropoda, Sauropodomorpha, Saurischia

PLEUROCOELUS

pliosauroids or **Pliosauroidea** (ply-uh-sawr-OY-dee-ah) "More Lizards" (Greek *pleion* = more + *sauros* = lizard.) Also called PLIOSAURS.

Not dinosaurs, but a suborder of short-necked, large-headed PLESIOSAURS. The smallest pliosauroids were about 10 feet (3 m) long, and the largest was 40 feet (12 m) long. It had a 12-foot (3.5-m) head. Pliosauroids had a small vertical tail fin. They cruised the oceans in MESOZOIC times, like sperm whales do today. They caught fish and other sea animals in their large mouths and dived for marine mollusks. KRONOSAURUS was a pliosauroid.

podokesaurids or **Podokesauridae** (po-doe-kee-SAWR-ih-dee) "Swift-footed Lizards" (Named after PODOKESAURUS.)

A primitive family of COELUROSAURS. This group had small heads; hollow bones; relatively short necks; very short, slender forelimbs; five fingers; and very long hind legs. They ranged between 24 inches (60 cm) to 10 feet (3 m) long. Podokesaurids lived during Late Triassic and possibly into the Early Jurassic times. They have been found in North America, South America, Europe, Africa, and Asia. COELOPHYSIS, HALTICOSAURUS, PODOKESAURUS, SALTOPUS, and TRIASSOLESTES were members of this family. Some people include DILOPHOSAURUS in this family instead of with the CARNOSAURS.

PODOKESAURUS (po-DOE-kee-sawr-us) "Swift-footed Lizard" (Greek *podokes* = swift-footed + *sauros* = lizard, because its long legs indicated it was a fast runner.)

A small Late Triassic or Early Jurassic COELUROSAUR of eastern North America. This BIPEDAL meat-eater was 5 feet (1.5 m) long and 2 feet (60 cm) tall. It was closely related to (or may even have been the same as) COELO-

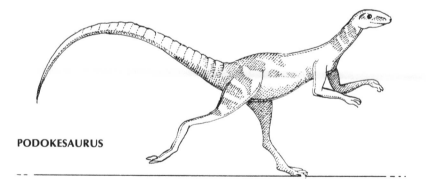

PODOKESAURUS

PHYSIS. *Podokesaurus* was lightly built and had a long tail, long hind legs, and a long, flexible neck. The only known specimen was found in Massachusetts.

Classification: Coelurosauria, Theropoda, Saurischia

POLACANTHUS (po-luh-KANTH-us) "Many Spines" (Greek *polys* = many + *akantha* = spine, referring to the spines on its back.)

Same as HYLAEOSAURUS. Since *Hylaeosaurus* is the older name, it is the preferred one, but this ANKYLOSAUR is also well-known as *Polacanthus,* the name given to a nearly complete skeleton found in England.

Classification: Nodosauridae, Ankylosauria, Ornithischia

PRENOCEPHALE (pren-uh-SEF-uh-lee) "Forward-bent Head" (Greek *prenes* = forward-bent + *kephale* = head, because it probably walked with its head bent forward.)

A small PACHYCEPHALOSAUR from Cretaceous Mongolia. This 7-foot (2-m) "dome-head" was related to STEGOCERAS. Its head was 10 inches (25 cm) long, and had a high, well-developed, solid dome. Nodes, or small bony knobs, decorated the back of the skull. The front teeth were long and sharp. *Prenocephale* was a BIPEDAL plant-eater and is known from a complete skull and most of a skeleton.

Classification: Pachycephalosauridae, Ornithopoda or Pachycephalosauria, Ornithischia

PROBACTROSAURUS (pro-BAK-truh-sawr-us) "Before Staff Lizard" (Greek *pro* = before + *bactros* = staff + *sauros* = lizard, because it was an earlier form than BACTROSAURUS.)

An IGUANODONT of Late Cretaceous times. This dinosaur was similar to *Bactrosaurus,* and scientists think it might be an ancestor of the HADROSAURS. Like all ORNITHOPODS, it was BIPEDAL and ate plants. It is known from a nearly complete skeleton found in Mongolia.

Classification: Iguanodontidae, Ornithopoda, Ornithischia

PROCHENEOSAURUS (pro-KEEN-ee-uh-sawr-us) "First Goose Lizard" (Greek *protos* = first + *cheneo* = goose + *sauros* = lizard, because it lived earlier than CHENEOSAURUS.)

A small, Late Cretaceous HADROSAUR (duck-billed dinosaur). This BIPED was 15 feet (4.5 m) long and had a small, bump-like crest on its head. It is considered by some to be the first hollow-crested hadrosaur or LAMBEOSAURINE. Others believe it is a juvenile form of CORYTHOSAURUS or LAMBEOSAURUS. Two nearly complete skeletons of this plant-eater have been found, one in Alberta, Canada, and one in Asia.

Classification: Hadrosauridae, Ornithopoda, Ornithischia

procompsognathids or **Procompsognathidae** (pro-komp-so-NAY-thih-dee) "Before Elegant Jaws" (Named after PROCOMPSOGNATHUS.)

The most primitive of the COELUROSAUR families. These little BIPEDAL meat-eaters were no more than 4 feet (1.2 m) long. They had very long necks and tails. Their hands had four fingers. They lived during the Late Triassic Period and have been found in Germany and China. LUKOUSAURUS and PROCOMPSOGNATHUS were members of this family.

PROCOMPSOGNATHUS (pro-komp-so-NAY-thus) "Before Elegant Jaw" (Greek *pro* = before + *kompos* = elegant + *gnathos* = jaw, because it was an earlier COELUROSAUR than COMPSOGNATHUS.)

A swift little coelurosaur of Late Triassic Germany. It

is one of the most primitive coelurosaurs that is known. It was 11.5 inches (29 cm) tall at the hips and 4 feet (1.2 m) long. It had hollow bones, a long flexible neck, long hind legs, and a long tail. The hands had four fingers, and the feet had three forward-pointing toes and a dewclaw. *Procompsognathus* ate insects and small animals. It is known from an incomplete skeleton.

Classification: Coelurosauria, Theropoda, Saurischia

PROCOMPSOGNATHUS

PROSAUROLOPHUS (pro-sawr-OL-uh-fus) "First Crested Lizard" (Greek *pro* = before + *sauros* = lizard + *lophos* = crest, because it was an earlier form than SAUROLO- PHUS.)

The earliest known solid-crested HADROSAUR. This duck-

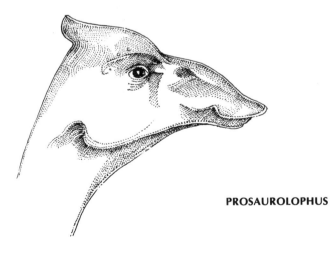

PROSAUROLOPHUS

bill was similar to ANATOSAURUS, but unlike *Anatosaurus,*
Prosaurolophus had a miniature crest that rose like small
knobs above the eyes and ended in a short, backward-
pointing spike. Its bill was smaller and shorter, and less
widely flared than that of *Anatosaurus.* Like all duckbills, this BIPEDAL plant-eater carried its body horizontally, balanced by a long crocodile-like tail. It probably
lived in plains regions. It is known from two skulls and a
partial skeleton found in Late Cretaceous sediments of
Alberta, Canada.

Classification: Hadrosauridae, Ornithopoda, Ornithischia

prosauropods or **Prosauropoda** (pro-sawr-uh-POD-ah) "Before Sauropods" (Greek *pro* = before + SAUROPODS, because they were thought to be the forerunners of sauropods.)

An infraorder of the SAUROPODOMORPHA. Most scientists
think that the ancestors of the sauropods may have come
from this suborder. However, not everyone agrees. A few
scientists think that the prosauropods are only related to
the sauropods through a common ancestor.

Early prosauropods were semi-QUADRUPEDAL. That is,
they were able to walk on either two or four legs. All
prosauropods were plant-eaters, but the earliest forms
probably also included meat (small ORNITHISCHIANS or
mammals) in their diets. These early groups had blade-
like teeth, as well as teeth suited for plant-eating. They
also had very light-weight bones. Later prosauropods
were entirely quadrupedal, had solid bones, and ate only
plants. All prosauropods had rather long necks and small
heads. They ranged in size from 8 to 40 feet (2.5 to 12 m)
long. They have been found almost everywhere in the
world and lived from the Middle Triassic to possibly very
early Jurassic.

Prosauropods have been divided into four families: the HERRERASAURIDAE were the smallest and most primitive. Some scientists think that the ancestors of all SAURISCHIANS came from this family. HERRERASAURIDS walked on either two or four legs, and ate both plants and meat. They lived during Middle Triassic times and have been found in Argentina. HERRERASAURUS and ISCHISAURUS were members of this family. Some scientists think that this family should be placed in the suborder PALEOPODA.

The ANCHISAURIDAE were somewhat more advanced than the Herrerasauridae, but were still quite primitive. They, too, were relatively small—8 to 10 feet (2.5 to 3 m) long. They were lightly built and had some hollow bones. They had long necks, long tails, and long slender fingers and toes. ANCHISAURIDS walked on either two or four legs, and may have eaten both meat and plants. They lived from Middle to Late Triassic and have been found almost all over the world. ANCHISAURUS, EFRAASIA, and THECODONTOSAURUS were members of this family.

The PLATEOSAURIDAE were more advanced than the anchisaurids, and were much larger; however, their heads were comparatively smaller. This group was also more quadrupedal. Their hands were fairly short; the fingers spread outward, indicating that they were used to support the weight much of the time. PLATEOSAURIDS had thicker and stronger bones than the earlier families. This group ate only plants; they did not have blade-like teeth. Plateosaurids were from 7 to 26 feet (2 to 8 m) long. They have been found in Late Triassic sediments on every continent except Australia and Antarctica. LUFENGOSAURUS, AMMOSAURUS, and PLATEOSAURUS were members of this family.

The MELANOROSAURIDAE were the largest and latest members of the prosauropods. They were from 20 to 40 feet (6 to 12 m) long. Their bodies were heavy and, unlike the earlier prosauropods, their bones were solid. These PROSAUROPODS were never BIPEDAL; their legs were massive like those of an elephant. The heads were very small, and the neck and tails quite long. Members of this family have been found in Late Triassic sediments in Africa and South America. MELANOROSAURUS and RIOJOSAURUS were MELANOROSAURIDS. VULCANODON, which was found in Early Jurassic sediments in Rhodesia, is sometimes placed in this family, but some scientists think it may be a very primitive sauropod rather than a prosauropod.

Proterosuchia (pro-tair-o-SOOK-ee-ah) "Earlier Crocodiles" (Greek *proteros* = earlier + *souchos* = crocodile, because they were an earlier form than crocodiles.)

Not dinosaurs, but a suborder of primitive THECODONTS that first appeared in the Late PERMIAN PERIOD. They became the largest Early Triassic creatures, and may have included the ancestors of the crocodiles. Many of this group lived in lakes and rivers in South Africa, but some were also land dwellers. Proterosuchia were CARNIVORES, and closely resembled crocodiles. They had a sprawling posture and bony plates on their backs. Some grew to be 13 feet (4 m) long.

PROTIGUANODON (pro-tuh-GWAN-uh-don) "First Iguana-tooth" (Greek *protos* = first + iguana + *odon* = tooth, because its finder thought it was an early IGUANODONT.)

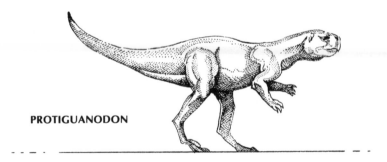

PROTIGUANODON

An Early Cretaceous ORNITHISCHIAN found in Mongolia. This 6-foot (1.8-m) plant-eater may have been related to PSITTACOSAURUS, but was not related to IGUANODON. It had a large skull, parrot-like jaws with teeth along the sides, and four fingers. Although it was mainly BIPEDAL, *Protiguanodon* probably walked on four legs some of the time. It may be an ancestor of the CERATOPSIANS. A complete skeleton of this animal has not been found.

Classification: Psittacosauridae?, Ornithopoda, Ornithischia

PROTOCERATOPS (pro-toe-SAIR-uh-tops) "First Horned Face" (Greek *protos* = first + *keratops* = horned face, because it is the earliest known true CERATOPSIAN.)

A pig-sized, four-legged, plant-eating dinosaur with a turtle-like beak and a small frill—the first of the true ceratopsians. Males had small bumps on their noses; females did not. Both males and females were about the same size, weighing about 900 pounds (410 kg) and measuring about 6 feet (1.8 m) from the tips of their snouts to the ends of their tails.

PROTOCERATOPS

This forerunner of the horned dinosaurs was the first dinosaur known from every stage of life—potato-shaped EGGS to full grown. Its eggs were the first dinosaur eggs ever found. Several of the NESTS contained hatchlings, and some of the eggs contained fragments of unhatched babies. Skulls and skeletons of adults were found nearby. Scientists had always assumed that dinosaurs were egg-laying reptiles. This discovery proved, for the first time, that this was true. The rough-shelled eggs were found in bowl-shaped nests that had been dug in sand. The eggs were 6 inches (15 cm) long and had been placed in rows around the sides of the bowl, then covered and separated by sand.

Protoceratops fossils have been found in Late Cretaceous deposits in Mongolia.

Classification: Protoceratopsidae, Ceratopsia, Ornithischia

protoceratopsians or **Protoceratopsidae** (pro-toe-sair-uh-TOPS-ih-dee) "First Horned Faces" (Named after PROTOCERATOPS.)

A family of CERATOPSIA. These were the most primitive of the true CERATOPSIANS. They were mainly QUADRUPEDAL plant-eaters, although some may have been partially BIPEDAL. They had relatively enormous heads with parrot-like beaks, well-developed frills (except for LEPTOCERATOPS), and very small horns, or none at all. Protoceratopsians ranged in size from 30 inches (76 cm) to 7 feet (2 m) long. They lived during Late Cretaceous times in North America and Asia. BAGACERATOPS, LEPTOCERATOPS, MICROCERATOPS, MONTANACERATOPS, and PROTOCERATOPS were protoceratopsians.

protorosaurs or **Protorosauria** (pro-toe-ro-SAWR-ee-ah) "First Lizards" (Greek *protos* = first + *sauros* = lizards, because they were the first known lizard-like reptiles.)

Not dinosaurs, but lizard-like reptiles. They preceded lizards and filled the same ecological niches that lizards do today. Small protorosaurs probably lived in the undergrowth, eating insects and small reptiles, but larger ones ate fish and lived near the sea. They, in turn, probably served as food for Triassic COELUROSAURS. Protorosaurs have been found in Europe. They lived during the PER-

MIAN and TRIASSIC PERIODS. They ranged from 2 to 20 feet (60 cm to 6 m) in length. TANYSTROPHEUS was a protorosaur.

Protosuchia (pro-toe-SOOK-ee-ah) "First Crocodiles" (Named for PROTOSUCHUS.)

Not dinosaurs, but the earliest true crocodiles. They were relatively small—about 3 feet (90 cm) long—and had rather short heads, but their arms and legs were like those of modern CROCODILIANS, and both their backs and bellies were covered with rows of bony plates. Animals belonging to this group have been found in Late Triassic or Early Jurassic deposits in North America, South America, and Africa. PROTOSUCHUS was a member of this group.

PROTOSUCHUS (pro-tuh-SOOK-us) "First Crocodile" (Greek *protos* = first + *souchos* = crocodile.)

Not a dinosaur, but the very first known crocodile. Except for its shorter head, it looked almost exactly like modern crocodiles, and probably lived like them. It had short legs and rows of bony plates protecting both the back and belly. Its fossils were found in Arizona where it lived from Late Triassic to Early Jurassic times.

pseudosuchians or **Pseudosuchia** (soo-doe-SOOK-ee-ah) "False Crocodiles" (Greek *pseudo* = false + *souchos* = crocodile, because they resembled crocodiles, but were not.)

Not dinosaurs, but a suborder of THECODONTS. Pseudosuchians lived during the Triassic Period in North America, South America, Europe, and Africa. Scientists think that the ancestors of dinosaurs were pseudosuchian thecodonts. In body build, most pseudosuchians resembled crocodiles, but were less sprawl-legged, and some were capable of running on two legs. They were probably OM-

NIVORES, eating both plants and meat. Their jaws were lined with sharp teeth. They ranged anywhere from rabbit-sized to 10 feet (3 m) long. EUPARKERIA, ORNITHOSUCHUS, RIOJASUCHUS, and SCLEROMOCHLUS were pseudosuchians.

psittacosaurs or **Psittacosauridae** (sit-uh-ko-SAWR-ih-dee) "Parrot Lizard" (Named for PSITTACOSAURUS.)

A family of ORNITHISCHIAN dinosaurs that are believed to be the ancestors of the CERATOPSIANS. These dinosaurs were mainly BIPEDAL, and are usually classed as ORNITHOPODS. However, some scientists now consider them to be the most primitive family of the CERATOPSIA. These planteaters probably grazed on all fours. They had large heads with parrot-like beaks. They were about 6 feet (1.8 m) long. Psittacosaurs lived during the Cretaceous Period and have been found in Mongolia. PSITTACOSAURUS and (according to some) PROTIGUANODON were members of this family.

PSITTACOSAURUS (SIT-uh-ko-sawr-us) "Parrot Lizard" (Greek *psittako* = parrot + *sauros* = lizard, because its skull was shaped like a parrot's.)

An ancestor of the CERATOPSIANS. *Psittacosaurus* had parrot-like jaws and the faintest hint of a bony frill. This 6.5-foot (1.9-m) plant-eater lived in early Late Cretaceous

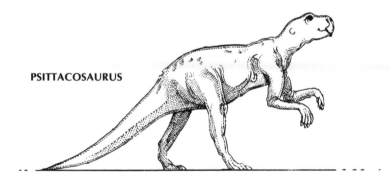

PSITTACOSAURUS

Mongolia and China. Unlike later ceratopsians, *Psittacosaurus* was mainly BIPEDAL, but probably walked on all fours when grazing. It is known from many complete skeletons in excellent condition.

A baby *Psittacosaurus,* about half the size of a pigeon, is one of the smallest dinosaurs found to date.

Classification: Psittacosauridae, Ornithopoda or Ceratopsia, Ornithischia

PTERANODON (tair-AN-o-don) "Winged and Toothless" (Greek *pteron* = wing + *anodontos* = toothless, because it could fly and was toothless.)

Not a dinosaur, but a tailless Late Cretaceous PTEROSAUR. It weighed 33 pounds (15 kg). It had a turkey-sized body, and a head that was 6 feet (1.8 m) long from the tip of its long, toothless beak to the end of a long, bony crest on the back of the head. In some, this crest doubled the length of the head. The purpose of the crest is unknown. Some specimens of *Pteranodon* had no crest, so perhaps it was a sex characteristic. It may have been used as a brake for landing, or it could have been a rudder, since the creature had no tail. Or it may simply have acted as a balance for the very long beak. Although *Pteranodon* had a 27-foot (8.2-m) wingspread, it could have flown only

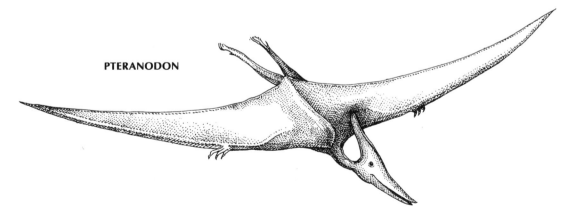

PTERANODON

in a light or moderate wind. It may have been a glider rather than a true flyer. This flying fish-eater may have fished on the wing. It was probably ENDOTHERMIC (warm-blooded) and may have had fur. Its fossils have been found in Kansas.

pterodactyls or **Pterodactyloidea** (tair-uh-dak-til-OY-dee-ah) "Wing Fingers" (Named after PTERODACTYLUS.)

Not a dinosaur, a suborder of PTEROSAURS that developed in the Late Jurassic times, 50 million years after the RHAMPHORHYNCHOIDEA. Early forms were small, no larger than a sparrow, but Cretaceous pterodactyls were huge, with up to 40-foot (12-m) wingspreads. All had long, curved necks and long faces. Some had few or no teeth, while others had closely spaced bristle-like teeth in their long jaws. They may have caught insects in flight or snatched fish from the water. They had either very short tails or none at all. Some had impressive crests. Pterodactyls have been found in North America, Europe, Africa, and Australia. PTERANODON, PTERODACTYLUS, and QUETZAL-COATLUS were pterodactyls.

PTERODACTYLUS (tair-uh-DAK-til-us) "Wing Finger" (Greek *pteron* = wing + *daktylos* = finger, because the fourth finger supported the wing.)

PTERODACTYLUS

Not a dinosaur, but a tailless PTEROSAUR. Some were as small as a sparrow; others were as large as a hawk. Their wingspread ranged from 12 to 30 inches (30 to 76 cm). These flying creatures were common along Late Jurassic shorelines in Europe and Africa. They probably caught insects in the air. Some authorities believe their legs were poorly adapted for land travel.

pterosaurs or **Pterosauria** (tair-uh-SAWR-ee-ah) "Winged Lizards" (Greek *pteron* = wing + *sauros* = lizard, referring to its leathery wings.)

Not dinosaurs, but the order of winged ARCHOSAURS capable of flying or gliding. They are classed as "flying reptiles" because of their very reptilian heads, teeth, and pelvises. Their hind feet were similar to those of dinosaurs or birds. Pterosaurs were lightly built, with hollow bones and small bodies. They had large BRAINS, which suggests that they had good maneuverability when flying. They probably could flap their wings slowly, but may have relied upon thermal updrafts (uprising columns of warm air) or light breezes to get off the ground. The smallest pterosaurs were the size of sparrows; the largest were giants with 40-foot (12-m) wingspreads.

A pterosaur's wing was formed by a leathery membrane that stretched from the side of its body to the tip of its fourth finger. This fourth finger was very long, and supported the front edge of the wing. The other fingers were short and were equipped with sharp claws.

Pterosaurs probably had a poor sense of smell, and no doubt they relied on keen eyesight for hunting. Their eyes were very large. Most were fish-eaters, and they may have fished on the wing. Some had throat pouches similar to those of modern pelicans. These probably fished from the surface of the seas. Some may have eaten insects. Still others had elongated, bristle-like teeth, resembling the baleen that modern whales use to strain plankton from seawater. These pterosaurs may have eaten plankton.

Pterosaurs were probably ENDOTHERMIC (warm-blooded). At least some are known to have had long, dense fur. Many had ridges or crests on their skulls. Some had long tails, others were tailless. Pterosaurs probably lived all over the world from Late Triassic through Late Cretaceous times. Two kinds are known. The RHAMPHORHYNCHOIDEA lived during the Triassic and Jurassic Periods. They were small in size and had long tails. The PTERODACTYLOIDEA lived from Late Jurassic to Late Cretaceous times. They probably had no tails. Some had long bony crests. Some grew to be huge.

Q

quadruped (KWAD-roo-ped) "Four-footed" (Latin *quadrupes* = four-footed.)

Any animal that stands or walks on four legs. Quadrupedal means "four-footed." ANKYLOSAURS, CERATOPSIANS, SAUROPODS, and STEGOSAURS were quadrupeds. Compare BIPED.

quadrupedal

See QUADRUPED.

QUETZALCOATLUS (ket-sol-ko-AT-lus) (Named after the Aztec feathered serpent god, Quetzalcoatl.)

Not a dinosaur, but a giant PTEROSAUR. *Quetzalcoatlus* is the largest known flying creature. One found in late Late Cretaceous rock in Texas had a 40-foot (12-m) wingspread. It had a small head and a long neck. Together they measured 8 feet (2.5 m) long. *Quetzalcoatlus* had a long, slender beak, and it may have probed in the mud for mollusks, or it may have been vulture-like and fed on carcasses. It probably lived on flat, low-lying ground, and it may have used thermal updrafts (uprising columns of warm air) to become airborne. This flying giant is known from parts of the wings of one individual, and scattered bones of a dozen smaller ones.

R

REBBACHISAURUS (reb-BAK-eh-sawr-us) "Rebbach Lizard" (Named for the territory of Rebbach, where the specimen was found + Greek *sauros* = lizard.)

A name given to a few SAUROPOD bones found in Morocco. These bones are similar to those of CAMARASAURUS, and this huge plant-eater may have resembled that dinosaur. Its discovery was important because it showed that sauropods lived in GONDWANALAND during the Early Cretaceous Period. Like all sauropods, *Rebbachisaurus* was QUADRUPEDAL and ate plants.

Classification: Sauropoda, Sauropodomorpha, Saurischia

reproduction
See EGGS; YOUNG.

reptiles or **Reptilia** (rep-TIL-ee-yah) "Creeping Animals" (Latin *reptilis* = creeping.)

A class of cold-blooded (ECTOTHERMIC), egg-laying, air-breathing animals with backbones. Most of these animals have a sprawling gait (or crawl on their bellies), three-chambered hearts, and bodies covered with horny plates or scales. Some reptiles live on land; others live in water. One class of reptiles (the DIAPSIDA) has two openings in the skull behind each eye socket. DINOSAURS, PTEROSAURS, and THECODONTS are placed in this class, because they had DIAPSID-type skulls. Snakes, lizards, turtles, and crocodiles are living reptiles.

RHABDODON (RAB-duh-don) "Rod Tooth" (Greek *rhab-dos* = rod + *odon* = tooth, referring to the shape of the teeth.)

Name given to jaw fragments and a few other bones of a Late Cretaceous ORNITHOPOD. *Rhabdodon* belonged to the IGUANODONT family, but was similar in appearance to CAMPTOSAURUS. Scientists estimate that this BIPEDAL plant-eater was 16 feet (5 m) long. Its fossils were found in France.

Classification: Iguanodontidae, Ornithopoda, Ornithischia

rhamphorhynchoids or **Rhamphorhynchoidea** (ram-fo-rink-OY-dee-ah) "Prow Beaks" (Named after RHAMPHORHYN-CHUS.)

Not dinosaurs, but the earliest of the PTEROSAURS. Some were no larger than sparrows; others were hawk-sized or larger. These animals were the first of the flying vertebrates. They lived from the Late Triassic through Jurassic times in Russia, Europe, Africa, and North America. They had short necks and long tails; some had small rudders on the tips of their tails. The wings were long and narrow. The jaws were well-developed, with numerous teeth. Some rhamphorhynchoids were probably fish-eaters; others may have been scavengers, eating carcasses. Some may have had fur. DIMORPHODON, RHAMPHORHYNCHUS, and SORDES are examples of this group.

RHAMPHORHYNCHUS (ram-fo-RINK-us) "Prow Beak" (Greek *rhamphos* = prow + *rhynchos* = beak, because its beak was curved.)

Not a dinosaur, but a small, long-tailed PTEROSAUR of Late Jurassic Europe and Africa. This flying fish-eater had a 4-foot (1.2-m) wingspan. Its body, including its tail, was only 18 inches (46 cm) long. The neck was short, but the head was long, and sharp teeth lined the long beak. *Rhamphorhynchus* had a small, flat membrane on the end of its very long, stiff tail. This membrane probably acted as a rudder.

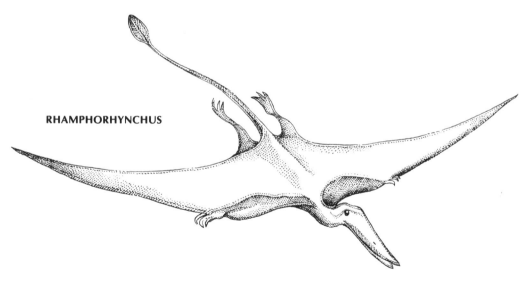

RHAMPHORHYNCHUS

RHOETOSAURUS (ROE-tuh-sawr-us) "Trojan Lizard" (Latin *rhoeteus* = Trojan + Greek *sauros* = lizard.)

One of the earliest known SAUROPODS. It was found in Early Jurassic rock in Australia. This huge four-legged plant-eater belonged to the CETIOSAURINAE family. It had a long neck and tail, and was similar to CETIOSAURUS. Its skull was larger than that of DIPLODOCUS, and the nostrils were high on its head. It had peg-like teeth. It is known from an incomplete skeleton. Its discovery was important, because it showed that sauropods lived in GONDWANALAND during Early Jurassic times.

Classification: Sauropoda, Sauropodomorpha, Saurischia

RHOETOSAURUS

RIOJASAURUS (ree-O-ha-sawr-us) "Rioja Lizard" (Named for La Rioja Province, Argentina, where it was found + Greek *sauros* = lizard.)

A 20-foot (6-m) Late Triassic PROSAUROPOD similar to MELANOROSAURUS. This dinosaur was a small-headed, long-necked HERBIVORE with a massive body and elephant-like legs. It was completely QUADRUPEDAL. A nearly complete skeleton of *Riojasaurus* was found in Argentina.

Classification: Prosauropoda, Sauropodomorpha, Saurischia

RIOJASUCHUS (ree-O-ha-sook-us) "Rioja Crocodile" (Named for La Rioja Province, Argentina, where it was found + Greek *souchos* = crocodile.)

Not a dinosaur, but an advanced THECODONT; some scientists think it was the first meat-eating dinosaur, but most think it was a thecodont. This animal was probably one of the most dangerous of the thecodonts. Its short, strong jaws had only a few teeth, but those were dagger-like. *Riojasuchus* was a rather small QUADRUPED. It weighed less than 100 pounds (45 kg). Its fossils have been found in Late Triassic of Argentina.

RUTIODON (ROO-tee-o-don) "Plant Tooth" (Latin *ruta* = a kind of plant + Greek *odon* = tooth, because it was first supposed that it ate plants.)

Not a dinosaur, but a typical PHYTOSAUR. This 12-foot (3.5-m) reptile has been found in Late Triassic deposits in North America, Europe, and Asia. It resembled a crocodile. It had a long skull and body, and bony plates (or scutes) covered its body. The nostrils were set far back—they were just in front of the eyes—and they were raised above the skull by cone-shaped bumps. This aggressive animal lived in lakes and streams, and preyed on small dinosaurs and any other animal it could catch. *Rutiodon* was the most dangerous animal of the Late Triassic Period.

RUTIODON

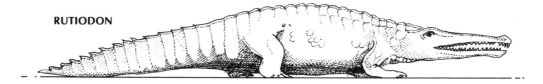

S

SAICHANIA (sye-CHAY-nee-ah) "Beautiful One" (Name derived from the Mongolian word for beautiful, perhaps because it was such an unusually fine specimen.)

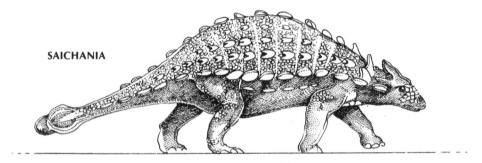

SAICHANIA

A Late Cretaceous ANKYLOSAUR. This armored dinosaur is the best-known of the Asian ankylosaurs. Many specimens have been found. One found in Mongolia had much of its armor plates in position, and the skull was very well-preserved. Its neck, back, and stomach were covered by rows of spikes and knobs on bony plates. *Saichania* was an ANKYLOSAURIDAE and had a heavy bony club on the end of its tail similar to that of ANKYLOSAURUS. Scientists estimate that this animal grew to be about 23 feet (7 m) long. Like all ankylosaurs, *Saichania* was QUADRUPEDAL and ate plants.

Classification: Ankylosauridae, Ankylosauria, Ornithischia

sails

See SPINES.

SALTASAURUS (salt-uh-SAWR-us) "Salta Lizard" (Named for Salta Province, Argentina, where it was found + Greek *sauros* = lizard.)

A Late Cretaceous SAUROPOD. This long necked, long tailed plant-eater measured 40 feet (12 m) from the tip of its snout to the end of its tail. It had massive, elephant-like legs and walked on all fours. It may have been capable of rearing up on two legs to reach the highest branches of tall trees. *Saltasaurus* was a TITANOSAURID. It is the earliest sauropod known to have had armor plates (or scutes) attached to its SKIN. It has been found in Argentina.

Classification: Sauropoda, Sauropodomorpha, Saurischia

SALTOPOSUCHUS (salt-o-po-SOOK-us) "Leaping Crocodile" (Latin *saltus* = leaping + Greek *souchos* = crocodile, though it was really more of a runner than a leaper.)

Not a dinosaur, but a PSEUDOSUCHIAN THECODONT. It looked very much like a small THEROPOD and was very lightly built with hollow bones. *Saltoposuchus* was probably capable of running swiftly on two legs. Its hind legs were long, but its front legs were short. Its tail (which was longer than the body) counterbalanced its large head. From the tip of its snout to the end of its tail, *Saltoposuchus* was 4 feet (1.2 m) long. Its jaws were lined with sharp

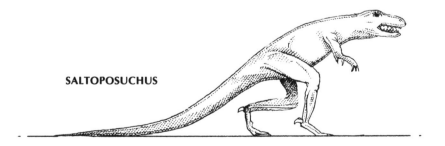

SALTOPOSUCHUS

teeth, indicating that it was a meat-eater. It lived in Europe during the Triassic Period.

SALTOPUS (SALT-o-pus) "Leaping Foot" (Latin *saltus* = leaping + Greek *pous* = foot, because the finder thought it was a leaper, but it was really a runner.)

A small COELUROSAUR of Triassic Europe. This BIPEDAL dinosaur was similar to PODOKESAURUS, but was smaller. It was an agile, little meat-eater about the size of a house cat. It stood only 8 inches (20 cm) high at the hips and weighed about 2 pounds (1 kg). Its hands had five fingers and were capable of grasping prey. *Saltopus* was a swift runner with sharp teeth, and it probably ate small lizards and other small animals. It had a long, swan-like neck and large eyes. It is known from partial skeletons found in Scotland.

Classification: Coelurosauria, Theropoda, Saurischia

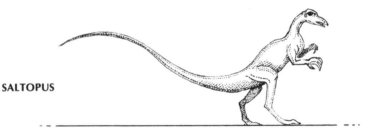

SALTOPUS

SARCOLESTES (sar-ko-LESS-teez) "Flesh Robber" (Greek *sarkos* = flesh + *lestes* = robber, the reason for this name is unknown.)

Name given to a partial lower left jaw found in Middle Jurassic of England. It was first thought to be a SCELIDOSAURID, but some authorities now think it might have been a NODOSAURID ANKYLOSAUR. The jaw is quite similar to the jaw of the nodosaur SAUROPELTA. It contained teeth and a large armor plate that was fused to the side of the jaw. If this dinosaur proves to be an ankylosaur, it will be the oldest one known.

Classification: Maybe Nodosauridae, Ankylosauria, Ornithischia

SARCOSAURUS (SAR-ko-sawr-us) "Flesh Lizard" (Greek *sarkos* = flesh + *sauros* = lizard, because it was a meat-eater.)

An Early Jurassic CARNOSAUR that was related to MEGALOSAURUS. It probably resembled that dinosaur. This big BIPEDAL meat-eater is known only from vertebrae, pelvis, and a hind leg found in England.

Classification: Carnosauria, Theropoda, Saurischia

SAURECHINODON (sawr-eh-KYE-nuh-don) "Lizard with Spiny Teeth" (Greek *sauros* = lizard + *echinatus* = spiny + *odon* = tooth.) A new name for ECHINODON.

A small Late Jurassic ORNITHOPOD whose fossils were found in England. It is known only from fragments of the upper and lower jaws. The jaws were similar to those of an earlier ornithopod, FABROSAURUS. *Saurechinodon* had a small head and a horny, beak-like jaw lined with teeth. Like all ornithopods, it walked on two legs and ate plants.

Classification: Fabrosauridae, Ornithopoda, Ornithischia

saurischians or **Saurischia** (sawr-ISS-kee-ah) "Lizard-hipped" (Greek *sauros* = lizard + *ischion* = hip, because their pelvises resembled those of lizards.)

One of the two orders of animals called DINOSAURS. Saurischians had lizard-like pelvises and clawed feet. Some were BIPEDAL, and others were QUADRUPEDAL. Some were meat-eaters; some were plant-eaters; while others ate both meat and plants. Saurischians lived all over the world from Middle Triassic times to the end of the Cretaceous Period. Some of them were no bigger than a chicken, while others were tall enough that they could have looked over a five-story building.

The saurischians have been divided into two suborders: The THEROPODA were bipedal meat-eaters and included both COELUROSAURS and CARNOSAURS. (It is from Theropoda that birds probably EVOLVED.) One group (the SEGNOSAURIDAE) currently classed as theropods were at least partially quadrupedal. However, this group needs more study. Some scientists think that they may actually be ORNITHISCHIANS. The SAUROPODOMORPHA were basically or entirely quadrupedal. All ate plants, a few may have included meat in their diets. This group included the PROSAUROPODS and the SAUROPODS. It is from this group that the largest and the smallest of the known dinosaurs have been found.

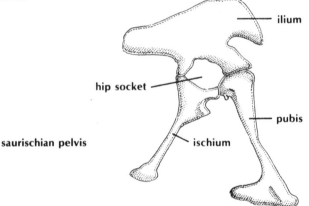

saurischian pelvis

SAUROLOPHUS (sawr-OL-o-fus) "Crested Lizard" (Greek *sauros* = lizard + *lophos* = crest, referring to the horn-like growth on its head.)

A solid-crested HADROSAUR of Late Cretaceous times. The crest of this duck-billed dinosaur was a spike-like horn that curved upward over the top of its skull. This BIPEDAL plant-eater was about 22 feet (6.5 m) long and 17 feet (5.2 m) tall. It had a long, spoon-shaped bill and its body resembled that of EDMONTOSAURUS. *Saurolophus* is known from complete skeletons found in western Canada and Mongolia.

Classification: Hadrosauridae, Ornithopoda, Ornithischia

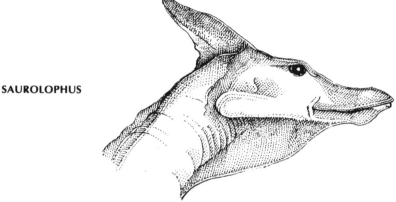

SAUROLOPHUS

SAUROPELTA (sawr-uh-PEL-tah) "Lizard with Shield" (Greek *sauros* = lizard + Latin *pelta* = shield, referring to its armor.)

The earliest known North American ANKYLOSAUR and one of the largest of the NODOSAURIDAE. It was 19 feet (5.8 m) long and weighed about 3 tons (2.7 metric tons). This Early Cretaceous plant-eater was a ponderous animal that walked on four short, stubby legs. Its back and club-less tail were covered with rounded horny plates. Long spikes lined its sides. *Sauropelta* is known from many incomplete skeletons found in several western states. HOPLITOSAURUS may be the same as this dinosaur.

Classification: Nodosauridae, Ankylosauria, Ornithischia

SAUROPLITES (sawr-uh-PLY-teez) "Stone-like Lizard" (Greek *sauros* = lizard + *op* = toward + *lites* = stone-like, referring to its hard back armor.)

The earliest known Asian ANKYLOSAUR and the oldest known ANKYLOSAURIDAE. It was found in very early Early Cretaceous rock near the Chinese-Mongolian border. It had a clubbed tail, walked on four legs, and ate plants. It has been estimated that this ankylosaur was at least 18 feet (5.5 m) long. *Sauroplites* is known from very fragmentary material—a small piece of pelvis and several dermal plates.

Classification: Ankylosauridae, Ankylosauria, Ornithischia

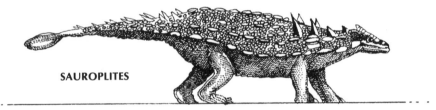

SAUROPLITES

sauropodomorphs or **Sauropodomorpha** (sawr-o-pod-ah-MORF-ah) "Lizard-footed Forms" (Greek *sauros* = lizard + *pod* = foot + *morphe* = form.)

A suborder of SAURISCHIAN dinosaurs. This group includes both the SAUROPODS and the PROSAUROPODS. Most were basically four-legged, and all ate plants; although some of the earlier prosauropods could also walk on two legs, and some probably ate meat as well as plants. Sauropodomorphs ranged in size from 7-foot (2-m) prosauropods to gigantic 100-foot (30-m) BRACHIOSAURS. They all had small heads, long necks, and long tails. Sauropodomorphs were very different from the other kind of saurischian dinosaurs, the THEROPODS. It is possible that sauropodomorphs and theropods EVOLVED from two different THECODONTS. Sauropodomorphs have been found on every continent except Antarctica. They lived from the Middle Triassic Period through the Cretaceous Period.

There were two infraorders of sauropodomorphs. The PROSAUROPODA were the more primitive of the two and lived during the Triassic Period. They included both semi-QUADRUPEDAL and completely quadrupedal types, and both OMNIVORES and HERBIVORES. The SAUROPODA were all quadrupedal herbivores. They lived during Jurassic and Cretaceous times.

SAUROPODOPUS (sawr-oh-POD-uh-pus) "Sauropod Foot" (Sauropod + Greek *pous* = foot.)

Name given to footprints found in South Africa that were made by a very early SAUROPODOMORPH that had elephant-like feet. These TRACKS were made in early Late Triassic times. No bones of the animal that made them have been found.

sauropods or **Sauropoda** (sawr-o-POD-ah) "Lizard-footed" (Greek *sauros* = lizard + *pod* = foot, because these animals had five toes like modern lizards.)

The infraorder of giant, four-legged, plant-eating SAURISCHIAN dinosaurs. This group included the largest known land animals. Sauropods had huge bodies, long necks, whip-like tails, and elephant-like legs. Their long necks enabled them to reach vegetation other animals could not reach, and gave them a good view of approaching danger, such as a pack of hungry CARNOSAURS. Sauropods had quite small BRAINS in comparison to their body size, but an auxiliary nerve center in the hip region controlled the hind legs and tail.

The size of sauropods varied greatly. Small CAMARASAURS were only 30 feet (9 m) long, while giants like "ULTRASAURUS" may have been as much as 100 feet (30 m) long. It is a mystery how these huge animals with such tiny heads could have eaten enough to stay alive. Most scientists doubt that sauropods could have been ENDOTHERMIC, because warm-blooded animals require more food than cold-blooded animals. However, scientists think that sauropods may have been HOMOIOTHERMIC. (Their huge bodies may have held enough heat at night to keep their body temperature fairly even.)

Sauropods lived on dry land or in swampy areas. It was once thought that sauropods were lake dwellers, because scientists believed sauropods were too heavy to walk on land. But recent bone studies show that their legs were perfectly capable of supporting their weight on land. It is also now known that these animals would not have been able to breathe if they were completely submerged in water—the pressure of the water on their lungs would have been too great. However, sauropods probably enjoyed an occasional dip in the water, just as modern elephants do. It was also once thought that sauropods ate only soft water plants, because sauropods had weak teeth. We now know that sauropods ate twigs and needles from tall pines, firs, and sequoias.

Fossil footprints indicate that sauropods traveled in HERDS with the YOUNG protected by a ring of adults. They traveled slowly, perhaps no faster than 4 miles (6.5 km) per hour.

Sauropods hatched from EGGS about twice the size of ostrich eggs. They may have lived for more than 100 years, and they may have never stopped growing as long as they lived. As a group, they existed from Early Jurassic times to the end of the Cretaceous Period. Sauropod fossils have been found on every continent except Antarctica. Some sauropods seem to have had bony plates embedded in their SKIN.

All scientists once thought that PROSAUROPODS were the ancestors of sauropods, because prosauropods were somewhat similar in body build to sauropods, and they lived at an earlier time period than did the sauropods. However, some scientists now consider it possible that these two groups of dinosaurs EVOLVED from a common ancestor.

There were two major groups, or families, of sauropods: those with peg-shaped teeth, and those with spatulate, or spoon-shaped, teeth. The spatulate group is called the BRACHIOSAURIDAE (a few call this family the CAMARASAURIDAE). The Brachiosauridae is divided into four subfamilies: the CETIOSAURINAE, the BRACHIOSAURINAE, the CAMARASAURINAE, and the EUHELOPODINAE.

The peg-toothed family is called the TITANOSAURIDAE (some call this family the ATLANTOSAURIDAE). This family is also divided into four subfamilies: the TITANOSAURINAE, the ATLANTOSAURINAE, the DIPLODOCINAE, and the DICRAEOSAURINAE.

Many recent discoveries have made it necessary to re-study the sauropods. When this study is completed, there may be some changes in the classification of sauropods. It is probable that some of the current subfamilies will be raised to family level. This has already been proposed for the DIPLODOCIDAE.

SAUROPUS (SAWR-o-pus) "Lizard Foot" (Greek *sauros* = lizard + *pous* = foot, because these prints resembled those of modern lizards.)

Name given to long, slender footprints found in Late Triassic rock in the Connecticut Valley of the eastern United States. Scientists believe these TRACKS were made by a primitive ORNITHOPOD that was similar to PISANOSAURUS. The footprints resemble the foot of *Pisanosaurus* quite closely, but no fossils of that dinosaur have been found in North America.

SAURORNITHOIDES (sawr-or-nith-OY-deez) "Bird-like Lizard" (Greek *sauros* = lizard + *ornithoides* = bird-like, because it had a bird-like build.)

A Late Cretaceous COELUROSAUR. This lightly built little BIPED was a close relative of DROMAEOSAURUS and STENONYCHOSAURUS. (It so closely resembled *Stenonychosaurus* that some scientists think it may have been the same GENUS.) *Saurornithoides* was 6.5 feet (1.9 m) long and had long grasping fingers, a small head with large eyes, powerful beak-like jaws, and a sickle-like claw on each foot. It had a large BRAIN and was probably one of the most intelligent of the dinosaurs—it might have been as intelligent as modern birds. It probably ate lizards, small dinosaurs, and rat-like mammals. *Saurornithoides* is known from a skull and several other bones found in Mongolia.

Classification: Coelurosauria, Theropoda, Saurischia

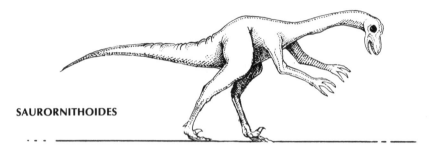

SAURORNITHOIDES

SAURORNITHOLESTES (saur-or-NITH-uh-les-teez) "Lizard Bird-robber" (Greek *sauros* = lizard + *ornithos* = bird + *lestes* = robber, because it resembled ORNITHOLESTES.)

A small DROMAEOSAURID COELUROSAUR recently discovered in Alberta, Canada. It is based on very scanty material, but it is believed that, like DROMAEOSAURUS, this small BIPEDAL meat-eater was a Late Cretaceous descendant of *Ornitholestes*.

Classification: Coelurosauria, Theropoda, Saurischia

scelidosaurid or **Scelidosauridae** (skel-ee-doe-SAWR-ih-dee) "Ribbed Lizards" (Named after SCELIDOSAURUS.)

A primitive family of ORNITHOPODS. Scelidosaurids had

small heads, weak jaws, and bony plates on their backs, necks, and tails. They were once considered ancestors of both the STEGOSAURS and ANKYLOSAURS. Scelidosaurids lived in England during the Early Jurassic Period. *Scelidosaurus* is the only known member of this family.

SCELIDOSAURUS (skel-EE-doe-sawr-us) "Ribbed Lizard" (Greek *skelidos* = rib + *sauros* = lizard, because a large number of ribs were recovered.)

One of the earliest known armored ORNITHISCHIANS. This 12-foot (3.5-m) plant-eater had rows of bony plates on its back, neck, and tail similar to those of ANKYLOSAURS. The plates that ran down the center were solid and shaped like a cone. Its head was quite small, and its jaws were weak, indicating that it was a plant-eater.

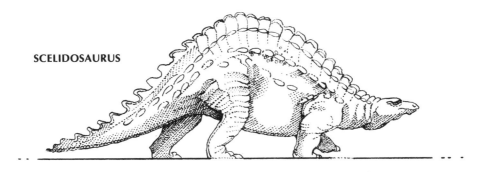

SCELIDOSAURUS

Some scientists consider this dinosaur to be an ancestor of STEGOSAURS; others suggest that it was a very early AN-KYLOSAUR, but recent studies indicate that it may have been an ORNITHOPOD (a BIPEDAL ornithischian) that somewhat resembled TENONTOSAURUS. It is known from two specimens found in Early Jurassic deposits in England. One is an almost complete skeleton.

Classification: Scelidosauridae, Ornithopoda, Ornithischia

SCLEROMOCHLUS (sklair-o-MO-klus) "Hard Jumper"
(Greek *scleros* = hard + *mochleuo* = to heave up, because it was presumed that it jumped like a kangaroo.)

Not a dinosaur, but a very advanced PSEUDOSUCHIAN. It
was so advanced that a few consider it to be a primitive
dinosaur. It was probably very closely related to the ancestor of the dinosaurs. *Scleromochlus* was 1 foot (30 cm)
long, lightly built, and BIPEDAL. This little meat-eater had
a small head, a short neck, a slender body, a long lizard-
like tail, and hollow bones. Several portions of the skeleton have been found in Late Triassic deposits in Scotland.

SCOLOSAURUS (SKO-luh-sawr-us) "Thorn Lizard" (Greek
scolos = thorn + *sauros* = lizard, referring to the long
spikes on its body.)

Name given to a nearly complete ANKYLOSAUR skeleton
found in Late Cretaceous deposits in Alberta, Canada.
This skeleton was 17 feet (5.2 m) long. The body—from the
head to the tip of its short, clubbed tail—was covered with
horny spikes. Two long spikes protruded from the tail.
Scolosaurus is now considered to be the same as EUO-
PLOCEPHALUS. Since *Euoplocephalus* is the older name, it
is the preferred name for this dinosaur.

Classification: Ankylosauridae, Ankylosauria, Ornithischia

SCUTELLOSAURUS (scoo-TEL-oh-sawr-us) "Little Shield
Lizard" (Latin *scutellum* = a little shield + Greek *sauros*
= lizard, referring to the many small scutes, or bony
plates, that covered this dinosaur.)

A small and very primitive Late Triassic (or very early
Jurassic) ORNITHOPOD. This FABROSAURID was recently
found in Arizona and is the earliest known ORNITHISCHIAN
of North America. It was not older, but was more primitive than PISANOSAURUS. Its toes had claws rather than the
hoof-like nails of later ornithischians. *Scutellosaurus*

was closely related to LESOTHOSAURUS and was similar in size—about 4 feet (1.2 m) long—but was different in several ways. It had a much longer tail—twice as long as the body and neck together. Its forelegs were longer, and its hind legs were shorter than those of *Lesothosaurus. Scutellosaurus* was covered by tiny bony plates, similar to those of EUOPLOCEPHALUS. Its feet indicate that this dinosaur was basically BIPEDAL and lived on land. However, its hands were large, which indicates that the weight of the armor may have occasionally forced it to walk on all fours. *Scutellosaurus* was a plant-eater; its teeth were triangular, serrated, and arranged in a single row. This dinosaur is known from one nearly complete skeleton and a partial skeleton of another individual.

Classification: Fabrosauridae, Ornithopoda, Ornithischian

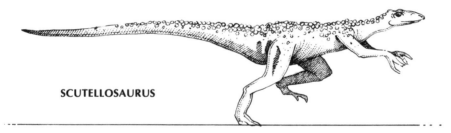

SCUTELLOSAURUS

SECERNOSAURUS (see-KER-nuh-sawr-us) "Severed Lizard" (Latin *secerno* = sever + Greek *sauros* = lizard, referring to its non-LAURASIAN origin; it was "cut-off" from other HADROSAURS.)

The second most primitive hadrosaur known. *Secernosaurus* has the distinction of being one of only two hadrosaurs ever discovered in GONDWANALAND. (The other one has not yet been named.) This Late Cretaceous duckbill was found in Argentina. It was a HADROSAURINE, and was crestless, but had some IGUANODONT features.

This BIPEDAL plant-eater is known from a partial braincase and a few other fossil bones.

Classification: Hadrosauridae, Ornithopoda, Ornithischia

SEGISAURUS (SEE-gih-sawr-us) "Segi Lizard" (Named for Segi Canyon in Arizona, where it was found + Greek *sauros* = lizard.)

A very late Late Triassic or Early Jurassic COELUROSAUR. Unlike other coelurosaurs, this rabbit-sized SAURISCHIAN had a collar bone and solid leg bones. It was a speedy little BIPED, and this was probably its best defense against larger predators. Its hands resembled those of ORNITHOLESTES. It probably ate small lizards and insects. *Segisaurus* fossils have been found in Arizona. A complete skeleton has not been found.

Classification: Coelurosauria, Theropoda, Saurischia

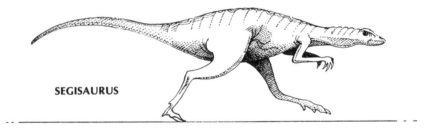

SEGISAURUS

segnosaurids or **Segnosauridae** (seg-no-SAWR-ih-dee) "Slow Lizards" (Named after SEGNOSAURUS.)

A new group of Late Cretaceous dinosaurs recently found in Mongolia. These dinosaurs are unlike any other known. They seem to represent a unique line of EVOLUTION. Perhaps they evolved from an animal that was a link between the two major orders of dinosaurs, the SAURISCHIA and the ORNITHISCHIA. They had unusual pelvises (called OPISTHOPUBIC PELVISES) that resembled neither the bird-hipped nor the lizard-hipped. These dinosaurs seem to have been meat-eaters, possibly preying on fish, and appear to have been at least partially QUADRUPEDAL. Their rather small heads had narrow, toothless beaks and small "cheek" teeth. Segnosaurids are currently classified as SAURISCHIAN THEROPODS, but some doubt this classification. It is possible that they may be ORNITHISCHIANS, but not enough remains have been found to establish this. Two kinds of segnosaurids have been described—SEGNOSAURUS and ERLIKOSAURUS. A third is known only from a pelvis.

SEGNOSAURUS (SEG-no-sawr-us) "Slow Lizard" (Latin *segnis* = slow + Greek *sauros* = lizard, possibly because it seems to be an evolutionary throwback.)

A strange new type of dinosaur found in Late Cretaceous deposits in Mongolia. This meat-eating dinosaur had a pelvis that was unlike either those of lizard-hipped or bird-hipped dinosaurs. It is called an OPISTHOPUBIC PELVIS. *Segnosaurus* had a relatively small head; its snout ended in a narrow, toothless beak. Twenty-four small

SEGNOSAURUS

teeth lined each side of the jaws. It probably ate fish. *Segnosaurus* had long arms and seems to have been at least partially QUADRUPEDAL. The short hands were three-fingered. The feet had four toes with long, thick, curved claws.

From the tip of its nose to the end of its tail, *Segnosaurus* was probably 30 feet (9 m) long and 8 feet (2.5 m) tall at the hips. Although it is currently classed as a SAURISCHIAN THEROPOD and seems to be a curious mixture of primitive and advanced saurischian features, some scientists think it may have been an ORNITHOPOD. *Segnosaurus* is known from a jaw, fore and hind limbs, pelvis, and several other bones.

Classification: Carnosauria?, Theropoda?, Saurischia?

sensory perception

Most dinosaurs had a well-developed sense of smell, good eyesight, and good hearing. Their ability to see, hear, and smell was probably the best defense of unarmed dinosaurs. By getting early warnings of approaching enemies they had ample time to escape.

Scientists can determine how good a dinosaur's vision was by the size of the eye sockets in the skull. The eyes of STENONYCHOSAURUS and DROMAEOSAURUS were very large, so these dinosaurs must have had extremely good vision. They should also have been able to judge distances quite accurately, because their eyes were spaced far apart and were on the front of their heads (rather than on the sides). They probably had good night vision, too.

There is evidence that HADROSAURS and SAUROPODS had excellent hearing. If dinosaurs had a good sense of hearing, they must also have been able to make sounds. We don't know what kind of sounds they made, but scientists think they may have bellowed like crocodiles. If so, a MESOZOIC forest must have been a noisy place!

Soft mud oozed into openings in the skulls of some dino-saurs and formed casts of their BRAINS. These show the roots of the nerves in the brain, and indicate that many dinosaurs had a keen sense of smell. The size of the nasal cavities also indicates that dinosaurs had a good sense of smell. Some scientists think that the purpose of the hollow CRESTS of LAMBEOSAURINE hadrosaurs was to lengthen the odor sensitive area of the nose lining and thus greatly improve the sense of smell.

short-frilled ceratopsians

See CERATOPSIANS.

SHANSHANOSAURUS (shan-SHAN-uh-sawr-us) "Shan-shan Lizard" (Named for the area of China, where it was found + Greek *sauros* = lizard.)

A small, Late Cretaceous CARNOSAUR about the size of DEINONYCHUS. This little BIPEDAL meat-eater is known from one nearly complete specimen found in China. It was probably a very agile animal and a fast runner.

Classification: Carnosauria, Theropoda, Saurischia

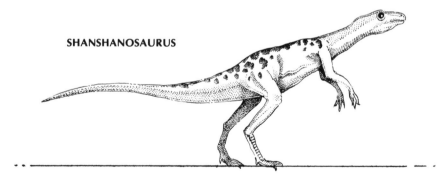

SHANSHANOSAURUS

SHANTUNGOSAURUS (shan-TUNG-o-sawr-us) "Shantung Lizard" (Named for Shantung, China, where it was discovered + Greek *sauros* = lizard.)

A duck-billed ORNITHISCHIAN recently found in Late Cretaceous deposits in China. This flat-headed HADROSAUR was a HADROSAURINAE somewhat resembling ANATOSAURUS. *Shantungosaurus* was BIPEDAL and ate plants.

Classification: Hadrosauridae, Ornithopoda, Ornithischia

SILVISAURUS (SIL-vuh-sawr-us) "Forest Lizard" (Latin *silva* = forest + Greek *sauros* = lizard, possibly referring to the place where it was found.)

A primitive Early Cretaceous ANKYLOSAUR. This NODOSAURID had a clubless tail and a longer neck than most. Spikes protected its sides, and bony plates protected its back and tail. *Silvisaurus* was 13 feet (4 m) long. This QUADRUPEDAL plant-eater is known from an incomplete skeleton found in Kansas.

Classification: Nodosauridae, Ankylosauria, Ornithischia

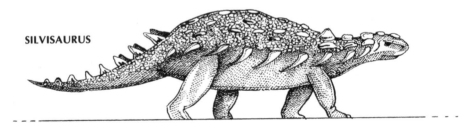

SILVISAURUS

SINOSAURUS (SYE-nuh-sawr-us) "Chinese Lizard" (Latin *sino* = Chinese + Greek *sauros* = lizard, referring to the country where it was found.)

A Late Triassic CARNIVORE. This animal was similar to ORNITHOSUCHUS. It was either a very primitive COELUROSAUR dinosaur or an advanced PSEUDOSUCHIAN. It is known only from jaw fragments found in China.

Classification: Coelurosauria?, Theropoda?, Saurischia?

size

Some dinosaurs were unbelievably huge—taller than a five-story building. Others were smaller than a chicken. They ranged from 2 feet (60 cm) to 90 feet (27 m) long.

Why did some dinosaurs get so large? Maybe they never stopped growing. It is possible that the largest lived to be more than 100 years old and never stopped growing in all that time. Many dinosaurs had large pituitary glands (glands that control growth); maybe that is why they became giants. Or maybe they got so large because solar radiation was greater during the MESOZOIC ERA than it is now, and *that* stimulated growth. Then again, maybe huge size was an adaptation for controlling the heat of their bodies (huge bodies cool more slowly than small ones). Scientists have many theories as to why dinosaurs grew so large, but we really don't know the answer.

The largest dinosaur we know about is a SAUROPOD called "ULTRASAURUS." It was probably 100 feet (30 m) long and 60 feet (18 m) tall, and may have weighed 80 tons (72 metric tons). The largest THEROPOD was the huge meat-eater, TYRANNOSAURUS, which was 50 feet (15 m) long and weighed 6 tons (5.5 metric tons). The largest HADROSAUR was LAMBEOSAURUS; some specimens of this duckbill were 40 feet (12 m) long. This dinosaur was also the largest known ORNITHISCHIAN. TRICERATOPS was the largest CERATOPSIAN; it was 25 feet (7.5 m) long, the same size of the largest STEGOSAUR, STEGOSAURUS. The largest ANKYLOSAUR, ANKYLOSAURUS reached a length of 25 feet (7.5 m).

The tiniest dinosaurs that have been found are a 30-inch (76-cm) long juvenile COMPSOGNATHUS; a 10-inch (25-cm) long baby PSITTACOSAURUS; and a robin-sized, newly hatched PROSAUROPOD called MUSSAURUS. The smallest known adult dinosaurs we know about are the

COELUROSAURS, *Compsognathus,* which was about the size of a chicken, and SALTOPUS, which was about the size of a house cat.

skin

Scientists have found several fossilized impressions of dinosaur skin. These show us what the skin of some of the dinosaurs was like. Most dinosaurs had tough, leathery skin covered with scales. Some scientists think it is possible that a few advanced dinosaurs, such as STENONY-CHOSAURUS, may have had insulating covering such as fur or feathers.

HADROSAURS had leathery skin with a pebbled surface similar to that of a football. Scientists have found two mummified skeletons of ANATOSAURUS that clearly show skin impressions. The skin of this duckbill was textured with small bumps (or tubercles), similar to the skin of a gila monster. The skin of CORYTHOSAURUS was covered with small polygonal bumps, but rows of larger, oval bumps covered the belly and pelvic area. The skin of LAM-BEOSAURUS was similar, but lacked the larger stomach bumps.

An impression of a small portion of the skin of a SAURO-POD shows that these animals had coarse, granular scales like some lizards of today. Skin impressions of the CERA-TOPSIAN CHASMOSAURUS show that this dinosaur was covered with rows of very large button-like tubercles. Some of these were 2 inches (5 cm) in diameter. They were set 5 inches (13 cm) apart and ran from the neck to the tail. The rows alternated with one another, and the area between the rows was covered by small scales.

ANKYLOSAURS and some sauropods had heavy bony armor plates embedded in their skin.

SORDES (SOR-deez) "Shaggy" (Latin *sordes* = shaggy clothes, because of its long, shaggy coat of fur.)

A RHAMPHORHYNCHOID that was found in Late Triassic

deposits in Russia. This PTEROSAUR was about the size of a pigeon. Impressions left in the fine limestone where it was discovered show that this creature had long, dense, and relatively thick hair. Only the long tail was bare. *Sordes* probably ate fish, but we have no evidence of this.

smell, sense of

See SENSORY PERCEPTION.

species (SPEE-sees)

See GENUS.

speed

Many people have the idea that all dinosaurs were slow creatures. Although some, such as the tank-like AN-KYLOSAURS and the huge SAUROPODS *were* slow, other dinosaurs were quite speedy. Sauropods probably moved no faster than 2 to 4 miles (3.2 to 6.5 km) per hour, whereas the ORNITHOMIMIDS could reach tremendous speeds. These were the "cheetahs" of the MESOZOIC world. Some probably could have outrun an ostrich, and ostriches have been clocked at 50 miles (80 km) per hour. STENONYCHOSAURUS was probably the swiftest dinosaur.

Scientists estimate the speed of dinosaurs from the length of their strides. Many fossilized dinosaur TRACK-WAYS have been found from which the stride can be measured. The faster an animal runs, the longer its strides. Scientists also can estimate the swiftness of an animal by comparing the length of its legs with known animals of comparable size. Up to a point, the longer and slenderer the legs, the faster the animal is able to run.

Some scientists estimate that ALLOSAURUS could run almost as fast as a man. TYRANNOSAURUS was somewhat slower. HADROSAURS probably could run about as fast as a modern horse. They may have been able to outrun *Tyrannosaurus,* but probably not ALBERTOSAURUS, which has generally been considered the swiftest of the large Late

Cretaceous CARNOSAURS. But the swiftest carnosaur may have been ACROCANTHOSAURUS. A trackway recently found in Texas, which is believed to have been made by that dinosaur, shows that this carnosaur was capable of running 25 miles (40 km) per hour. A CERATOPSIAN could charge an attacker at speeds of up to 20 miles (32 km) per hour.

spines

Several prehistoric animals had long spines on their backbones. It is assumed that these spines supported a SKIN fold or fin similar to that of modern sailfish. These fins, or "sails," may have helped control the body temperature of the animals. If the animal stood in full sun, the fin would have warmed up quickly; in the shade, the fin would have cooled the animal more rapidly. These fins were rigid, not collapsible.

The best-known of the ancient sail-backed animals is not a dinosaur, but a PERMIAN reptile named DIMETRODON. However, three dinosaurs did have similar fins on their backs. The fin of SPINOSAURUS was supported by spines 6 feet (1.8 m) high. OURANOSAURUS and ALTISPINAX also had very long spines on their vertebrae, but theirs were not as long as those of *Spinosaurus*. ACROCANTHOSAURUS had spines up to 17 inches (43 cm) long, but these probably were embedded in a thick ridge of muscles instead of supporting a fin.

spinosaurids or Spinosauridae (spy-nuh-SAWR-ih-dee)
"Spiny Lizards" (Named after SPINOSAURUS.)

A family of CARNOSAURS characterized by very long spines on the vertebrae. Some of the spines were as much as 6 feet (1.8 m) long. Scientists believe that these spines may have supported a skin fold shaped like the fin of a fish, that ran along the dinosaur's back. Spinosauridae lived in North Africa during the Cretaceous Period. SPINOSAURUS is the only positively known member of this group, although some people include the very poorly known ALTISPINAX.

SPINOSAURUS (SPY-nuh-sawr-us) "Spiny Lizard" (Latin *spinous* = spiny + Greek *sauros* = lizard, referring to the very long spines on its vertebrae.)

A large CARNOSAUR of Late Cretaceous Egypt. *Spinosaurus* was 40 feet (12 m) long. It had spines 6 feet (1.8 m) tall on its back. It is assumed that these spines supported a huge fan-like sail or fin that stretched from the middle of the neck to just behind the hips. This fin probably helped to control the body temperature of the animal. *Spinosaurus* had a huge head and strong teeth. This BIPEDAL meat-eater is known from an incomplete skeleton, which,

SPINOSAURUS

unfortunately, was destroyed during World War II.
Classification: Carnosauria, Theropoda, Saurischia

STAGONOLEPIS
See AETOSAURS.

staurikosaurids or Staurikosauridae (stor-ik-uh-SAWR-ih-dee) "Cross Lizards" (Named after STAURIKOSAURUS.)

The most primitive family of THEROPODS. The
staurikosaurids lived during the mid part of the Triassic
Period in Brazil. They had long jaws and long, slender
legs. Their bodies somewhat resembled those of the
PROSAUROPODS. *Staurikosaurus* is the only known member
of this family.

STAURIKOSAURUS (stor-IK-uh-sawr-us) "Cross Lizard" (Greek *staurikos* = of a cross + *sauros* = lizard, referring to the Southern Cross constellation, because its fossils were found in the southern hemisphere.)

A primitive THEROPOD of Middle Triassic or early Late
Triassic times. It is the earliest known theropod. This
long-jawed CARNOSAUR had very long, slender legs and a
body somewhat similar to that of a PROSAUROPOD.
Staurikosaurus belonged to the TERATOSAURID family.
Like all carnosaurs it was a BIPEDAL meat-eater. It is
known from lower jaws, vertebrae, pelvis, and hind legs
found in Brazil.
Classification: Carnosauria, Theropoda, Saurischia

STEGOCERAS (steg-OSS-air-us) "Covered Horn" (Greek *steganos* = covered + *keras* = horn, perhaps because the finder thought the "dome" covered a horn.) Originally called TROÖDON.

A small to medium-sized Late Cretaceous PACHYCEPH-
ALOSAUR. The rather large BRAIN of this "dome-headed"
dinosaur was covered by 3 inches (8 cm) of solid bone. The

dome was divided into two parts, and males had larger and thicker domes than females. Small spikes fringed the back of the head, but the sides of the skull did not have the wart-like nodes found on PACHYCEPHALOSAURUS, a much larger pachycephalosaur. *Stegoceras* may have lived like wild goats of today, and males may have butted heads to defend territories or to win a mate.

Stegoceras was a BIPEDAL plant-eater about the size of a goat—5 to 6 feet (1.5 to 1.8 m) long, and 22 inches (56 cm) tall at the hips. It is known from nearly complete remains. Its fossils have been found in Wyoming and Montana; in Alberta, Canada; and in northwestern China.

Classification: Pachycephalosauridae, Ornithopoda or Pachycephalosauria, Ornithischia

STEGOCERAS

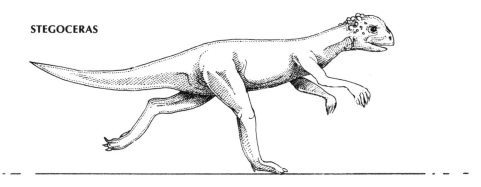

STEGOPELTA (steg-uh-PEL-ta) "Plated Shield" (Greek *stegos* = covered; plated + *pelte* = shield, referring to its bony armor.)

Same as NODOSAURUS. This name was given to a fragmentary specimen that was found in Early Cretaceous deposits in Wyoming. Since *Nodosaurus* is the older name, it is the correct one to use.

Classification: Nodosauridae, Ankylosauria, Ornithischia

stegosaurs or **Stegosauria** (steg-uh-SAWR-ee-ah) "Plated Lizards" (Named after STEGOSAURUS.)

The suborder of ORNITHISCHIAN dinosaurs that had rows of plates and spikes running down their backs. Stegosaurs had small heads and tiny BRAINS (the brain of the largest was only about the size of a golf ball). The forelegs were short and the hind legs were long. Stegosaurs carried their heads close to the ground and probably ate low ground plants. They had beak-like jaws and weak teeth. These dinosaurs ranged from 15 to 25 feet (4.5 to 7.5 m) long and weighed up to 2.25 tons (2 metric tons). The arrangement of plates and spikes varied from one stegosaur to another, and no one knows exactly what the plates and spikes were for. Maybe they helped attract mates. Or perhaps they protected the stegosaur from large CARNOSAURS such as ALLOSAURUS. Some scientists think that the plates may have been temperature control devices. The plates had many blood vessels running through them. Sun shining on the plates would have warmed the blood flowing through them; wind blowing around the plates would have cooled the blood.

Only eight kinds of stegosaurs are known. It was once thought that these four-legged plant-eaters were failures because they were short lived. However, as a group, stegosaurs lived for more than 50 million years and that actually is a pretty good record. The oldest stegosaur lived during the Middle Jurassic, and the latest lived in late Early Cretaceous or early Late Cretaceous. DACENTRURUS, DRAVIDOSAURUS, KENTROSAURUS, LEXOVISAURUS, and STEGOSAURUS were stegosaurs.

STEGOSAURUS (STEG-uh-sawr-us) "Plated Lizard" (Greek *stegos* = covered or plated + *sauros* = lizard, referring to the plates on its back.)

The only plated dinosaur ever found in North America. It has also been found in Europe. This four-legged plant-eater was 11 feet (3.3 m) tall at the hips and 25 feet (7.5 m) long. Its body was about the size of an Asian elephant. *Stegosaurus* had a ridiculously small head and a golf-ball-sized BRAIN. Its hindquarters were controlled by an enlargement of the spinal cord above the hips. (Some people think this was a second brain, but it was not.)

Stegosaurus was high at the hips and low at the shoulders, causing it to carry its head low. It probably ate low ground plants. Its long, heavy tail was armed with four spikes, each about 1 foot (30 cm) long. Two rows of large, thin, leaf-like, bony plates, arranged alternately (rather than in pairs), ran down its neck and back and part way down its tail. The largest plates were 2 feet (60 cm) wide and 2 feet (60 cm) tall. These were situated over the hips. No one knows the purpose of these plates. They might have been used to attract a mate, or as a defense mechanism—perhaps they made the animal look larger. The most recent theory is that they helped control the body temperature. (Wind flowing around the plates would have cooled the blood flowing through them.)

STEGOSAURUS

Stegosaurus lived during the Late Jurassic Period. Many skeletons of this dinosaur have been found in Colorado, Utah, and Wyoming. One skeleton was a baby about the size of a German shepherd dog. Another was found with its plates in position.

Classification: Stegosauridae, Stegosauria, Ornithischia

STENONYCHOSAURUS (sten-ON-ik-uh-sawr-us) "Narrow-clawed Lizard" (Greek *stenos* = narrow + *onychos* = claw + *sauros* = lizard, referring to the sickle-like claw on each foot.)

A very advanced COELUROSAUR of Late Cretaceous western Canada. Although this BIPEDAL meat-eater was only 6 feet (1.8 m) long, it was probably one of the most dangerous of the Late Cretaceous animals. It closely resembled DROMAEOSAURUS, and like *Dromaeosaurus* it had hollow bones, a large BRAIN, and large eyes. Its eyes were spaced far apart, so it was probably able to judge distances accurately. Scientists think it was the most intelligent of the dinosaurs.

Stenonychosaurus was an active predator. It was a swift runner and probably could have outrun any other dinosaur. Its feet were equipped with sickle-like claws, and its hands had grasping fingers. Its claws indicate it may have caught prey larger than itself. It probably hunted in packs.

Some scientists think *Stenonychosaurus* must have been warm-blooded, because it was so active. Some even think it might have developed an insulating covering

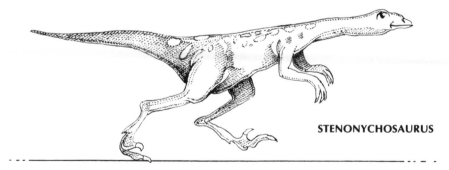

STENONYCHOSAURUS

such as feathers; if it did, it could have hunted at night.

A complete skeleton of *Stenonychosaurus* was found in Alberta, Canada. This dinosaur so closely resembled SAURORNITHOIDES of Mongolia that some scientists think they may be the same.

Classification: Coelurosauria, Theropoda, Saurischia

STENOPELIX (sten-o-PEL-ix) "Narrow Helmet" (Greek *stenos* = narrow + *pelex* = helmet or cap, possibly referring to the shape of the pelvis.)

A small ORNITHISCHIAN. It was related to PSITTACOSAURUS. This primitive CERATOPSIAN is known only from very fragmentary material (a pelvis and hind legs) found in Early Cretaceous deposits in Germany. It was a plant-eater and probably walked on two legs.

Classification: Psittacosauridae, Ornithopoda or Ceratopsidae, Ornithischia

STOKESOSAURUS (STOKES-uh-sawr-us) "Stokes's Lizard" (Named in honor of Lee Stokes, American paleontologist + Greek *sauros* = lizard.)

A short-snouted Late Jurassic CARNOSAUR. It is estimated that this BIPEDAL meat-eater was only 13 feet (4 m) long and 5 feet (1.5 m) tall. Like all carnosaurs, *Stokesosaurus* had long serrated teeth. It may have been related to ALBERTOSAURUS, but it was not a TYRANNOSAUR, because it lived in the Jurassic Period. It is known from fragments found in Utah.

Classification: Carnosauria, Theropoda, Saurischia

stomach stones

See GASTROLITHS.

STRUTHIOMIMUS (strooth-ee-uh-MY-mus) "Ostrich Mimic" (Greek *strouthion* = ostrich + *mimos* = mimic, because it resembled an ostrich.)

A Late Cretaceous ORNITHOMIMID—one of the "ostrich dinosaurs." Like an ostrich, *Struthiomimus* had a long neck; long, slender—but powerful—legs; and a small head. A horny toothless beak covered its jaws. Its eyes were quite large, as was its BRAIN.

Although *Struthiomimus* so closely resembled ORNITHOMIMUS that many scientists consider them to be the same, *Struthiomimus* was a bit smaller and had a longer tail. It stood 7 feet (2 m) tall and was 12 feet (3.5 m) long. Its tail was 3 feet (90 cm) longer than its very short body.

Struthiomimus had grasping fingers that were equipped with long, bear-like claws. The claws may have been used to rip open logs to get at insects. This little BIPED may have been OMNIVOROUS like ostriches. It may have eaten small reptiles, eggs, and fruit, as well as insects. It is known from at least one complete skeleton and several partial ones found in Alberta, Canada. COELUROSAURUS may be the same as this dinosaur.

Classification: Coelurosauria, Theropoda, Saurischia

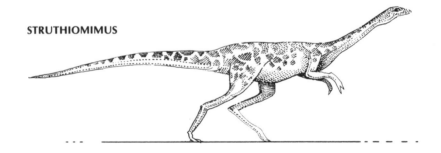

STRUTHIOMIMUS

STRUTHIOSAURUS (STROOTH-ee-o-sawr-us) "Harsh Lizard" (Greek *struthnos* = harsh + *sauros* = lizard, possibly referring to its rough cranium.)

The smallest known ANKYLOSAUR. This four-legged plant-eater was only 5 or 6 feet (1.5 or 1.8 m) long. *Struthiosaurus* was probably the last of the NODOSAURIDAE. It is known only from incomplete material found in Late Cretaceous deposits in Austria. Its head was unarmed, but since *Struthiosaurus* was a NODOSAURID, its sides were probably protected by large spikes, and its tail was clubless.

Classification: Nodosauridae, Ankylosauria, Ornithischia

STYRACOSAURUS (sty-RAK-uh-sawr-us) "Spiked Lizard" (Greek *styrax* = spike + *sauros* = lizard, referring to the spikes on its frill.)

STYRACOSAURUS

A short-frilled CERATOPSIAN with six long spikes along the edge of its frill. A straight horn nearly 2 feet (60 cm) long and 6 inches (15 cm) thick grew on its nose, but only stumps grew above its eyes. Like all ceratopsians, it was a four-legged plant-eater with a bulky body and a relatively short, thick tail. *Styracosaurus* was 18 feet (5.5 m) long and 6 feet (1.8 m) tall. It probably weighed 3 tons (2.7 metric tons). Some scientists believe it was a good runner —it may have been capable of going 20 miles (32 km) per hour. *Styracosaurus* is known from several skulls and a complete skeleton found in Late Cretaceous deposits in Alberta, Canada.

Classification: Ceratopsidae, Ceratopsia, Ornithischia

Sundance Sea (Named for the Sundance Rock formation of the Rocky Mountain area.)

Name given to a long, narrow arm of sea that stretched down across North America from the Arctic Ocean to southern Utah during the early part of the Late Jurassic Period. On the west side of the sea a narrow finger of highlands separated the sea from the ocean; on the east side were vast lowlands; and to the south were extensive sand dunes. Near the end of the Jurassic Period the sea retreated to the Arctic Ocean.

"Supersaurus" (SOO-per-sawr-us) (So nicknamed because it obviously was a very large dinosaur. It has not yet received an official scientific name.)

An enormous Late Jurassic SAUROPOD. It was probably closely related to BRACHIOSAURUS, but was even larger than that dinosaur. It is known only from a few gigantic bones found in Colorado: a pair of shoulder blades 8 feet (2.5 m) long, a pelvis 6 feet (1.8 m) wide, neck vertebrae 4.5 feet (1.4 m) long, and ribs 10 feet (3 m) long. "Supersaurus" may have been 90 feet (27 m) long and may have towered 50 feet (15 m) tall. It could have weighed 75 tons (67.5 metric tons). Like all sauropods, it walked on four legs and ate plants. Its front legs were probably longer than the hind, so that its back sloped like a giraffe's.

Classification: Sauropoda, Sauropodomorpha, Saurischia

synapsid (sin-AP-sid) "Fused Arch" (Greek *syn* = fused + *apsid* = arch.)

synapsid skull

Any animal with only one opening low on each side of its skull behind the eye sockets. The mammal-like reptiles of the late PALEOZOIC and early MESOZOIC ERAS were synapsids, as are present-day mammals. DIMETRODON was a synapsid.

SYNTARSUS (sin-TAR-sus) "Fused Ankle" (Greek *syn* = fused + *tarsus* = ankle, because some bones of the ankle were fused together.)

A very primitive Late Triassic COELUROSAUR related to COELOPHYSIS. Its four-fingered hands resembled those of *Coelophysis,* but its four-toed feet and fused ankles were more similar to those of an early ORNITHOPOD, HETERODON-TOSAURUS. *Syntarsus* weighed only 65 pounds (30 kg) and was about 2 feet (60 cm) tall. Some scientists think it may have been insulated with primitive feathers. This very early BIPEDAL meat-eater probably ate small lizards and mammals. It is known from most of a skeleton found in Zimbabwe.

Classification: Coelurosauria, Theropoda, Saurischia

SYNTARSUS

SYRMOSAURUS (SEER-mo-sawr-us) "Trail Lizard" (Greek *syrma* = anything trailed along + *sauros* = lizard, because it was presumed that it dragged its tail.)

Most of a skeleton of this ANKYLOSAUR was found in Mongolia. It is now known to be the same as PINACOSAU-RUS.

Classification: Ankylosauridae, Ankylosauria, Ornithischia

T

tails

Dinosaurs had long, heavy, reptilian-type tails. Some BIPEDAL dinosaurs may have used their tails as braces when standing upright, but not all could have done this. For example, the tails of some, such as DEINONYCHUS and TENONTOSAURUS were held out rigidly behind by bundles of bony, rod-like tendons that lay along each side of the vertebrae. Such rigidity improved the use of the tail as a counterbalance when the animal ran. HADROSAURS had flat tails, similar to those of alligators. This flatness may have been useful in swimming, but the main purpose of their tails (as it was with all BIPEDAL dinosaurs—both OR-NITHOPODS and THEROPODS), was to balance the bodies when walking or running.

QUADRUPEDAL dinosaurs did not need long tails to balance their bodies while walking or running. The tails of CERATOPSIANS were relatively short, but thick and heavy. The SAUROPODOMORPHS needed long tails to counterbalance their long necks. Several SAUROPODS had whip-like tails, which could have been used as defense weapons. Some of the ANKYLOSAURS and the STEGOSAURS undoubtedly used their tails as weapons. The tails of the AN-KYLOSAURIDAE were armed with heavy, mace-like clubs or spikes. Stegosaurs had long spikes on the ends of their tails.

Some scientists think that the quadrupedal dinosaurs extended their tails when running, the same as the bipedal dinosaurs did. Others are convinced that the sauropods, at least, always dragged their tails on the ground. Sauropods with quite short tails and long legs have recently been discovered. These seem to support the theory that at least some sauropods extended their tails. It is hard to see how these dinosaurs could have dragged their tails.

TALARURUS (tah-lah-ROO-rus) "Basket-like" (Greek *talaros* = basket. The reason for this name is unknown, but may be because the finder thought its ribs resembled the ribs of a basket.)

An early Late Cretaceous ANKYLOSAUR—the second oldest ANKYLOSAURID known. This armored dinosaur was about 17 feet (5.2 m) long. It walked on four short legs and browsed on low ground plants. Its back, hips, and clubbed tail were covered with 2-inch (5-cm) thick bony scutes (plates) and rows of sharp spikes. Its back was flexible instead of being rigid like a turtle's back. *Talarurus* is known from several partial skeletons and a partial skull found in Mongolia.

Classification: Ankylosauridae, Ankylosauria, Ornithischia

TANIUS (TAN-ee-us) (Named for the Chinese province where it was discovered.)

A Late Cretaceous HADROSAUR (duck-billed dinosaur) closely related to ANATOSAURUS. Like *Anatosaurus*, *Tanius* was BIPEDAL and ate plants. It was a HADROSAURINE and had a flat, broad head. There was a low dome or hump between its eyes similar to the hump found on the snout of KRITOSAURUS. This duckbill is known from a nearly complete skeleton found in eastern China.

Classification: Hadrosauridae, Ornithopoda, Ornithischia

TANIUS

TANYSTROPHEUS (tan-ee-STRO-fee-us) "Long Vertebrae" (Greek *tanyo* = long + *stropheus* = vertebra, referring to the vertebrae of its neck.)

TANYSTROPHEUS

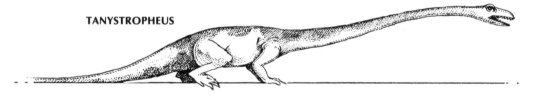

Not a dinosaur, but a 20-foot (6-m) long PROTOROSAUR that lived in Europe during the Middle Triassic Period. This predecessor of modern lizards was almost all neck. Its body was only 3.5 feet (1 m) long, and its tail was 6.5 feet (2 m) long. The neck of this incredible animal was 10 feet (3 m) long, but it had only ten vertebrae. Adult *Tanystropheus* ate fish and probably lived near the sea, but the YOUNG lived inland and ate plants or insects.

TARBOSAURUS (TAR-bo-sawr-us) "Terrible Lizard" (Greek *tarbo* = terrible + *sauros* = lizard, because it was a fearsome dinosaur.)

A large Late Cretaceous CARNOSAUR very similar to TYRANNOSAURUS. Some grew to be 46 feet (14 m) in length and 20 feet (6 m) or more tall. *Tarbosaurus* ran on powerful hind legs with its body parallel to the ground and its heavy tail extended. It had a 4-foot (1.2-m) skull and 6-inch (15-cm) dagger-like teeth. Its arms were short; the hands had two fingers ending in 2-inch (5-cm) claws. The claws on the three-toed feet were 4 inches (10 cm) long. This giant meat-eater is known from ten complete skeletons found in the Gobi Desert of Mongolia.

Classification: Carnosauria, Theropoda, Saurischia

TARBOSAURUS

TARCHIA (TAR-kee-a) (Name derived from the Mongolian word for BRAIN, because the first specimen found was a skull.)

A Late Cretaceous ANKYLOSAUR found in the Gobi Desert of Mongolia. This armored dinosaur was an AN-KYLOSAURIDAE. It had a triangular head, which was covered completely by bony plates, and it had spines above and behind the eyes. *Tarchia* is the latest and one of the largest ankylosaurs known from Asia. It may have grown to be 18 feet (5.5 m) long. Its jaws were lined with 18 teeth. Spikes protruded from the corners of the mouth and rows of spikes ran down its back and clubbed tail. This QUAD-RUPEDAL plant-eater is known from skulls, vertebrae columns, spikes, plates, ribs, and other material of two separate species.

Classification: Ankylosauridae, Ankylosauria, Ornithischia

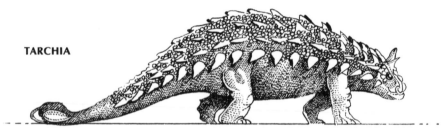

TARCHIA

teeth

The dinosaurs never had a dental problem. As soon as one of their teeth became old or worn, it dropped out and a new one grew in its place. This continued throughout their lives. Every dinosaur tooth is quite distinctive, and scientists can usually tell by looking at a fossil tooth which kind of dinosaur it had belonged to. Scientists can tell whether the animal was a plant-eater or a meat-eater, and sometimes they can get a good idea of the size of the animal from the size of the tooth.

Meat-eating dinosaurs had sharp, pointed, blade-like teeth. CARNOSAURS had dagger-like teeth with edges that were serrated like a steak knife. The largest carnosaurs had teeth that were 6 inches (15 cm) long. COELUROSAURS had small, thin, pointed teeth with serrated edges.

Some PROSAUROPODS had both blade-shaped teeth and flat leaf-shaped teeth (molars), indicating that they ate both plants and meat. Others had only the leaf-shaped teeth of plant-eaters.

The teeth of the plant-eating dinosaurs varied a great deal, even within the same kinds of dinosaurs. For example, some SAUROPODS had weak, peg-shaped teeth that were slightly pointed on the end. Others had spatulate (spoon-shaped) teeth. Sauropods had no molars, nor grinding teeth. They probably swallowed their food whole.

The teeth of the CERATOPSIANS chopped plant food instead of grinding it. The lower teeth closed inside the upper, cutting tough tree branches like a pair of scissors cutting paper. ANKYLOSAURS and STEGOSAURS had small, weak teeth on the sides of the jaws. These teeth were suited only for eating tender ground plants.

The ORNITHOPODS had the most varied teeth of all the dinosaurs. Some had triangular cutting teeth to the tip of their snouts, others had only grinding teeth in their cheek region. They used their beaks to snip off branches. The HETERODONTS had both cutting teeth and grinding teeth; they had canine teeth, as well. Most ornithopods had teeth arranged in single rows, but the HADROSAURS had banks of several rows of sharp, rod-like teeth packed closely together. Some species had as many as 280 teeth on each side of the upper and lower jaws—1120 teeth altogether! These teeth were especially suited for grinding coarse plant fibers.

TELMATOSAURUS (tel-MAT-o-sawr-us) "Marsh Lizard" (Greek *telmatos* = marsh + *sauros* = lizard, perhaps because it was thought to be a marsh dweller.)
Name given to a primitive HADROSAUR skull found in

Hungary. It is the only positively known European representative of the duck-billed dinosaurs. This duckbill was crestless, and was a BIPEDAL plant-eater. It lived during Late Cretaceous times. A fossilized leg bone found in Holland may also be a *Telmatosaurus.*

Classification: Hadrosauridae, Ornithopoda, Ornithischia

TENONTOSAURUS (ten-ON-tuh-sawr-us) "Tendon Lizard" (Greek *tenontos* = sinew + *sauros* = lizard, referring to the ossified tendons along its backbone.)

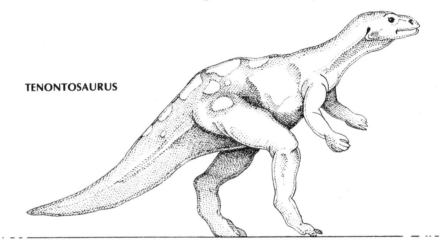

TENONTOSAURUS

An ORNITHOPOD of Early Cretaceous North America. This 20-foot (6-m) BIPEDAL plant-eater weighed 2 tons (1.8 metric tons) or more. It probably resembled IGUANODON, but did not have spiked thumbs. Its tail was equipped with bony, rod-like tendons that held the tail rigid when *Tenontosaurus* ran. *Tenontosaurus* probably roamed vast areas—partial skeletons have been found in Montana, Wyoming, Texas, and Oklahoma.

Classification: Iguanodontidae, Ornithopoda, Ornithischia

teratosaurids or **Teratosauridae** (teh-rat-uh-SAWR-ih-dee) "Monster Lizards" (Named after TERATOSAURUS.)

The most primitive family of CARNOSAURS. These meat-eaters grew to be 20 feet (6 m) long. They had massive builds, large heads, and dagger-like teeth. Their forelimbs were about three-fourths the length of the hind and had three-fingered hands. Teratosaurids lived in Europe and South America during the Triassic Period. STAURIKOSAURUS and TERATOSAURUS were teratosaurids.

TERATOSAURUS (teh-RAT-uh-sawr-us) "Monster Lizard" (Greek *teratos* = monster + *sauros* = lizard, referring to its monstrous teeth.)

The largest of the Late Triassic CARNOSAURS. It was perhaps 20 feet (6 m) long and weighed more than half a ton. This BIPEDAL meat-eater was similar to MEGALOSAURUS. It had a large head and dagger-like teeth. Its hands had three fingers that were armed with long, curved claws. *Teratosaurus* is known from most of a skeleton found in Germany.

Classification: Carnosauria, Theropoda, Saurischia

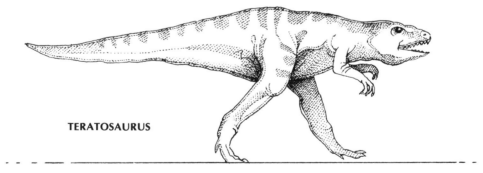

TERATOSAURUS

Tertiary (TER-she-er-ee) **Period** (From Latin *tertius* = third. When this period was named, geological time was divided into three parts. The Tertiary was the third, or last of these periods.)

The first of the two periods of the CENOZOIC ERA. The Tertiary Period is the geologic time that immediately followed the Cretaceous Period (the last period of the MESOZOIC ERA). It lasted from 65 million years ago to 2 million years ago. No dinosaur fossils have been found in rocks of this age. They had disappeared along with the PTERO-SAURS, PLESIOSAURS, AMMONITES, and many kinds of plant forms at the end of the Mesozoic Era. During the Tertiary Period, mammals became the dominant life form.

Tethys (TETH-iss) **Sea** (Named after Tethys—in Greek mythology, daughter of Oceanus.)

Name of the sea or waterway that separated the two great supercontinents, LAURASIA and GONDWANALAND during the MESOZOIC ERA. During the PERMIAN and Triassic Periods, before the breakup of PANGAEA, Tethys was only an arm of the ocean that reached into the eastern shoreline. By the Late Jurassic Period, 140 million years ago, it had completely separated the two supercontinents.

TETRAPODITE (teh-tra-poe-DYE-tee) "Four-footed" (Greek *tetra* = four + *podite* = footed.)

Name given to a rare type of dinosaur footprint. These footprints were found in British Columbia and Alberta, Canada. Scientists believe that they were made by a CERA-TOPSIAN. Ceratopsians had rather massive, four-toed hind feet and five-toed forefeet. Both the hind feet, and the forefeet had blunt claws.

TETRASAUROPUS (tet-ruh-SAWR-uh-pus) "Four Lizard Foot" (Greek *tetra* = four + *sauropous* = lizard foot, referring to the number of toes.)

Name given to four-toed footprints made by an unknown PROSAUROPOD. The footprints were found in Late Triassic rock in South Africa. They resemble the footprints named NAVAHOPUS. The dinosaur that made these

TRACKS was QUADRUPEDAL and took short strides. It had four toes on both its forefeet and its hind feet. The hind feet were long-soled. The forefeet were much smaller and had claws on the first and third fingers.

THECODONTOSAURUS (thee-kuh-DON-tuh-sawr-us)
"Socket-toothed Lizard" (THECODONT + Greek *sauros* = lizard, because its teeth were set in sockets like those of thecodonts.)

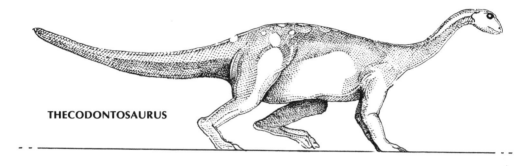

THECODONTOSAURUS

A very early PROSAUROPOD similar to ANCHISAURUS, but more primitive. It is one of the earliest prosauropods known. Its fossils have been found in several regions of the world, including a tooth from North America. It lived during Middle and Late Triassic times. *Thecodontosaurus* was relatively small—only 10 feet (3 m) long— and was lightly built. Its head was small, and its teeth were serrated. Those in front were cone-shaped like those of thecodonts, but the jaw teeth were flat like the teeth of HERBIVORES. *Thecodontosaurus* probably ate both meat and plants. Its neck and tail were long, but its legs and feet were slender. *Thecodontosaurus* was QUADRUPEDAL, but could also walk on its hind legs.

Classification: Prosauropoda, Sauropodomorpha, Saurischia

thecodonts or **Thecodontia** (thee-koh-DON-tee-ah) "Socket-toothed" (Greek *theka* = socket + *odontos* = teeth, because their teeth grew in sockets in the jaws.)

Not dinosaurs, but an order of Triassic reptiles. This is the group from which DINOSAURS, CROCODILIANS, PTEROSAURS, and possibly birds arose. Thecodonts and their descendants are called ARCHOSAURS. Most thecodonts ate meat, but some were OMNIVOROUS, eating both meat and plants. Most were QUADRUPEDAL, some were capable of running on two legs, and a few may have been completely BIPEDAL.

There were four suborders of thecodonts—the AETOSAURIA, the PHYTOSAURIA, the PROTEROSUCHIA, and the PSEUDOSUCHIA. Scientists think that the pseudosuchia is the only group that could have produced the ancestors of the dinosaurs. They were the most advanced thecodonts.

Thecodonts ranged from rabbit-sized pseudosuchians to 30-foot PHYTOSAURS.

therapsids or **Therapsida** (thair-AP-sid-ah) "Beast Opening" (Greek *theros* = beast or mammal + *apsides* = opening, because the openings in their skulls were like those in the skulls of mammals.)

Not dinosaurs, but the mammal-like reptiles from which mammals arose. These beasts lived during Late PALEOZOIC and Early MESOZOIC times. The therapsids dominated animal life on earth for 40 million years before the rise of the dinosaurs. There were more than 300 GENERA of therapsids. They ranged from the size of a rat to the size of a rhinoceros. Some were CARNIVOROUS, and some were HERBIVOROUS; all were four-legged. They lived all over the world. MOSCHOPS was a therapsid.

THERIZINOSAURUS (thee-RIZ-in-o-sawr-us) "Scythe Lizard" (Greek *therizino* = scythe + *sauros* = lizard, referring to its sickle-like claws.)

A Late Cretaceous CARNOSAUR relative of DEINOCHEIRUS. It is known only from a gigantic arm and several sickle-shaped claws. The arm was 8 feet (2.5 m) long, and the claws were 2 and 3 feet (60 and 90 cm) long. The arm was shorter, but more massive than the arms of *Deinocheirus.* The fossils of this BIPEDAL meat-eater were found in Mongolia.

Classification: Carnosauria, Theropoda, Saurischia

theropods or **Theropoda** (thair-uh-PODE-ah) "Beast-footed" (Greek *theros* = beast or mammal + *podos* = foot. Mis-named—the feet were actually more bird-like than beast-like.)

A suborder of SAURISCHIAN dinosaurs. Members of this group were meat-eaters that walked on strong hind legs with their bodies held horizontally, or parallel to the ground, and their tails outstretched to counterbalance their bodies. Most had short forelimbs with clawed hands that could be used for grasping. Their bird-like feet had three long, forward-pointing toes and a backward-pointing dewclaw. The smallest theropods were chicken-sized; the largest were 50-foot (15-m) giants. They lived almost worldwide from mid-Triassic through Cretaceous times.

Theropods included both toothed and toothless kinds. The toothless theropods may have been OMNIVOROUS, probably eating fruit as well as meat. Toothed theropods had blade-like teeth that were serrated like a steak knife.

Scientists think that theropods were ENDOTHERMIC (warm-blooded), because they were very active and most were swift runners.

There were two major kinds of theropods: CARNOSAURS and COELUROSAURS. The carnosaurs were the large, heavily built meat-eaters. ALLOSAURUS, ALBERTOSAURUS, and TYRANNOSAURUS were carnosaurs. Coelurosaurs were small predators with hollow bones. COELOPHYSIS and

COMPSOGNATHUS were members of this group. Some scientists suggest the addition of the DEINONYCHOSAURS, which would include DEINONYCHUS and DROMAEOSAURUS.

Because many recent theropod discoveries do not fit neatly into these classifications, some scientists propose abolishing the COELUROSAURIA and CARNOSAURIA designations and classifying all meat-eaters in families under Theropoda.

Scientists describe theropods as small, medium, or large, depending on their overall length from snout to the tip of the tail. They call theropods that are 0 to 5 feet (0 to 1.5 m) long very small. Those 5 to 10 feet (1.5 to 3 m) are called small; 10 to 23 feet (3 to 7 m) are medium; 23 to 35 feet (7 to 10.5 m) are large; 35 to 50 feet (10.5 to 15 m) long are very large; and over 50 feet (15 m) long are extremely large.

THESCELOSAURUS (THESS-uh-lo-sawr-us) "Marvelous Lizard" (Greek *theskelos* = marvelous + *sauros* = lizard, referring to the excellent condition of the first specimen found.)

A Late Cretaceous ORNITHOPOD that closely resembled PARKSOSAURUS and CAMPTOSAURUS. Although it was basically BIPEDAL, this plant-eater probably walked on four legs part of the time. It was 12 feet (3.5 m) long from its snout to the tip of its tail. It legs were rather short, its body was plump, and its head was small. The hands had five

THESCELOSAURUS

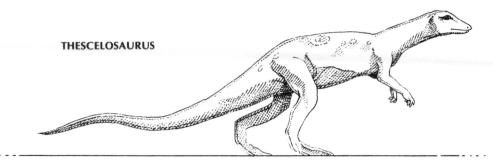

fingers, and the feet had four toes. Their claws were hoof-like, but sharp. *Thescelosaurus* may have had armor plates. It is known from a nearly complete skeleton. Its fossils have been found in Wyoming, Montana, South Dakota, and in Alberta and Saskatchewan, Canada.

Classification: Thescelosauridae, Ornithopoda, Ornithischia

THESPESIUS (thes-PE-see-us) "Divine Lizard" (Greek *thespesios* = divine. The reason for this name is unknown.)

A Late Cretaceous HADROSAUR. This flat-headed duckbill is known only from a partial skull and other incomplete skeletal material found in South Dakota. The skull closely resembles those of ANATOSAURUS or EDMONTOSAURUS, and some think *Thespesius* may be the same as one of them.

Classification: Hadrosauridae, Ornithopoda, Ornithischia

TICINOSUCHUS (teh-CHIN-uh-sook-us) "Ticino Crocodile" (Named for the place in Switzerland where it was first found + Greek *souchos* = crocodile.)

Not a dinosaur, but a 10-foot (3-m) PSEUDOSUCHIAN THECODONT. It was a close relative of MANDASUCHUS and probably resembled that pseudosuchian. It was basically QUADRUPEDAL, but could probably run on two legs. It had sharp teeth and was probably a meat-eater. This thecodont is believed by some to be the ancestor of the plant-eating SAURISCHIAN dinosaurs. Its fossils have been found in Late Triassic deposits in Austria and Switzerland.

TIENSHANOSAURUS (tih-en-SHAN-o-sawr-us) "Tien Shan Lizard" (Named for the Tien Shan Mountains in China, near which it was found + Greek *sauros* = lizard.)

An Early Cretaceous SAUROPOD that resembled EUHELOPUS in size and shape. This four-legged plant-eater is known from much of a skeleton found in China. It had a small head, a long neck, and a long tail. Its forelegs and hind legs were nearly equal in length.

Classification: Sauropoda, Sauropodomorpha, Saurischia

titanosaurids or **Titanosauridae** (tye-tan-uh-SAWR-ih-dee) "Large Lizards" (Named after TITANOSAURUS.)

The preferred name for the family of large, peg-toothed SAUROPODS (those with pencil-shaped teeth). This major division had shorter front legs than hind legs. They were large four-legged plant-eaters, 50 to 90 feet (15 to 27 m) long. They flourished in North America, South America, Europe, Asia, and Africa from Middle Jurassic through Late Cretaceous times. This group is also called ATLANTOSAURIDAE. It is divided into four subfamilies: the TITANOSAURINAE, the ATLANTOSAURINAE, the DIPLODOCINAE, and the DICRAEOSAURINAE.

A new study of sauropods combines the Titanosaurinae with the Atlantosaurinae, and the Diplodocinae with the Dicraeosaurinae, and raises the latter to family level, under the name of DIPLODOCIDAE.

titanosaurs or **Titanosaurinae** (tie-tan-uh-SAWR-ih-nee) "Large Lizards" (Named after TITANOSAURUS.)

A subfamily of Titanosauridae dinosaurs. This group was very much like the DIPLODOCINAE, but had six vertebrae in the pelvic area instead of five. Some had armor plates. They ranged in size from 50 to 60 feet (15 to 18 m) long. They lived during the Cretaceous Period and have been found in Africa, Europe, India, South America, and the United States. HYPSELOSAURUS, LAPLATOSAURUS, SALTASAURUS, and TITANOSAURUS were members of this subfamily.

TITANOSAURUS (tye-TAN-uh-sawr-us) "Large Lizard" (Named after the Titans, a family of giants in Greek mythology + Greek *sauros* = lizard, because it was a large dinosaur.)

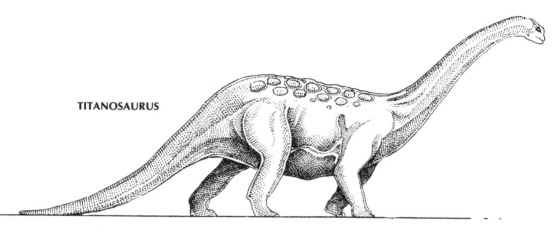

TITANOSAURUS

A Late Cretaceous SAUROPOD. This four-legged meat-eater resembled DIPLODOCUS, but was smaller, heavier, and had six vertebrae in the pelvic area instead of five. Its neck and tail were more like those of CAMARASAURUS. *Titanosaurus* was one of the last of the sauropods and it may have had armor plates. It is known from many fossils found in India, Europe, Africa, and Mongolia. A nearly complete skeleton found in Argentina lacked only a skull. *Titanosaurus* was 60 to 66 feet (18 to 20 m) long.

Classification: Sauropoda, Sauropodomorpha, Saurischia

TORNIERIA (tor-NAIR-ee-a) (Named in honor of T. Tornier, German paleontologist.)

A Late Jurassic SAUROPOD of the TITANOSAURINAE subfamily. It is known only from fragments found in Tanzania. The size of these fossils suggests that this four-legged plant-eater was a *very* large creature—its height at the shoulders may have reached 20 feet (6 m). *Tornieria's* forelimbs were the same length as the hind.

Classification: Sauropoda, Sauropodomorpha, Saurischia

TOROSAURUS (TOR-o-sawr-us) "Piercing Lizard" (Greek *toros* = piercing + *sauros* = lizard, referring to its horns.)

One of the last of the CERATOPSIANS. Its frill was longer than that of any other ceratopsian. Its skull, from the tip of the horny beak to the back edge of the frill, was 8.7 feet (2.6 m) long. The frill was 5.5 feet (1.7 m) wide, and extended well back of the animal's shoulders. This dinosaur's head was larger in proportion to the size of the body than that of any other known land animal.

Torosaurus was probably 20 feet (6 m) long and weighed about 5 tons (4.5 metric tons). Its nose-horn was small, but the horns on its brow were 2 feet (60 m) long. *Torosaurus* walked on four legs and ate low vegetation, which it chopped with scissor-like teeth.

Torosaurus lived in Late Cretaceous North America and endured to the very end of the period. Its fossils have been discovered in Wyoming, Texas, and Alberta, Canada, but a complete skeleton has not been found.

Classification: Ceratopsidae, Ceratopsia, Ornithischia

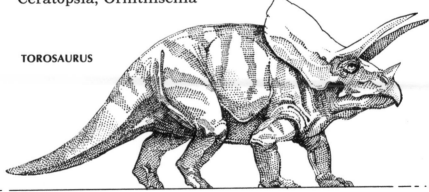

TOROSAURUS

TORVOSAURUS (TOR-vuh-sawr-us) "Savage Lizard" (Latin *torvus* = savage + Greek *sauros* = lizard, referring to its lethal claws and teeth.)

A large and heavily built Late Jurassic CARNOSAUR. It was about 35 feet (10.5 m) long and may have weighed as much as 6 tons (5.5 metric tons). *Torvosaurus* was different from other known meat-eaters. It was more massive than the other Jurassic carnosaurs, and its arms were shorter—about the length of a man's arms. However, the arms were much longer than those of the TYRANNOSAURS, and were more powerful. The hands had three short, stout fingers equipped with wicked 12-inch (30-cm) claws that were longer than the claws of any other Jurassic THEROPOD. It had shorter and more massive jaws than any other carnosaur. They were lined with enormous teeth. *Torvosaurus* resembled MEGALOSAURUS more than it did any other theropod. Like TYRANNOSAURUS, *Torvosaurus* probably could not run swiftly because of its weight, and it was probably a scavenger. This BIPEDAL meat-eater is known from an incomplete skeleton found in Colorado.

Classification: Carnosauria, Theropoda, Saurischia

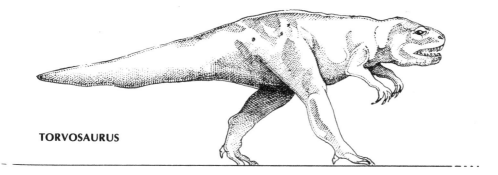

TORVOSAURUS

TRACHODON (TRAK-o-don) "Rough Tooth" (Greek *trachys* = rough + *odon* = tooth, referring to the rough surface formed by dozens of tiny denticles on the tooth crown.)

Name given to a single HADROSAUR tooth found in Late Cretaceous rock in Montana. *Trachodon* is now considered to be the same as ANATOSAURUS. Since the name *Anatosaurus* is based on more complete information, it is the preferred one.

Classification: Hadrosauridae, Ornithopoda, Ornithischia

trachodont (TRAK-o-dont) "Rough Tooth" (Named after TRACHODON.)

Any duck-billed dinosaur; a name sometimes used in place of HADROSAUR.

tracks, trackways

Scientists have discovered thousands of dinosaur tracks that were left in MESOZOIC mud. These fossilized footprints tell many things about the animals that made them. From tracks scientists have learned things they could not have learned in any other way.

Tracks have been found that show when dinosaurs sat or rested. Others show the animals swimming or floating. A recent discovery shows that a THEROPOD had been floating in water, pushing itself along with one foot. This provides evidence that theropods sometimes went into water. Scientists once thought that SAUROPODS and HADROSAURS could escape predators by taking to the water, but perhaps this was not true. In England whole trackways of MEGALOSAURUS have been found. Scientists have learned almost as much about this dinosaur from its tracks as from its fossil bones.

From tracks scientists can tell whether an animal was BIPEDAL or QUADRUPEDAL. They can determine whether the animal sprawled like an alligator, or walked erect like an elephant. By measuring the distance between footprints scientists can estimate how fast the dinosaur was going. Long strides indicate the animal was traveling rapidly. Gigantic three-toed CARNOSAUR tracks found in a coal mine in Colorado show that the animal that made them had a very long stride. Three-toed footprints recently uncovered by a flash flood in Texas reveal that 15 large carnosaurs that passed that way in Early Cretaceous times were in a great hurry. The strides are the longest known. By using a formula based on the distance between the tracks and the size of them, a scientist has estimated that these dinosaurs were running nearly 25 miles (40 km) per hour. We can't be sure what dinosaur made the tracks, but it is thought that they were made by ACROCANTHOSAURUS, a carnosaur whose fossils have been found in similar rock nearby. Whether these animals were chasing something, running from something, or were just romping cannot be determined.

Some tracks give clues to the way dinosaurs lived. Tracks in Canada indicate that carnosaurs hunted in packs. A sauropod trackway in Texas shows that 23 individuals were traveling in the same direction. Smaller individuals were most often in the center of the group. This indicates HERDING and also suggests that adult sauropods protected their YOUNG. (See PARENTAL CARE.) Another trackway in Texas shows the prints of a sauropod that was being followed by a three-toed carnosaur. The carnosaur footprints are impressed on top of those of the sauropod. Scientists think that the carnosaur may have been stalking the sauropod. Still another group of tracks shows herding in COELUROSAURS. These footprints are in the Connecticut Valley in eastern United States. They indicate that several members of the same SPECIES were traveling together. Long trackways left by hadrosaurs in Canada show that hadrosaurs traveled in herds and that they walked side by side. Young hadrosaurs appear to have herded in groups of similar-sized individuals.

Scientists can't be exactly sure which kind of dinosaur made a footprint or trackway unless they find a fossil skeleton nearby that has feet that match the footprints. But scientists can determine whether the track was made by a sauropod, a carnosaur, a coelurosaur, or a hadrosaur, because they know what kind of foot each of these types of dinosaurs had. (See FEET.)

Triassic (try-ASS-ik) **Period** (From Latin *trias* = triad, referring to the three successive series of rocks in Germany that are of this age.)

The first of the three periods of the MESOZOIC ERA. This geological time period began 225 million years ago and ended 190 million years ago. Dinosaurs appeared in the middle of this period. Other major land animals of the period were amphibians and THERAPSIDS. The THECODONTS were the dominant life form. ICHTHYOSAURS and NOTHOSAURS inhabited the oceans. During the Late Triassic, the first mammals and earliest CROCODILIANS and turtles appeared.

TRIASSOLESTES (tri-ass-o-LESS-teez) "Triassic Robber" (Triassic + Greek *lestes* = robber, referring to the strata in which it was found.)

A small COELUROSAUR that lived in Argentina during the earliest part of the Late Triassic Period. This little BIPEDAL

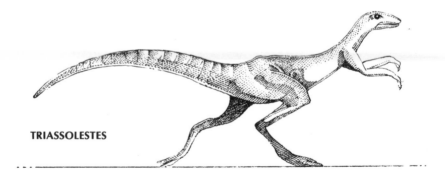

TRIASSOLESTES

meat-eater was about the size of Podokesaurus and probably closely resembled that dinosaur. It is known from an incomplete skull, lower jaw, and cervical vertebrae.

Classification: Coelurosauria, Theropoda, Saurischia

TRICERATOPS (try-SAIR-uh-tops) "Three-horned Face" (Greek *tri* = three + *keratops* = horned face, because it had three horns.)

The largest and heaviest of the CERATOPSIANS. It was 25 feet (7.5 m) long and 9.5 feet (2.9 m) tall. It weighed 5 tons (4.5 metric tons). It had a smooth, solid frill; a short, thick nose-horn; and two enormous 40-inch (102-cm), forward-curved brow horns. This four-legged plant-eater lived in western North America during Late Cretaceous times.

Triceratops was one of the very last of the horned dinosaurs to develop and one of the last of the dinosaurs to become extinct. (See EXTINCTION.) It had no real enemies. It was an aggressive animal and was well protected by its horns, frill, and tough, leathery skin.

TRICERATOPS

Triceratops had a turtle-like beak and scissor-like teeth. Large numbers of *Triceratops* must have roamed western North America, because several whole skeletons have been found in Montana, Wyoming, and Alberta, Canada.

Classification: Ceratopsidae, Ceratopsia, Ornithischia

TROÖDON (TROO-o-don) "Wound Tooth" (Greek *troo* = to wound + *odon* = tooth, referring to its serrated teeth.)

A small Late Cretaceous CARNIVOROUS dinosaur. This was one of the first dinosaurs named in North America. The name was given to a single tooth found in Montana. Later a jaw lined with similar teeth was found. Until recently this was all that was known of this dinosaur.

The type of dinosaur that *Troödon* is has been the subject of much debate. It was once thought to be a dome-headed dinosaur, now known as STEGOCERAS, but the teeth do not resemble those of that dinosaur. More recently it was thought that *Troödon* was a THEROPOD, because the back teeth are blade-shaped and serrated and the front teeth are cylindrical, like those of the DEINODONTS. Furthermore, bands of color on the tooth enamel and the areas of wear on the teeth are similar to those on the teeth of theropods and unlike the teeth of ORNITHOPODS. Then too, *Troödon's* jaw was U-shaped and did not have a horny beak, again indicating that this dinosaur was not an ornithopod.

In 1980 scientists made an important discovery in Montana. They found several NESTS, EGGS, juveniles, and adults of a dinosaur which they believe are specimens of *Troödon.* Scientists are still studying this find, but these fossils seem to indicate that *Troödon* was an ornithopod after all —but a very unusual one. Its teeth and long limbs show that it was an agile predator. If it does prove to be an ornithopod, it will be the only known flesh-eating ORNITHISCHIAN. The large number of nests and juveniles found near adults suggests that *Troödon* took care of its YOUNG.

Classification: Uncertain at this time.

TSINTAOSAURUS (chin-TAY-o-sawr-us) "Chinese Lizard" (Chinese *Tsintao* = China + Greek *sauros* = lizard, referring to the country where it was found.)

A Late Cretaceous HADROSAUR whose fossils were found in China. This LAMBEOSAURINE duckbill had a hollow, spike-like crest that projected upward and slightly forward like a horn. However, it seems to have been covered by SKIN instead of horn covering, so it probably was not a weapon. Some scientists think that maybe a flap of skin stretched from the crest to the middle of the nose. It may have been a sex display device. This BIPEDAL plant-eater is known from a nearly complete skeleton.

Classification: Hadrosauridae, Ornithopoda, Ornithischia

TUOJIANGOSAURUS (too-HWANG-o-sawr-us) "Tuojiang Lizard" (Named for the place where it was found + Greek *sauros* = lizard.)

A STEGOSAUR of Late Jurassic China. This plated dinosaur resembled STEGOSAURUS. It had rows of plates down the middle of its back, and spikes on its tail. Like all stegosaurs, it was a four-legged plant-eater. It is known from incomplete material.

Classification: Stegosauridae, Stegosauria, Ornithischia

TYLOCEPHALE (tye-lo-SEF-uh-lee) "Knob Head" (Greek *tylos* = knob + *kephale* = head, referring to its domed head.)

A recently discovered PACHYCEPHALOSAUR. This dome-headed dinosaur is known only from a partial skull and several other skeletal parts found in Mongolia. The skull was thick and decorated with small spikes similar to those on the skull of STEGOCERAS. Like all pachycephalosaurs, *Tylocephale* walked on two legs and ate plants.

Scientists estimate that this animal was about 7 feet (2 m) long.

Classification: Pachycephalosauridae, Ornithopoda or Pachycephalosauria, Ornithischia

TYLOSAURUS (TYE-lo-sawr-us) "Knot Lizard" (Greek *tylos* = knot or knob + *sauros* = lizard. The reason for this name is not known.)

Not a dinosaur, but one of the largest known of the MOSASAURS. This seagoing lizard lived in the NIOBRARA SEA during the Late Cretaceous Period. It was 20 to 40 feet (6 to 12 m) long and had a long, slim body. It had huge jaws; sharp, cone-like teeth; and flipper-like hands and feet. It was a savage hunter and ate fish and shellfish. *Tylosaurus* fossils have been found in Kansas.

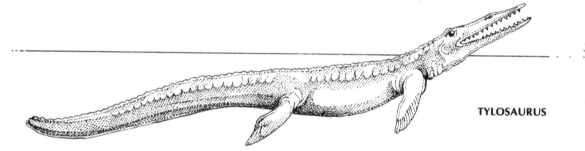

TYLOSAURUS

TYPOTHORAX
See AETOSAURS.

tyrannosaurids or **Tyrannosauridae** (tye-ran-uh-SAWR-ih-dee) "Tyrant Lizards" (Named after TYRANNOSAURUS.) Also called TYRANNOSAURS.

The family of Late Cretaceous CARNOSAURS. The tyrannosaurs were the largest and the last of the meat-eaters. They had huge heads, long teeth, very short arms, and two short fingers with long claws. Tyrannosaurs had heavier, more powerful bodies than earlier carnosaurs. Some weighed as much as 6 tons (5.5 metric tons), and the largest were 50 feet (15 m) long. They probably could not run swiftly due to their great weight. It is possible that they were scavengers, eating carcasses. They have been found in North America, Mongolia, India, and Japan. ALBERTOSAURUS, ALECTROSAURUS, DASPLETOSAURUS, TARBOSAURUS, and TYRANNOSAURUS were tyrannosaurs.

tyrannosaurs (tye-RAN-uh-sawrz)
See TYRANNOSAURIDS.

TYRANNOSAURUS (tye-RAN-uh-sawr-us) "Tyrant Lizard" (Greek *tyrannos* = tyrant + *sauros* = lizard, because of its great size, and wicked teeth and claws.)

The last and largest known CARNOSAUR. This huge meat-eater measured up to 50 feet (15 m) from the tip of its enormous jaws to the end of its tail. It was 18.5 feet (5.6 m) tall and weighed 6 tons (5.5 metric tons). It ran with its massive tail extended to balance its 4-foot (1.2-m) head. Its

TYRANNOSAURUS

monstrous 3-foot (90-cm) jaws were lined with 60 dagger-like teeth that were 3 to 6 inches (8 to 15 cm) long. *Tyrannosaurus* had long, strong hind legs, and its huge feet were equipped with 8-inch (20-cm) talons. However, its arms were very short—only about 30 inches (76 cm) long. They were so short *Tyrannosaurus* could not even scratch its chin! But the hands, like the feet, were armed with long, strong claws.

This ferocious BIPEDAL dinosaur stalked its prey across western North America during Late Cretaceous times. It probably preferred to eat young duckbills or other prey that was easy to catch, because it was much too heavy to run swiftly. A complete skeleton of *Tyrannosaurus* was found in Montana. Its fossils have also been found in Wyoming. A close relative, TARBOSAURUS, lived in Mongolia.

Classification: Carnosauria, Theropoda, Saurischia

U

"Ultrasaurus" (UL-truh-sawr-us) (So nicknamed because of its enormous size. It has not yet received an official scientific name.)

The largest known dinosaur. "Ultrasaurus" was a huge, Late Jurassic SAUROPOD. It is known from a 9-foot (2.7-m) shoulder blade (the largest dinosaur bone ever found), 5-foot (1.5-m) vertebrae, and a few other bones found in Colorado. The shoulder blade of "Ultrasaurus" was 25 percent larger than that of BRACHIOSAURUS. This means "Ultrasaurus" may have been 100 feet (30 m) long, 50 or 60 feet (15 or 18 m) tall, and may have weighed 80 tons (72 metric tons). That is 15 times as large as an African elephant! If "Ultrasaurus" was as large as scientists think it was, then it was the largest known land creature that ever existed on earth. It was taller than a five-story building. If "Ultrasaurus" was built like *Brachiosaurus,* with its forelegs longer than its hind legs, its forelegs would have been 20 feet long, which is as long as a giraffe is tall. Like all sauropods, this BIPEDAL plant-eater had elephant-like legs, a small head, a long neck, and a long tail.

Classification: Sauropoda, Sauropodomorpha, Saurischia

V

VALDOSAURUS (VAL-doe-sawr-us) "Wealden Lizard" (Latin *valdo* = wealden + Greek *sauros* = lizard, referring to the Wealden rock formation where it was found.)

An ORNITHOPOD of Early Cretaceous England. This BIPEDAL plant-eater was closely related to and resembled DRYOSAURUS, and was probably a descendant of that dinosaur. It is known only from very fragmentary material.

Classification: Hypsilophodontidae, Ornithopoda, Ornithischia

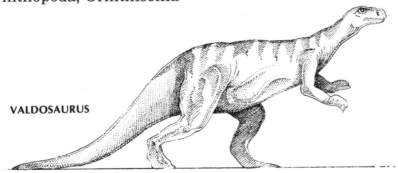

VALDOSAURUS

VECTISAURUS (VEK-tuh-sawr-us) "Spike Lizard" (Latin *vectis* = spike + Greek *sauros* = lizard. The reason for this name is not known.)

An Early Cretaceous ORNITHOPOD. *Vectisaurus* was an IGUANODONT and probably resembled IGUANODON. Like all ornithopods, it was a BIPEDAL plant-eater. It is known only from fragmentary material found on the Isle of Wight.

Classification: Iguanodontidae, Ornithopoda, Ornithischia

VELOCIRAPTOR (veh-loss-ih-RAP-tor) "Swift Robber" (Latin *velocis* = swift + *raptor* = robber, referring to its speed and its grasping hands.)

A COELUROSAUR similar to DEINONYCHUS, but this fierce little meat-eater lived several million years later, during the Late Cretaceous Period. *Velociraptor* was about the size of a man. It had long, three-fingered hands and sickle-like talons on each foot. Like *Deinonychus,* this BIPED had long, slender legs and could run swiftly. Its fossils were found in Mongolia, where it had died in a death struggle—its hands were gripping the skull of a PROTOCERATOPS, and one of its awful claws was embedded in the belly of its prey.

Classification: Coelurosauria, Theropoda, Saurischia

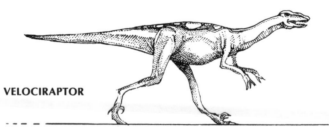

VELOCIRAPTOR

VOLKHEIMERIA (volk-HYE-mer-ee-ah) (Named in honor of Wolfgang Volkheimer, Argentine paleontologist.)

A Middle Jurassic SAUROPOD. This dinosaur was similar to CETIOSAURUS, but was more primitive. In fact, it is one of the most primitive sauropods known. Like all sauropods, it walked on four pillar-like legs, ate plants, and had a long neck and tail. It is known from an incomplete skeleton found in Argentina. This is a very recent discovery and has not yet been thoroughly studied.

Classification: Sauropoda, Sauropodomorpha, Saurischia

VULCANODON (vul-CAN-o-don) "Fire Tooth" (Named after Valcanus, the Roman god of fire + Greek *odon* = tooth, because it was found in sandstone between two lava flows.)

An Early Jurassic PROSAUROPOD resembling MELANOROSAURUS. This four-legged plant-eater was found in Zimbabwe. It is one of the last and largest of the prosauropods. In fact, some believe it was a primitive SAUROPOD instead of a prosauropod. It was 40 feet (12 m) long from the tip of the snout to the end of its long tail. It probably weighed more than an elephant. Like all prosauropods, *Vulcanodon* had a small head and a long neck. It also had elephant-like legs.

Classification: Prosauropoda, Sauropodomorpha, Saurischia

W

WUERHOSAURUS (WER-ho-sawr-us) "Wuerhkohsiehte Lizard" (Named for the village in China near the site where it was found + Greek *sauros* = lizard.)

Until recently, the only positively identified STEGOSAUR

of the Cretaceous age. Until its discovery, it was thought that the stegosaurs had become extinct by the end of the Jurassic Period. It was found in Early Cretaceous rock in northwestern China. It is known only from fragments. Like all stegosaurs, it was a QUADRUPEDAL plant-eater.

Classification: Stegosauridae, Stegosauria, Ornithischia

Y

YALEOSAURUS   (YALE-ee-o-sawr-us) "Yale's Lizard" (Named in honor of Yale University + Greek *sauros* = lizard.)

Name given to several PROSAUROPOD fossils found in Late Triassic rock in Connecticut. They are now known to be the same as those of ANCHISAURUS, and since the name *Anchisaurus* was given first, it is the preferred name for this dinosaur.

Classification: Prosauropoda, Sauropodomorpha, Saurischia

YANGCHUANOSAURUS   (yang-CHWAWN-uh-sawr-us) "Yang-ch'uan Lizard" (Named for Yang-ch'uan, China, where it was found + Greek *sauros* = lizard.)

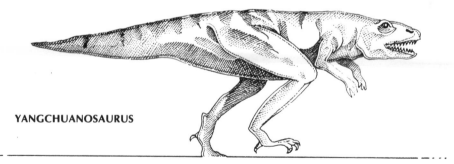

YANGCHUANOSAURUS

A Late Jurassic or Early Cretaceous CARNOSAUR. *Yangchuanosaurus* was closely related to MEGALOSAURUS. It was about 26 feet (8 m) long and had a 32-inch (82-cm) skull. It had short arms and three-fingered hands. It walked on two strong legs with its heavy tail extended to balance its huge head. The jaws of this large meat-eater were lined with dagger-like teeth. A nearly complete skeleton of *Yangchuanosaurus* was found in China.

Classification: Carnosauria, Theropoda, Saurischia

YAVERLANDIA (yah-ver-LAND-ee-ah) Named for Yaverland Battery on the Isle of Wight, where it was found.)

A very primitive PACHYCEPHALOSAUR (dome-headed dinosaur) discovered in Early Cretaceous rock on the Isle of Wight. The skull cap of this turkey-sized ancestor of STEGOCERAS had thickened into two small, rather flat domes. Otherwise *Yaverlandia's* head resembled that of a HYPSILOPHODONT. It is known only from a skull cap. Like all PACHYCEPHALOSAURS, it was a BIPEDAL plant-eater.

Classification: Pachycephalosauridae, Pachycephalosauria, Ornithischia

young

Little is known about baby dinosaurs. Discoveries of their remains are extremely rare. Their immature bones were too fragile to fossilize readily. However, enough young dinosaurs have been found to give us some idea of dinosaur development. The fossil record seems to indicate that specialized traits did not develop until the animals were half-grown.

PROTOCERATOPS is one dinosaur that is known from every stage of development. EGGS, hatchlings, half-grown, and adult individuals of this dinosaur have been found. Young *Protoceratops* had very poorly developed frills. The frills did not become fully developed until the animals were about half-grown. Skeletons of several other young CERATOPSIANS show that their horns were not well developed until they were half-grown, either.

MAIASAURA (a HADROSAUR) is also known from hatchlings to adults. The hatchlings were 18 inches (46 cm) long. Month old babies were about 3 feet (1 m) long or about one-tenth of the size of the adults, while "adolescents" were half the adult size. Young hadrosaurs did not develop crests until they were half-grown. In immature hadrosaurs, the bills were less broad than in adults, and there were fewer rows of teeth. Similarly, young PACHYCEPHALOSAURS had more shallow domes than the adults, and baby STEGOSAURUS did not have plates.

Young CARNOSAURS had larger heads, bigger eyes, and longer legs in comparison to their body size and to the adults. These characteristics probably improved their ability to catch prey and to escape larger predators. Several half-grown ALBERTOSAURUS have been found and ALLOSAURUS is known from juveniles 10 feet (3 m) long to full-grown adults. These young individuals were about one-fifth of adult size, and were well past the hatchling stage. Hatchlings were probably no more than 30 inches (76 cm) long (or about one-tenth of adult size).

Several young SAUROPODS have been found. The most complete and smallest CAMARASAURUS skeleton ever discovered was a 16-foot (4.8-m) juvenile. This animal was about one-fourth the size of a full-grown adult. Hatchlings are unknown, but from the size of known sauropod eggs, hatchlings could not have been more than 30 inches (80 cm) long or weighed more than 17 pounds (7.7 kg).

The smallest and youngest known dinosaur to date is a newly hatched PROSAUROPOD called MUSSAURUS. This tiny dinosaur was about the size of a robin. It had a tiny head, a long neck, a long tail, and heavy legs. The second smallest dinosaur is a baby PSITTACOSAURUS. Wear on its teeth indicate it was not a hatchling. This tiny dinosaur was only about 10 inches (25 cm) long—its body was half the size of a pigeon's. It had enormous eyes and a large brain-case.

Other known juvenile dinosaurs include a turkey-sized CAMPTOSAURUS, and a 30-inch (75-cm) long COMPSOGNA-THUS. Several very young COELOPHYSIS are also known.

YOUNGOOLITHUS (yung-oo-LITH-us) "Young's Stone Eggs" (Named in honor of C. C. Young, Chinese paleon-tologist + Greek *oion* = egg + *lithos* = stone.)

Name given to dinosaur EGGS and a footprint found in China. The eggs were in a clutch of 16. A three-toed left footprint was clearly impressed upon three of the eggs. Scientists think the footprint was made by the dinosaur that laid the eggs. The eggs were elongated and nearly pointed on each end. They were found in Cretaceous rock.

Z

ZATOMUS (zah-TOE-mus) "Very Sharp" (Greek *za* = very + *tomos* = sharp, referring to the character of the tooth.)

Name given to a single CARNOSAUR tooth found in North Carolina. This tooth is similar to those of TERATOSAURUS. It is the only evidence, other than footprints, that large THEROPODS lived in eastern North America during the Late Triassic Period.

Classification: Carnosauria, Theropoda, Saurischia

ZEPHYROSAURUS (ZEF-ear-o-sawr-us) "West Wind Liz-ard" (Named after Zephyros, god of the west wind in Greek mythology + Greek *sauros* = lizard, because it was discovered in western North America.)

An Early Cretaceous ORNITHOPOD recently found in

Montana. It was closely related to HYPSILOPHODON. *Ze-phyrosaurus* was 6 to 8 feet (1.8 to 2.5 m) long. Its skull was 6 inches (15 cm) long. This animal was a BIPEDAL plant-eater. It is known from a partial skull that included the braincase and a jaw, a few ribs, and broken vertebrae.

Classification: Hypsilophodontidae, Ornithopoda, Ornithischia

ZIGONGOSAURUS (sih-GON-guh-sawr-us) "Zigong Lizard" (Named for Zigong, China, near where it was found + Greek *sauros* = lizard.)

A BRACHIOSAURID SAUROPOD found in Late Jurassic deposits of China. This four-legged plant-eater probably grew to be 50 feet (15 m) long and weighed about 20 tons (18 metric tons). It is known from partial skeletons of different sized individuals.

Classification: Sauropoda, Sauropodomorpha, Saurischia

For Further Reading

Charig, Alan J. *A New Look at the Dinosaurs.* New York: Mayflower Books, 1979.

Colbert, Edwin H. *The Age of Reptiles.* New York: W. W. Norton & Co., 1965.

_____. *The Year of the Dinosaur.* New York: Charles Scribner's Sons, 1977.

Desmond, Adrian J. *The Hot-Blooded Dinosaurs.* New York: Warner Books, 1977.

Gould, Stephen Jay. "The Great Dying." *Natural History,* October 1974, pp. 22–27.

_____. "Were Dinosaurs Dumb?" *Natural History,* May 1978, pp. 9–16.

Horenstein, Sydney. *Dinosaurs and Other Prehistoric Animals.* New York: Strawberry Books, 1978.

Jacobs, Louis L., Ed. *Aspects of Vertebrate History.* Flagstaff: Museum of Northern Arizona Press, 1980.

Kielan-Jaworowska, Zofia. *Hunting for Dinosaurs.* Cambridge: The MIT Press, 1969.

Kurtén, Björn. *The Age of the Dinosaurs.* New York: McGraw-Hill Book Co., 1968.

Langston, Wann, Jr. "Pterosaurs." *Scientific American,* February 1981, pp. 122–136.

Long, Robert. *The Last of the Dinosaurs.* San Francisco: Bellerophon Books, 1978.

Long, Robert A. and Welles, Samuel P. *All New Dinosaurs.* San Francisco: Bellerophon Books, 1975.

McIntosh, John S. *Dinosaur National Monument.* Phoenix: Constellation Phoenix, Inc., 1977.

McLoughlin, John C. *Archosauria: A New Look at the Old Dinosaur.* New York: The Viking Press, 1979.

Moody, Richard. *A Natural History of Dinosaurs.* London: Chartwell, 1977.

———. *The World of Dinosaurs.* New York: Grosset & Dunlap, 1977.

Olshevsky, George. "Dinosaur Renaissance." *Science Digest,* August 1981, pp. 34–43.

Ostrom, John H. *The Strange World of Dinosaurs.* New York: G. P. Putnam's Sons, 1964.

———. "A New Look at Dinosaurs." *National Geographic,* August 1978, pp. 152–85.

Russell, Dale A. *A Vanishing World.* Ottawa: National Museum of Natural Sciences, 1977.

———. "The Mass Extinctions of the Late Mesozoic." *Scientific American,* January 1982, pp. 58–65.

Sattler, Helen Roney. *Dinosaurs of North America.* New York: Lothrop, Lee & Shepard Books, 1981.

Stout, William. *The Dinosaurs.* New York: Bantam Books, 1981.

Tweedie, Michael. *The World of Dinosaurs.* New York: William Morrow & Co., 1977.

Wadsworth, Nelson. "Colorado's 100-foot Dinosaur! Is It the World's Largest?" *Science Digest,* April 1973, pp. 77–81.

West, Susan. "Dinosaur Hunt." *Science News,* vol. 116, pp. 314–315.

Reference, by Location, of Dinosaur Discoveries

HELEN RONEY SATTLER has been an elementary school teacher and a children's librarian. She was born in Iowa but is now a resident of Bartlesville, Oklahoma, where her husband is a chemical engineer. They have two children and two grandchildren. It was their grandson's fascination with dinosaurs that sparked Mrs. Sattler's interest in the subject. Her research has now spanned several years and taken the form of trips to dinosaur excavations and interviews and correspondence with paleontologists, in addition to extensive reading of scientific papers about recent theories and discoveries.

"My aim," she says, "is to incorporate the latest evidence and theories about these highly successful creatures and, at the same time, to correct many long-held misconceptions about them." The critical acclaim from both scientists and nonscientist reviewers of her previous book, *Dinosaurs of North America,* attests to how well Mrs. Sattler has been able to achieve this aim. She has reached the same high standard of excellence in her work on *The Illustrated Dinosaur Dictionary.*